Library of Presidential Rhetoric

Martin J. Medhurst, General Editor

D1525604

WOODROW WILSON'S WESTERN TOUR

Woodrow Wilson's Western Tour

Rhetoric, Public Opinion,

and the League of Nations

J. MICHAEL HOGAN

Texas A&M University Press : College Station

The paper used in this book meets the minimum requirements
of the American National Standard for Permanence
of Paper for Printed Library Materials, z39.48–1984.
Binding materials have been chosen for durability.

Frontispiece: In the first real test of the "magnivox," a crude electronic public
address system, Woodrow Wilson addresses a crowd of nearly 50,000 in
San Diego on September 19, 1919. Photo courtesy of the
Library of Congress, #LC-USZ62-101026.

Woodrow Wilson's Pueblo Address is reprinted with the permission of
Princeton University Press.

Wilson, Woodrow. "An Address in the City Auditorium in Pueblo, Colorado."
In *The Papers of Woodrow Wilson*, ed. Arthur S. Link, John E. Little, Manfred F.
Boemeke, and L. Kathleen Amon, vol. 63: 500–513.
Princeton: Princeton University Press, 1990.

Library of Congress Cataloging-in-Publication Data

Hogan, J. Michael, 1953–
Woodrow Wilson's western tour : rhetoric, public opinion, and the League
of Nations / J. Michael Hogan.— 1st ed.
    p. cm. — (Library of presidential rhetoric)
Includes bibliographical references and index.
ISBN-13: 978-1-58544-524-0 (cloth : alk. paper)
ISBN-10: 1-58544-524-X (cloth : alk. paper)
ISBN-13: 978-1-58544-533-2 (pbk. : alk. paper)
ISBN-10: 1-58544-533-9 (pbk. : alk. paper)
    1. Wilson, Woodrow, 1856–1924—Oratory.   2. United States—Politics and
government—1913–1921.   3. Rhetoric—Political aspects—United
States—History—20th century.   4. League of Nations—
I. Title. II. Series.
E767.1H84   2006
973.91'3—dc22   2005037458

For Lisa and her menagerie:

Leo, Bella, and Haley

Contents

Acknowledgments

I owe the idea of this small book to the general editor of the Library of Presidential Rhetoric, Martin J. Medhurst. The task proved bigger than the book, but I do not hold that against Marty, nor is he responsible for any errors of interpretation or fact. James R. Andrews, himself a model of Wilsonian statesmanship, also provided inspiration and insight, teaching me about Wilson's early life and his contributions to American nationalism. Jennifer Young Abbott, now at Wabash College, served as my graduate research assistant, tracking down newspaper coverage of the Western tour and making useful suggestions. Another graduate research assistant, Jill Weber, helped with the final stages of the manuscript's preparation. Many other colleagues and graduate students at Penn State also contributed to the project by providing material support or by shaping my thinking about rhetoric and politics. I am particularly grateful to Glen Williams at Southeast Missouri State University, who provided encouragement and welcome diversions during the writing of this book.

Like all students of Woodrow Wilson, I owe a great debt to the late Arthur S. Link and his team of editors, whose superbly edited sixty-nine-volume edition of Wilson's papers has set the standard for such collections. For assistance with other materials, I thank the staffs of the Pattee and Paterno Libraries at the Pennsylvania State University and the Library of Congress in Washington, D.C.

Woodrow Wilson: "An Address in the City Auditorium in Pueblo, Colorado," September 25, 1919

Mr. Chairman and fellow citizens: It is with a great deal of genuine pleasure that I find myself in Pueblo, and I feel it a compliment that I should be permitted to be the first speaker in this beautiful hall. One of the advantages of this hall, as I look about, is that you are not too far away from me, because there is nothing so reassuring to men who are trying to express the public sentiment as getting into real personal contact with their fellow citizens.

I have gained a renewed impression as I have crossed the continent this time of the homogeneity of this great people to whom we belong. They come from many stocks, but they are all of one kind. They come from many origins, but they are all shot through with the same principles and desire the same righteous and honest things. So I have received a more inspiring impression this time of the public opinion of the United States than it was ever my privilege to receive before.

The chief pleasure of my trip has been that it has nothing to do with my personal fortunes, that it has nothing to do with my personal reputation, that it has nothing to do with anything except the great principles uttered by Americans of all sorts and of all parties which we are now trying to realize at this crisis of the affairs of the world.

But there have been unpleasant impressions as well as pleasant impressions, my fellow citizens, as I have crossed the continent. I have perceived more and more that men have been busy creating an absolutely false impression of what the treaty of peace and the Covenant of the League of Nations contain and mean. I find, moreover, that there is an organized propaganda against the League of Nations and against the treaty proceeding from exactly the same sources that the organized propaganda proceeded from which threatened this country here and there with disloyalty. And I want to say—I cannot say it too often—any man who carries a hyphen about with him carries a dagger that he is ready to plunge into the vitals of this republic whenever he gets the chance. (applause) If I can catch any man with a hyphen in this great contest, I will know that I have caught an enemy of the republic. My fellow citizens, it is only certain bodies of foreign sympathies, certain bodies of sympathy with foreign nations that are organized against this great document, which the American representatives have brought back from Paris. Therefore, it is in order to clear away the mists, in order to remove misapprehensions, in order to do away with false impressions that have clustered around this great subject, that I want to tell you a few simple things about these essential things—the treaty and the Covenant of the League of Nations.

Don't think of this treaty of peace as merely a settlement with Germany. It is that. It is a very severe settlement with Germany, but there is not anything in it that she did not earn. (applause) Indeed, she earned more than she can ever be able to pay for, and the punishment exacted of her is not a punishment greater than she can bear. And it is absolutely necessary in order that no other nation may ever plot such a thing against humanity and civilization.

But the treaty is so much more than that. It is not merely a settlement with Germany; it is a readjustment of those great injustices which underlay the whole structure of European and Asiatic societies. Of course this is only the first of several treaties. They are all constructed on the same plan. The Austrian treaty follows the same lines. The treaty with

Hungary follows the same lines. The treaty with Bulgaria follows the same lines. The treaty with Turkey, when it is formulated, will follow the same lines.

What are those lines? They are based on the principle that every government dealt with in this great settlement is put in the hands of the people and taken out of the hands of coteries and sovereigns who had no right to rule over the people. (applause) It is a people's treaty, that accomplishes by a great sweep of practical justice the liberation of men who never could have liberated themselves. And the power of the most powerful nations has been devoted, not to their aggrandizement, but to the liberation of people whom they could have put under their control if they had chosen to do so. Not one foot of territory is demanded by the conquerors, not one single item of submission to their authority is demanded by them. The men who sat around that table in Paris knew that the time had come when the people were no longer going to consent to live under masters, but were going to live their lives as they chose to live and under such governments as they chose to erect. That is the fundamental principle of this great settlement.

And we did not stop with that. We added a great international charter for the rights of labor. (applause) Reject this treaty, impair it, and this is the consequence to the laboring men of the world—there is no international tribunal which can bring the moral judgments of the world to bear upon the great labor questions of the day. What we need to do with regard to the labor questions of the day, my fellow countrymen, is to lift them into the light, is to lift them out of the haze and distraction of passion, of hostility, into the calm spaces where men look at things without passion. The more men you get into a great discussion the more you exclude passion. Just so soon as the calm judgment of the world is directed upon the question of justice to labor, labor is going to have a forum such as it never was supplied with before. And men everywhere are going to see that the problem of labor is nothing more nor less than the problem of the elevation of humanity. (applause) We must see that all the questions which have disturbed the world, all the questions which have eaten into the confidence of men toward their governments, all the questions which have disturbed the processes of industry, shall be brought out where men of all points of view, men of all attitudes of mind, men of all kinds of experience, may contribute their part to the settlement of the great questions which we must settle and cannot ignore.

But at the front of this great treaty is put the Covenant of the League of Nations. It will also be at the front of the Austrian treaty and the Hungarian treaty and the Bulgarian treaty and the treaty with Turkey. Every one of them will contain the Covenant of the League of Nations, because you cannot work any of them without the Covenant of the League of Nations. Unless you get the united, concerted purpose and power of the great governments of the world behind this settlement, it will fall down like a house of cards.

There is only one power to put behind the liberation of mankind, and that is the power of mankind. It is the power of the united moral forces of the world. And in the Covenant of the League of Nations, the moral forces of the world are mobilized. For what purpose? Reflect, my fellow citizens, that the membership of this great League is going to include all the great fighting nations of the world, as well as the weak ones. It is not for the present going to include Germany, but for the time being Germany is not a great fighting country. (applause) But all the nations that have power that can be mobilized are going to be members of this League, including the United States. And what do they unite for? They enter into a solemn promise to one another that they will never use their power against one another for aggression; that they never will impair the territorial integrity of a neighbor; that they will never interfere with the political independence of a neighbor; that they will abide by the principle that great populations are entitled to determine their own destiny and that they will not interfere with that destiny; and that, no matter what differences arise amongst them, they will never resort to war without first having done one or other of two things—either submitting the matter of controversy to arbitration, in which case they agree to abide by the result without question, or, having submitted it to the consideration of the Council of the League of Nations, laying before that Council all the documents, all the facts, agreeing that the Council can publish the documents and the facts to the whole world. You understand that there are six months allowed for the mature consideration of these facts by the Council, and, at the expiration of these six months, even if they are not then ready to accept the advice of the Council with regard to the settlement of the dispute, they will still not go to war for another three months.

In other words, they consent, no matter what happens, to submit every matter of difference between them to the judgment of mankind. And, just so certainly as they do that, my fellow citizens, war will be in the far background, war will be pushed out of that foreground of terror in which it has kept the world for generation after generation, and men will know that there will be a calm time of deliberate counsel.

The most dangerous thing for a bad cause is to expose it to the opinion of the world. The most certain way that you can prove that a man is mistaken is by letting all his neighbors know what he thinks, by letting all his neighbors discuss what he thinks, and, if he is in the wrong, you will notice that he will stay at home, he will not walk on the streets. He will be afraid of the eyes of his neighbors. He will be afraid of their judgment of his character. He will know that his cause is lost unless he can sustain it by the arguments of right and of justice. The same law that applies to individuals applies to nations.

But you say, "We have heard that we might be at a disadvantage in the League of Nations." Well, whoever told you that either was deliberately falsifying or he had not read the Covenant of the League of Nations. I leave him the choice. I want to give you a very simple account of the organization of the League of Nations and let you judge for yourselves. It is a very simple organization. The power of the League, or rather the activities of the League, lie in two bodies. There is the Council, which consists of one representative from each of the Principal Allied and Associated Powers—that is to say, the United States, Great Britain, France, Italy, and Japan, along with four other representatives of the smaller powers chosen out of the general body of the membership of the League. The Council is the source of every active policy of the League, and no active policy of the League can be adopted without a unanimous vote of the Council. That is explicitly stated in the Covenant itself.

Does it not evidently follow that the League of Nations can adopt no policy whatever without the consent of the United States? The affirmative vote of the representative of the United States is necessary in every case.

Now, you have heard of six votes belonging to the British Empire. Those six votes are not in the Council. They are in the Assembly, and the interesting thing is that the Assembly does not vote. (applause) I must qualify that statement a little, but essentially it is absolutely true. In every matter in which the Assembly is given a vote—and there are only four or five—its vote does not count unless concurred in by the representatives of all the nations represented on the Council. So that there is no validity to any vote of the Assembly unless in that vote also the representative of the United States concurs. That one vote of the United States is as big as the six votes of the British Empire. (applause) I am not jealous for advantage, my fellow citizens, but I think that is a perfectly safe situation. There isn't validity in a vote, either by the Council or the Assembly, in which we do not concur. So much for the statements about the six votes of the British Empire.

Look at it in another aspect. The Assembly is the talking body. The Assembly was created in order that anybody that purposed anything wrong would be subjected to the awkward circumstance that everybody could talk about it. This is the great assembly in which all the things that are likely to disturb the peace of the world or the good understanding between nations are to be exposed to the general view. And I want to ask you if you think it was unjust, unjust to the United States, that speaking parts should be assigned to the several portions of the British Empire? Do you think it unjust that there should be some spokesman in debate for that fine little stout republic down in the Pacific, New Zealand? Do you think it unjust that Australia should be allowed to stand up and take part in the debate—Australia, from which we have learned some of the most useful progressive policies of modern time, a little nation only five million in a great continent, but counting for several times five in its activities and in its interest in liberal reform.

Do you think it unjust that that little republic down in South Africa, whose gallant resistance to being subjected to any outside authority at all we admired for so many months, and whose fortunes we followed with such interest, should have a speaking part? Great Britain obliged South Africa to submit to her sovereignty, but she immediately after that felt that it was convenient and right to hand the whole self-government of that colony over to the very men whom she had beaten.

The representatives of South Africa in Paris were two of the most distinguished generals of the Boer army, two of the most intelligent men I ever met, two men that could talk sober counsel and wise advice along with the best statesmen in Europe. To exclude General Botha and General Smuts from the right to stand up in the parliament of the world and say something concerning the affairs of mankind would be absurd.

And what about Canada? Is not Canada a good neighbor? I ask you, is not Canada more likely to agree with the United States than with Great Britain? Canada has a speaking part. And then, for the first time in the history of the world, that great voiceless multitude, that throng hundreds of millions strong in India, has a voice among the nations of the world. And I want to testify that some of the wisest and most dignified figures in the peace conference at Paris came from India, men who seemed to carry in their minds an older wisdom than the rest of us had, whose traditions ran back into so many of the unhappy fortunes of mankind that they seemed very useful counselors as to how some ray of hope and some prospect of happiness could be opened to its people. I, for my part, have no jealousy whatever of those five speaking parts in the Assembly. Those speaking parts cannot translate themselves into five votes that can in any matter override the voice and purpose of the United States.

Let us sweep aside all this language of jealousy. Let us be big enough to know the facts and to welcome the facts, because the facts are based upon the principle that America has always fought for, namely, the equality of self-governing peoples, whether they were big or little—not counting men, but counting rights, not counting representation, but counting the purpose of that representation.

When you hear an opinion quoted you do not count the number of persons who hold it; you ask, "Who said that?" You weigh opinions, you do not count them. And the beauty of all democracies is that every voice can be heard, every voice can have its effect, every voice can contribute to the general judgment that is finally arrived at. That is the object of democracy. Let us accept what America has always fought for, and accept it with pride—that America showed the way and made the proposal. I do not mean that America made the proposal in this particular instance. I mean that the principle was an American principle, proposed by America.

When you come to the heart of the Covenant, my fellow citizens, you will find it in Article X, and I am very much interested to know that the other things have been blown away like bubbles. There is nothing in the other contentions with regard to the League of Nations, but there is something in Article X that you ought to realize and ought to accept or reject. Article X is the heart of the whole matter.

What is Article X? I never am certain that I can from memory give a literal repetition of its language, but I am sure that I can give an exact interpretation of its meaning. Article X provides that every member of the League covenants to respect and preserve the territorial integrity and existing political independence of every other member of the League as against external aggression.

Not against internal disturbance. There was not a man at that table who did not admit the sacredness of the right of self-determination, the sacredness of the right of any body of people to say that they would not continue to live under the government they were then living under. And under Article XI of the Covenant, they are given the privilege to say whether they will live under it or not. For following Article X is Article XI, which makes it the right of any member of the League at any time to call attention to anything, anywhere, that is likely to disturb the peace of the world or the good understanding between nations upon which the peace of the world depends. I want to give you an illustration of what that would mean.

You have heard a great deal—something that was true and a great deal that was false—about that provision of the treaty which hands over to Japan the rights which Germany enjoyed in the province of Shantung in China. In the first place, Germany did not enjoy any rights there that other nations had not already claimed. For my part, my judgment, my moral judgment, is against the whole set of concessions. They were all of them unjust to China, they ought never to have been exacted, they were all exacted by duress from a great body of thoughtful and ancient and helpless people. There never was any right in any of them. Thank God, America never asked for any, never dreamed of asking for any.

But when Germany got this concession in 1898, the government of the United States made no protest whatsoever. That was not because the government of the United States was not in the hands of high-minded and conscientious men. It was. William McKinley was President and John Hay was Secretary of State—as safe hands to leave the honor of the United States in as any that you can cite. They made no protest because the state of international law at that time was that it was none of their business unless they could show that the interests of the United States were affected, and the only thing that they could show with regard to the interests of the United States was that Germany might close the doors of Shantung Province against the trade of the United States. They, therefore, demanded and obtained promises that we could continue to sell merchandise in Shantung. And what good that would be for the independence of China, it is very difficult to see.

Immediately following that concession to Germany, there was a concession to Russia of the same sort—of Port Arthur, and Port Arthur was handed over subsequently to Japan on the very territory of the United States. Don't you remember that, when Russia and Japan got into war with one another, the war was brought to a conclusion by a treaty written at Portsmouth, New Hampshire? And in that treaty, without the slightest intimation from any authoritative sources in America that the government of the United States had any objection, Port Arthur, Chinese territory, was turned over to Japan.

I want you distinctly to understand that there is no thought of criticism in my mind. I am expounding to you a state of international law. Now, read Article X and XI. You will see that international law is revolutionized by putting morals into it. Article X says that no member of the League, and that includes all these nations that have done these things unjustly to China, shall impair the territorial integrity or the political independence of any other member of the League. China is going to be a member of the League. Article XI says that any member of the League can call attention to anything that is likely to disturb the peace of the world or the good understanding between nations, and China is for the first time in the history of mankind afforded a standing before the jury of the world.

I, for my part, have a profound sympathy for China, and I am proud to have taken part in an arrangement which promises the protection of the world to the rights of China. The whole atmosphere of the world is changed by a thing like that, my fellow citizens. The whole international practice of the world is revolutionized.

But, you will say, "What is the second sentence of Article X? That is what gives very disturbing thoughts." The second sentence is that the Council of the League shall advise what steps, if any, are necessary to carry out the guarantee of the first sentence, namely, that the members will respect and preserve the territorial integrity and political independence of the other members. I do not know any other meaning for the word "advise" except "advise." The Council advises, and it cannot advise without the vote of the United States. Why gentlemen should fear that the Congress of the United States would be advised to do something that it did not want to do, I frankly cannot imagine, because they cannot even be advised to do anything unless their own representative has participated in the advice.

It may be that that will impair somewhat the vigor of the League, but, nevertheless, the fact is so—that we are not obliged to take any advice except our own, which to any man who wants to go his own course is a very satisfactory state of affairs. Every man regards his own advice as best, and I dare say every man mixes his own advice with some thought of his own interest. Whether we use it wisely or unwisely, we can use the vote of the United States to make impossible drawing the United States into any enterprise that she does not care to be drawn into.

Yet Article X strikes at the taproot of war. Article X is a statement that the very things that have always been sought in imperialistic wars are henceforth forgone by every ambitious nation in the world.

I would have felt very lonely, my fellow countrymen, and I would have felt very much disturbed if, sitting at the peace table in Paris, I had supposed that I was expounding my own ideas. Whether you believe it or not, I know the relative size of my own ideas; I know how they stand related in bulk and proportion to the moral judgments of my fellow countrymen. And I proposed nothing whatever at the peace table at Paris that I had not sufficiently certain knowledge embodied the moral judgment of the citizens of the United States. I had gone over there with, so to say, explicit instructions.

Don't you remember that we laid down fourteen points which should contain the principles of the settlement? They were not my points. In every one of them I was conscientiously trying to read the thought of the people of the United States. And, after I uttered those points, I had every assurance given me that could be given me that they did speak the moral judgment of the United States and not my single judgment. Then, when it came to that critical period just a little less than a year ago, when it was evident that the war was coming to its critical end, all the nations engaged in the war accepted those fourteen principles explicitly as the basis of the Armistice and the basis of the peace.

In those circumstances, I crossed the ocean under bond to my own people and to the other governments with which I was dealing. The whole specification of the method of settlement was written down and accepted beforehand, and we were architects building on those specifications. It reassures me and fortifies my position to find how, before I went over, men whose judgment the United States has often trusted were of exactly the same opinion that I went abroad to express. Here is something I want to read from Theodore Roosevelt:

"The one effective move for obtaining peace is by an agreement among all the great powers in which each should pledge itself not only to abide by the decisions of a common tribunal, but to back its decisions by force. The great civilized nations should combine by solemn agreement in a great world league for the peace of righteousness; a court should be established. A changed and amplified Hague Court would meet the requirements, composed of representatives from each nation, whose representatives are sworn to act as judges in each case and not in a representative capacity." Now, there is Article X. He goes on and says this: "The nations should agree on certain rights that should not be questioned, such as territorial integrity, their right to deal with their domestic affairs, and with such matters as whom they should admit to citizenship. All such guarantee each of their number in possession of these rights."

Now, the other specification is in the Covenant. The Covenant in another portion guarantees to the members the independent control of their domestic question. There is not a leg for these gentlemen to stand on when they say that the interests of the United States are not safeguarded in the very points where we are most sensitive. You do not need to be told again that the Covenant expressly says that nothing in this Covenant shall be construed as affecting the validity of the Monroe Doctrine, for example. You could not be more explicit than that.

And every point of interest is covered, partly for one very interesting reason. This is not the first time that the Foreign Relations Committee of the Senate of the United States has read and considered this Covenant. I brought it to this country in March last in a tentative, provisional form, in practically the form that it now has, with the exception of certain additions which I shall mention immediately. I asked the foreign relations committees of both houses to come to the White House, and we spent a long evening in the frankest discussion of every portion that they wished to discuss. They made certain specific suggestions as to what should be contained in this document when it was to be revised. I carried those suggestions to Paris, and every one of them was adopted.

What more could I have done? What more could have been obtained? The very matters upon which these gentlemen were most concerned were the right of withdrawal, which is now expressly stated; the safeguarding of the Monroe Doctrine, which is now accomplished; the exclusion from action by the League of domestic questions, which is now accomplished. All along the line, every suggestion of the United States was adopted after the Covenant had been drawn up in its first form and had been published for the criticism of the world. There is a very true sense in which I can say this is a tested American document.

I am dwelling upon these points, my fellow citizens, in spite of the fact that I dare say to most of you they are perfectly well known, because, in order to meet the present situation, we have got to know what we are dealing with. We are not dealing with the kind of document which this is represented by some gentlemen to be. And, inasmuch as we are dealing with a document simon-pure in respect of the very principles we have professed and lived up to, we have got to do one or other of two things—we have got to adopt it or reject it. There is no middle course. You cannot go in on a special-privilege basis of your own. I take it that you are too proud to ask to be exempted from responsibilities which the other members of the League will carry. We go in upon equal terms or we do not go in at all. And if we do not go in, my fellow citizens, think of the tragedy of that result—the only sufficient guarantee of the peace of the world withheld! Ourselves drawn apart with that dangerous pride, which means that we shall be ready to take care of ourselves. And that means that we shall maintain great standing armies and an irresistible navy; that means we shall have the organization of a military nation; that means we shall have a general staff, with the kind of power that the General Staff of Germany had, to mobilize this great manhood of the nation when it pleases, all the energy of our young men drawn into the thought and preparation for war.

What of our pledges to the men that lie dead in France? We said that they went over there, not to prove the prowess of America or her readiness for another war, but to see to it that there never was such a war again.

It always seems to make it difficult for me to say anything, my fellow citizens, when I think of my clients in this case. My clients are the children; my clients are the next generation. They do not know what promises and bonds I undertook when I ordered the armies of the United States to the soil of France, but I know. And I intend to redeem my pledges to the children; they shall not be sent upon a similar errand.

Again and again, my fellow citizens, mothers who lost their sons in France have come to me and, taking my hand, have shed tears upon it, not only that, but they have added, "God bless you, Mr. President!" Why, my fellow citizens, should they pray God to bless me? I advised the Congress of the United States to create the situation that led to the death of their sons. I ordered their sons overseas. I consented to their sons being put in the most difficult parts of the battle line, where death was certain, as in the impenetrable difficulties of the forest of Argonne.

Why should they weep upon my hand and call down the blessings of God upon me? Because they believe that their boys died for something that vastly transcends any of the immediate and palpable objects of the war. They believe, and they rightly believe, that their sons saved the liberty of the world. They believe that, wrapped up with the liberty of the world, is the continuous protection of that liberty by the concerted powers of all civilized people. They believe that this sacrifice was made in order that other sons should not be called upon for a similar gift—the gift of life, the gift of all that died.

And, if we did not see this thing through, if we fulfilled the dearest present wish of Germany and now dissociated ourselves from those alongside whom we fought in the war, would not something of the halo go away from the gun over the mantelpiece, or the sword? Would not the old uniform lose something of its significance? These men were crusaders. They were not going forth to prove the might of the United States. They were going forth to prove the might of justice and right. And all the world accepted them as crusaders, and their transcendent achievement has made all the world believe in America as it believes in no other nation organized in the modern world. There seems to me to stand between us and the rejection or qualification of this treaty the serried ranks of those boys in khaki—not only those boys who came home, but those dear ghosts that still deploy upon the fields of France.

My friends, on last Decoration Day, I went to a beautiful hillside near Paris, where was located the cemetery of Suresnes, a cemetery given over to the burial of the American dead. Behind me on the slopes was rank upon rank of living American soldiers. And, lying before me upon the levels of the plain, was rank upon rank of departed American soldiers. Right by the side of the stand where I spoke, there was a little group of

French women who had adopted these boys—they were mothers to these dear boys—putting flowers every day upon those graves, taking them as their own sons, their own beloved, because they had died to save France. France was free, and the world was free because America had come! I wish that some men in public life who are now opposing the settlement for which these men died could visit such a spot as that. I wish that that feeling which came to me could penetrate their hearts. I wish that they could feel the moral obligation that rests upon us not to go back on those boys, but to see the thing through, to see it through to the end and make good their redemption of the world. For nothing less depends upon us, nothing less than the liberation and salvation of the world.

You will say, "Is the League an absolute guarantee against war?" No, I do not know any absolute guarantee against the errors of human judgment or the violence of human passion. But I tell you this: with a cooling space of nine months for human passion, not much of it will keep hot.

I had a couple of friends who were in the habit of losing their tempers, and, when they lost their tempers, they were in the habit of using very unparliamentary language. Some of their friends induced them to make a promise that they never swear inside the town limits. When the impulse next came upon them, they took a streetcar to go out of town to swear, and by the time they got out of town, they did not want to swear. They came back convinced that they were just what they were—a couple of unspeakable fools, and the habit of losing their tempers and of swearing suffered great inroads upon it by that experience.

Now, illustrating the great by the small, that is true of the passions of nations. It is true of the passions of men, however you combine them. Give them space to cool off. I ask you this: if this is not an absolute insurance against war, do you want no insurance at all? Do you want nothing? Do you want not only no probability that war will not recur, but the probability that it will recur? The arrangements of justice do not stand of themselves, my fellow citizens. The arrangements of this treaty are just, but they need the support of the combined power of the great nations of the world. (applause) And they will have that support.

[15]

Now that the mists of this great question have cleared away, I believe that men will see the truth, eye to eye and face to face. There is one thing that the American people always rise to and extend their hand to, and that is the truth of justice and of liberty and of peace. We have accepted that truth, and we are going to be led by it, and it is going to lead us, and, through us, the world, out into pastures of quietness and peace such as the world never dreamed of before. (applause)

Introduction

Woodrow Wilson's Western Tour

*It is not wise, it is not possible, to guide national policy
under the impulse of passion.*
PITTSBURGH, PENNSYLVANIA, JANUARY 29, 1916

Monday, September 22, 1919. "The flags are out, the bunting is flying,
the hotels are jammed, the streets are crowded, the people are chat-
tering, the big search lights have been tested, the acoustics have been
arranged—for it is President's day in Reno." Thus did the *Nevada State
Journal* report on the morning of September 22, 1919, as Reno prepared
for the arrival of President Wilson. It was to be the only visit of the
nation's twenty-eighth chief executive to the sparsely populated state,
and people from around Nevada traveled to Reno for the celebration.
When the president arrived at 8 P.M. aboard his special train car, the
Mayflower, he was met "by joyful dignitaries and a jubilant crowd." He
then proceeded by motorcade to the Rialto Theater, where he was to
deliver the twenty-ninth major address of his Western tour. Introduced
with three cheers and interrupted frequently by applause, the president
spoke for an hour and fifteen minutes. By one historian's account,
"Wilson was at his rhetorical best in Reno," and the next day his speech
was published in full in newspapers across the state.[1]

Yet despite the warm welcome, despite the cheers and applause, despite the fact that some Nevadans had "nothing but praise for the chief executive's oratorical brilliance," Reno's two daily newspapers had little good to say about the president's visit. The city's morning paper, the *Nevada State Journal*, accused Wilson of conducting a propaganda campaign and called the president "a poor prophet and a man of extremely bad judgment." The city's evening newspaper, the *Reno Evening Gazette*, went even further, declaring the president's visit to Reno a complete waste of time. The president, editorialized the *Gazette*, had not "altered the opinion of a single man or woman" on the question of whether the treaty should be ratified without reservations.[2]

Wilson's day in Reno represents, in microcosm, the president's legendary Western tour on behalf of the League of Nations. Coming near the end of the twenty-two-day, 8,000-mile trip, it reflected, on the one hand, the enthusiasm, even the adulation of the crowds that greeted Wilson, especially in the Far West. At some venues the crowds rivaled those that cheered the president during his triumphal parades through European capitals after World War I. On the other hand, Reno's two newspapers reflected the stubbornness, even passionate hostility, of Wilson's critics. For many who opposed Wilson and his plan for a League of Nations, the Western tour was not just about the treaty. It was, instead, yet another demonstration of the president's partisanship or worse—a reflection of his megalomania and delusions of grandeur.

Historians have been no less divided in their assessments of Wilson's Western tour. For his admirers, as John Milton Cooper Jr. has noted, the tour was Wilson's "finest hour," a "noble act of self-sacrifice" for an equally noble cause. In their view, Wilson felt such an obligation to those who had fought and died in the war—and he had such faith in the League's ability to prevent future wars—that he "willingly, knowingly risked his health, indeed his life, in the effort to persuade Americans to adopt his program." The Western tour, at least to his admirers, "represented the purest and best in Woodrow Wilson." To his detractors, Wilson's Western tour was a "willful, ill-conceived act of vanity and desperation." Driven by "self-righteous egotism, bordering on a messiah complex," Wilson embarked upon the tour in a fit of anger, and he took such a rigid stand toward his opponents that "he fell prey to delusions of grandeur about his own persuasive powers and even to a wish for martyrdom in a holy cause."[3] In the view of his critics, Wilson got just what he deserved. Seeking to bully the Senate into ratifying the treaty without amendments or reservations, he suffered a humiliating defeat when the Senate refused to ratify it at all.

Whatever their assessment of Wilson's motives, character, or even his mental health, historians generally agree with Thomas Bailey that, in the final analysis, the Western tour proved a "disastrous blunder."[4] Not only did Wilson fail to win ratification in the Senate, but he also destroyed his own health, leaving him but "a shell of a man, incompetent to occupy the office of President." Instead of rallying the public behind ratification of the treaty, the Western tour left Wilson incapacitated, unable to carry on the fight once he returned to Washington. Instead of securing his legacy as "one of the keenest intellects ever to ponder affairs of state," the Western tour brought Woodrow Wilson's "great political career" to "a pitiful end."[5]

Why did Wilson decide to tour in the first place? And why did he so stubbornly refuse to compromise with the mild reservationists in the Senate? These questions have driven the historical scholarship on Wilson's Western tour. Yet the answers remain elusive. For many historians, Wilson's physical and mental health best explain his seemingly irrational behavior.[6] Some critics—largely discredited now—have even attributed his behavior to a serious personality disorder rooted in a troubled relationship with his father.[7] Few historians have taken seriously what most observers at the time considered the best explanation for Wilson's actions: his faith in the power of his own oratory to influence public opinion. In a great debate over America's role in the world, Wilson had every confidence that he could rally public opinion behind the League of Nations. And he had faith that, in the end, public opinion would force the Senate to surrender to his uncompromising position.

As president, Wilson earned a reputation as a principled and effective public speaker, "a spellbinder during a time when the American people admired oratory above all other political skills."[8] Indeed, many of Wilson's contemporaries viewed him as the greatest speaker of his day—an orator skilled not just on the platform but also in the give-and-take of discussion and debate. Unlike Theodore Roosevelt, Wilson did not oversimplify ideas for public consumption; he had "great confidence in his ability to convey complicated ideas to the public."[9] A man of broad learning with a record of service to the nation, Wilson was widely perceived as the very incarnation of the ideal orator: a man who used the power of eloquence to advance truth and the common good; a man of high ethical principles and prophetic vision; the "good man skilled at speaking." In an era of widespread nostalgia for the golden age of American oratory, Wilson "embodied the cultural ideal of the educated and principled orator who could be trusted as a steward of the public interest."[10]

Wilson had effectively appealed to public opinion before when battling with an uncooperative Congress. In the first two years of his presidency he overcame opposition to his New Freedom initiatives with careful appeals to public opinion, and in 1916 he prevailed in the great debate over preparedness by taking his case to the people. As Robert C. Hilderbrand has suggested, Wilson had every confidence in his "personal support among the American people" and in "his ability to win them over with a personal appeal."[11] Even more confident was his personal secretary and chief planner of the tour, Joseph Tumulty. Urging Wilson to take his case to the people, Tumulty predicted that a speaking tour would bring irresistible public pressure on the Senate to ratify the treaty. "It would be a great stimulant," Tumulty declared; it would mean "the utter rout of your political enemies." In remarkably similar language, Wilson's son-in-law and former secretary of the treasury William Gibbs McAdoo also advocated the tour. "A good many of your best friends are very eager to have you make argumentative speeches, in your irresistible style, to the people when you go to the country on the League of Nations," McAdoo wrote to the president on July 11, 1919. "I believe that such speeches from you would rout the opposition."[12]

Yet there was more behind Wilson's decision to tour than confidence that he would prevail. The tour also reflected Wilson's views on the character of true statesmanship, the obligations of presidential leadership, and the role of public opinion in the democratic process. As a scholar of politics and government, Wilson had long advocated reforms in the American political system to promote more robust public debate. For many years he advocated a British-style cabinet government as the best means of reinvigorating democratic deliberation. By the first decade of the twentieth century, however, he had abandoned the British model and had begun to imagine how a rhetorical presidency might promote both national unity and more vigorous political debate. In *Constitutional Government in the United States* (1908), Wilson observed that the nation had "grown more and more inclined . . . to look to the President as the unifying force in our complex system, the leader of both his party and of the nation," and he envisioned the president serving as the spokesman for public opinion in great national debates. Rather than promote some narrow partisan agenda, Wilson's rhetorical president assumed the obligation to educate, interpret, and give expression to public opinion. He did not manipulate or even persuade public opinion, but rather served as a "spokesman for the real sentiment and purpose of the country."[13]

Given his background and political views, the great mystery surrounding the debate over the League of Nations is not why Wilson chose to tour in the first place. As in Wilson's own day, the real mystery is why the tour failed to produce the desired results. Why, on this occasion, was Wilson unable to duplicate his earlier oratorical triumphs? Why was he unable to rally public opinion and pressure the Senate to ratify the treaty? Was the tour doomed from the start, as some historians have suggested?[14] Or did it reveal the limits of the modern, rhetorical presidency, as Jeffrey Tulis has argued?[15] Or did Wilson simply make the wrong rhetorical choices, choosing the wrong arguments or failing to exercise the same "discretion" in leading public opinion that he had in his earlier, more successful public campaigns?[16]

Answering these questions requires a different approach to Wilson's Western tour, an approach that closely scrutinizes the campaign in terms of prevailing views of oratory, presidential leadership, and public opinion. It requires that we ask the questions that a student of oratory and debate—a student like the young Woodrow Wilson himself—might have asked at the time: How did Wilson make the case for the treaty? How did he mobilize those already sympathetic to his cause, and how did he respond to the concerns and questions of those skeptical or critical of the agreement? In addition, we must ask about the role of public opinion in the outcome of the debate. What difference did public opinion make in the outcome of the debate? Indeed, what did public opinion mean in the days before polling? What effects did the Western tour have on public opinion, and what impact, if any, did public opinion have on the Senate's decision?

Wilson's own writings provide a starting point for answering these questions, for throughout his career he reflected at great length on questions of leadership, political deliberation, and public opinion. In works ranging from his schoolboy reflections on great orators to his most mature scholarly works, Wilson grappled with one central problem: how might the federal government respond energetically and efficiently to modern challenges, yet still retain its democratic character? Early in his career Wilson concluded that only a British-style parliamentary system could provide what he called "responsible" government. Later he came to see a dynamic, rhetorical presidency—one that both led and gave voice to public opinion—as the solution to the various ills he perceived in the Founders' constitutional order. According to Tulis, Wilson's rhetorical presidency has had a number of deleterious effects on American politics, including an "erosion of the processes of deliberation" and a "decay of political discourse." In Tulis's view, Wilson failed to take seriously the threat of demagoguery.[17] Yet Wilson actually worried a great deal about demagoguery, and he devoted much of his career to championing what he saw as the surest protections against demagogues: an enlightened class of political leaders combined with a well-informed and freely deliberating public. Tulis is wrong to blame Wilson for the excesses of today's rhetorical presidency. Wilson envisioned a rhetorically active presidency, but one constrained by the ethical and rhetorical standards of the neoclassical tradition.

Wilson's Western tour came at a transitional moment in the history of American public address. At the end of World War I, a Progressive renaissance in oratory and public deliberation had begun to give way to a new age of propaganda and scientific "opinion management." While public education and civic engagement had been dominant themes of the Progressive Era, the public relations and advertising industries of the 1920s inspired a new, more cynical view of public debate and mass persuasion. Perhaps more than any other speaker of his day, Woodrow Wilson embodied this tension between the old and the new. At times, he played the role of the orator-statesman, rising above personal and partisan interests and engaging his fellow citizens in "common counsel." At other times, he gave in to the frustrations of one embroiled in a bitter political debate, lashing out at his critics and trying to manipulate public opinion. Even over the course of his Western tour, as Mary McEdwards has suggested, Wilson descended "somewhat awkwardly" from the "detached, austere" style of a "dedicated, high-principled idealist" to the "level of the grass-roots politician." Resorting to a rhetorical style "long familiar" to most politicians but "abhorrent to him," he ultimately turned his League of Nations campaign into a "personal crusade," using "any and all methods" to win the debate and marshaling "every rhetorical weapon at his command."[18]

Historians, of course, have celebrated the final speech of the Western tour—Wilson's famous address in Pueblo, Colorado—as among the best of his career. Rhetorical scholars also have canonized the speech, counting it among the "top 100 speeches" of the twentieth century in a recent survey.[19] In many ways, however, the Pueblo speech epitomized Wilson's drift toward demagoguery, as he struck a defiant pose and resorted to maudlin emotionalism in an effort to rally public support for his uncompromising position. Claiming a public mandate, Wilson accused all who opposed him of betraying the boys who had died in the Great War. In doing so, he not only distorted public opinion but also sidestepped the real issues in the debate. Historians and even rhetorical scholars may proclaim the speech eloquent. But that only testifies to how completely we have lost touch with the neoclassical tradition that Wilson himself celebrated in his scholarly writings.

Establishing the context for my reappraisal of Wilson's Western tour, I begin by reviewing Wilson's scholarly writings on government, oratory, and presidential leadership. Recounting the evolution of his views on government from his earliest celebrations of the British parliamentary model to his more mature reflections upon what Tulis has called the rhetorical presidency, I show how Wilson helped lay the groundwork for the oratorical renaissance of the Progressive Era by imagining a classical rhetoric for the modern age. I then show how, for the most part, Wilson embodied his own ideals of oratorical statesmanship during his first term as president. Committed to reinvigorating public discussion, Wilson took his case for New Freedom reforms to the people, and later he promoted military preparedness with a "swing around the circle." In both cases, Wilson lived up to his own neoclassical principles and his vision of an active yet responsible rhetorical presidency.

In chapter 2, I begin my reexamination of the Western tour by recounting how, during the first leg of the tour, Wilson generally lived up to his own principles of oratorical statesmanship. Crossing the Midwest and upper Great Plains during his first ten days on the road, Wilson delivered wide-ranging surveys of the peace settlement and the proposed League of Nations, engaging his audiences in "common counsel" by explaining the principles embodied in the agreement and locating those principles in American public opinion. From the very first day, however, press coverage of the tour emphasized the president's attacks on his critics, and by the second week newspaper reporters began to lose interest in Wilson's elaborate explanations of the treaty. As a result, Wilson's speeches during this initial leg of the tour have not received as much attention as the more passionate and combative addresses he delivered later. They are the "forgotten speeches" of Wilson's Western tour.

In chapter 3, I show how a change in speech-making strategy seemed to pay off in California, as Wilson attracted huge and wildly enthusiastic audiences in the Golden State with a more aggressive style suggested by Joseph Tumulty. In San Francisco, Wilson effectively responded to Chinese and Irish American critics of the peace settlement. In San Diego, he rallied the largest crowd ever to gather in that city with one of the most passionate addresses of the tour, and in Los Angeles he was so warmly received that some reporters declared the debate over. All that might explain why, as he neared the end of the tour, Wilson himself claimed victory and issued an ultimatum to the Senate: either ratify the treaty without reservations or he would kill it himself. Wilson's new, more defiant tone proved a hit with the crowds. Yet it also hurt his chances of compromise with the Senate, particularly with those he most needed to persuade: the nineteen or twenty mild reservationists who held the balance of power.

In chapter 4, I examine how Wilson's drift toward demagoguery culminated in the most celebrated speech of the Western tour, his famous address in Pueblo, Colorado. Picking up the story with his remarkably combative address in Salt Lake City, I show how Wilson became even more belligerent in the two speeches leading up to the Pueblo address—in Cheyenne and in Denver. Next, I offer one of the few close readings of what Wilson actually said in Pueblo, showing how that address was neither original nor strategically astute. Waving the bloody shirt and attacking his critics, Wilson's speech in Pueblo not only destroyed whatever chances still remained for compromise but also portended some of the worst tendencies of the modern, rhetorical presidency. The Pueblo speech lives on in history and public memory as a "great" presidential address, but that may only be because of what happened afterward. By Wilson's own standards of oratorical states-manship, the Pueblo speech was among the worst of the tour.

Wilson's rhetorical choices may not entirely explain why he lost the League of Nations debate. But this study does offer a counterpoint to those, like Tulis, who have paid little attention to what Wilson actu-ally said during his Western tour. It also sheds light on an important transitional moment in the history of American public address. With electronic media and public opinion polling on the horizon, the Progressive Era had come to an end. The Progressives' celebration of democratic eloquence, public deliberation, and civic engagement was giving way to an age of public relations and scientific advertising. Wilson's Western tour reflected both the old and the new at this mo-ment of transition. After the Western tour, the rhetorical presidency would no longer be constrained by the neoclassical rhetorical tradition.

Nor would it reflect the Progressive Era's celebration of civic engagement and democratic deliberation. Reflecting the cultural ethos of the modern mass media, the rhetorical presidency eventually would bring the focus groups and "spin" machines of the "permanent campaign."[20] The oratorical renaissance of the Progressive Era has given way to the Age of Propaganda.

CHAPTER 1

The Rhetorical Presidency and Public
Deliberation in the Progressive Era

... the wisest thing to do with a fool is to encourage him
to hire a hall and discourse to his fellow citizens. Nothing
chills nonsense like exposure to the air; nothing dispels
folly like its publication.
CONSTITUTIONAL GOVERNMENT
IN THE UNITED STATES, 1908

Writing in his shorthand diary during his freshman and sophomore years at Princeton, "Tommy" Wilson reflected on baseball, the "fairer sex," and the character of the professors and students he met during these important, formative years of his life. Along the way, he also wrote about oratory, politics, and the future of the American republic. In brief yet surprisingly bold political commentaries, Wilson predicted that the American republic, as conceived by the Founders, would "never celebrate another centennial," at least not "under its present Constitution and laws." In 1876, he even marked Independence Day by proclaiming the "English form of government" the "only true one" and by again predicting that America would "never celebrate another centennial" under its existing Constitution: "How much happier [?] she would be now if she had England's form of government instead of the miserable delusion of a republic. A republic too founded upon the notion of abstract liberty!"[1]

No wonder historian Richard Hofstadter branded Wilson a "thorough Anglophile."[2] Yet Wilson's embrace of the British model was but his first answer to a question that he struggled with throughout his career: How might the federal government be both energized and made more accountable to the people? Convinced that the Founders had impractically separated the legislative and executive branches, Wilson sensed that Congress had become too absorbed in administrative tasks to perform its most important purpose: debating the great issues of the day "in the presence of the whole country." A British-style cabinet government would respond more efficiently to pressing national problems yet still remain accountable to the voters. Moreover, it would assure that only the best men—genuine "orator-statesmen"—would rise to positions of leadership. As Wilson wrote in one of his most famous schoolboy reflections: "The cardinal feature of Cabinet government . . . is responsible leadership—the leadership and authority of a small body of men who have won the foremost places in their party . . . by evidence of high ability upon the floor of Congress in the stormy play of debate."[3]

Wilson later abandoned the British model and instead imagined a uniquely American solution to the problem of a government dominated by Congress: an active, *rhetorical* president who presided over great national debates and served as the voice of "the whole people." Inspired by the example of Theodore Roosevelt, Wilson envisioned the president as a leader and interpreter of public opinion who, in great national debates, would speak both *to* and *for* the American people. Rising above partisan politics, Wilson's rhetorical president would be an "orator-statesman," upholding neoclassical standards of "responsible" speech and engaging the public in "common counsel." According to Jeffrey Tulis, Wilson's vision of a more energetic and rhetorically active president—Wilson's "rhetorical presidency"—departed so radically from the Founders' plan that it constituted, in effect, a "second constitution." More importantly, in Tulis's view, it had a number of deleterious effects on the American political system, including an "erosion" of the deliberative process and the unrealistic expectation that all presidents would be great orators.[4]

In blaming Wilson for the modern rhetorical presidency, Tulis not only exaggerated Wilson's influence but also the magnitude of the "revolution" that he brought to the presidency. As Richard Ellis has argued, recent historical research has shown that the popularization of various forms of presidential discourse—acceptance speeches, inaugural addresses, and campaign speeches, to name just a few— actually began long before Wilson arrived on the scene. A number of Wilson's predecessors, including Andrew Jackson, Andrew Johnson, Grover Cleveland, and William McKinley, did not hesitate to "go public," and at least one president who came later, Franklin Delano Roosevelt, arguably did more than Wilson to shape the modern rhetorical presidency. At most, Wilson represented the "culmination" of a number of changes in the "rhetorical patterns" of the presidency that had been evolving for years, according to Ellis. He just happened to be in office when "all the pieces" came together in a "recognizably modern" pattern.[5]

Nor did Wilson envision today's rhetorical presidency—the presidency of "sound bites," focus groups, and poll-driven speeches. To the contrary, Wilson shared Tulis's concern with demagoguery, and he complained about many of the same trends in popular speech that troubled Tulis. Like Tulis, Wilson worried that an overly popular style of presidential leadership might degrade public discourse and subvert deliberation.[6] Wilson envisioned a president who gave voice to public opinion, yet who also moderated "the heats and the hastes, the passions and the thoughtless impulses" of the people.[7] In addition, Wilson never advocated that presidents routinely go "over the head" of Congress. To the contrary, he was "centrally concerned with safeguarding traditional institutional arrangements against the very sort of demagogic populist leaders and appeals that so trouble Tulis."[8] Far from encouraging the excesses of the modern rhetorical presidency, Wilson upheld standards of responsible speech grounded in the neoclassical tradition—a tradition that was "at base an ethical tradition that required its adherents to live up to an exalted code of conduct."[9]

During his first term as president, Wilson embodied that neoclassical tradition. Pushing his New Freedom legislation, Wilson carefully balanced his appeals to public opinion with constructive bargaining with Congress. Wilson again modeled what he had in mind in his academic writings as he campaigned for preparedness in 1916. During his first "swing around the circle" as president, Wilson eschewed the passionate, partisan appeals of the "spellbinders" of the era and instead cast himself as the facilitator of a great national debate and a spokesman for the "whole people." When war came, of course, the Wilson administration launched the most massive propaganda campaign in history, betraying the president's commitment to public deliberation by silencing dissent and manipulating public opinion. For the most part, however, Wilson's presidency reflected the ideals of his scholarly writings. In general, Wilson strove to be the orator-statesman of the neoclassical tradition.

This chapter establishes the context for my reexamination of Woodrow Wilson's Western tour by revisiting the theory and practice of Wilsonian politics. Examining both his scholarly writings and the theory implicit in his political leadership, I outline the attitudes toward oratory, presidential leadership, and pubic deliberation that defined Wilson's vision of a responsible rhetorical presidency. First, I examine how, in his earliest reflections on politics, Wilson grappled with the question of how the American system might be made both more energetic and more accountable to public opinion. As a student of politics in the Gilded Age, Wilson wrote and spoke prolifically about the need for oratorical leadership and a revival of public deliberation. Imagining a revival of oratory and debate under a cabinet-style government in America, he also cultivated his own rhetorical skills in anticipation of the role he might someday play in American politics. Second, I examine how, in the context of the Progressive Era, Wilson revised his earlier reform program and developed his theory of a rhetorical presidency. Taking a close look at his most mature scholarly work, *Constitutional Government in the United States* (1908), I show how Wilson actually anticipated many of the objections to today's rhetorical presidency and proposed something quite different: a presidency that transcended partisanship, eschewed personal and passionate appeals to public opinion, and instead aimed to educate, unite, and give voice to the people through a process of "common counsel." Finally, I examine how Wilson, as president, generally embodied his own vision of a responsible rhetorical presidency. Recalling Wilson's campaign for New Freedom legislation and his "swing around the circle" on behalf of preparedness in 1916, I argue that during his first term Wilson generally lived up to his ideal of a president who both led and followed public opinion. As a wartime president, however, Wilson would betray his own principles by presiding over one of the most notorious propaganda campaigns in history: the Committee on Public Information's efforts to build a prowar consensus.

Oratory, Statesmanship, and Public Deliberation

In a prize-winning oration that he delivered as a student at Princeton on January 30, 1877, Woodrow Wilson painted a famous portrait of the "Ideal Statesman." Declaring that there was "no worthier ambition," Wilson described the "True Statesman" as "a man of conspicuous business ability and a profound lawyer," but also a man of principle. "No *partizan* can be a statesman," Wilson declared, for unless he could "rise above party and act from broad and fixed principles" he could not "aspire to the exalted name of statesman." The "true statesman" possessed Shakespeare's "divine insight into human nature," along with Benjamin Franklin's "deep sympathy with all the efforts and strivings of the common mind." He had to leave "self out of every question," always upholding the common good over selfish interests. In addition, the ideal statesman was "in advance of his age," pointing "the true way" with his "prophetic finger." This prophetic insight—this ability to foresee the future—was "one of the most important" characteristics of Wilson's "ideal statesman." Above all, however, the true statesman was an orator; he displayed "an orator's soul, an orator's words, an orators actions."[10] For Wilson that meant something much different, something much more, than it might to the modern reader. Drawing upon the classical tradition, Wilson's ideal orator was a man of broad liberal learning and high moral character. Wilson's orator-statesman was Quintilian's "good man skilled in speaking."

The story of the young "Tommy" Wilson's own remarkable efforts to make himself into an orator-statesman has been told many times. The son of a Presbyterian minister renowned for his preaching, Wilson began studying the great British and American orators in history at a young age. His father, the Reverend Joseph Ruggles Wilson, taught rhetoric at Jefferson College and "sacred oratory" at Columbia Theological Seminary. Nostalgic for "the bygone era when oratory had a more central place in American society," the elder Wilson "never tired of telling how he had seen the great Webster speak in person, nor of bemoaning the fallen state of contemporary public discourse."[11] The Reverend Wilson believed (as his son would later argue) that all young men aspiring to leadership should train in oratory and debate, and for him that meant much more than developing a pleasing style or an effective delivery. For the Reverend Wilson, there was a strong philosophical and ethical component to the study of rhetoric. In his view, oratory was a "lifelong vocation," and the orator had to strive not only to appear to be but actually to *be* the "good man skilled in speaking."[12]

Wilson drilled incessantly to develop his own speaking skills, and he spent many hours studying the great orators in history. In late adolescence, he could be found practicing his elocution by reading great speeches aloud in his father's empty church.[13] As a student at Davidson College, Wilson was elected to the Eumenean Society, a college debating club,[14] and he began to more seriously pursue his life's ambition: to "make himself into an oratorical statesman of the first rank—an American Gladstone."[15] Wilson would later claim that his intellectual awakening came during his freshman year at Princeton, but as historian John Milton Cooper Jr. has noted, his "realization of his interests and abilities" appears to have been more gradual and "occurred particularly during the two years before he entered Princeton," when he was a student at Davidson.[16]

At Princeton (then the College of New Jersey), Wilson's study of oratory became a more serious scholarly pursuit, as well as the focus of his extracurricular activities. While pursuing his regular studies, Wilson read Aristotle's *Rhetoric*,[17] and he copied passages from the speeches of Edmund Burke, John C. Calhoun, and Webster, among others, into his

Index Rerum.[18] During his first two years, he also was very active in the American Whig Society, one of two literary and debating societies at Princeton, and he helped found the Liberal Debating Club by drafting a constitution based on the British parliamentary model.[19] Wilson also kept a shorthand diary in which he commented on orators and oratory, as well as on his own "efforts to improve his style in writing and speaking."[20] Typical of Wilson's diary entries was his commentary on one of the rhetoric texts he had read, Louis Bautain's *The Art of Extempore Speaking:* "Read good deal of Bautain's Art of Extempore Speaking. It is an excellent book and I enjoyed reading it more than I have enjoyed any book in some time. The style is extremely pleasing and every page contains advice which every speaker would do well to follow to the letter."[21]

Wilson became a campus leader at Princeton and, "within decorous limits, a bit of a rebel."[22] In 1877, he wrote a series of editorials complaining that "very little attention" was paid to oratory at Princeton and calling for a "systematic course of instruction" in the "Ciceronian art."[23] In one editorial, he even criticized Princeton's only professor of elocution for dividing his time between Princeton and "several preparatory schools and young ladies' seminaries." Calling for the hiring of "some eminent professor of declamation and voice-training," Wilson concluded that "systematic and intelligent training" was "all important" to the development of the orator.[24] In his editorials at Princeton, Wilson wrote mostly about the practical skills of composing and delivering a speech, but before long he would place more emphasis on issues of character, leadership, and democratic deliberation.

In his final year at Princeton, 1878–79, Wilson published a prize-winning essay on William Earl Chatham, "the first of Parliamentary orators,"[25] as well as an essay frequently cited as the culmination of his early political thought: "Cabinet Government in the United States." In some ways, "Cabinet Government" was more about rhetoric than politics, and it marked the beginning of Wilson's long scholarly journey toward a comprehensive theory of rhetoric and political culture. Proclaiming "*debate* . . . the essential function of a popular representative body," Wilson introduced the central issue in much of his scholarship over the next decade: How might the American constitutional system be reformed to assure "responsible government," government that legislated "in the presence of the whole country," in an atmosphere of "open and free debate." Insisting that the "very life of free, popular institutions" depended on their "breathing the bracing air of thorough, exhaustive, and open discussions," Wilson complained that there was "little real deliberation" in the Congress of his day. He then proposed a radical solution: a British-style cabinet government. Proclaiming the "most despotic government under the control of wise statesmen" preferable to "the freest ruled by demagogues," Wilson concluded that only a cabinet-style government could restore genuine debate and attract "men of real ability" to public service:

> The cardinal feature of Cabinet government . . . is responsible leadership,—the leadership and authority of a small body of men who have won the foremost places in their party . . . by evidence of high ability upon the floor of Congress in the stormy play of debate. None but the ablest can become leaders and masters in this keen tournament in which arguments are the weapons, and the people the judges. . . . To keep men of the strongest mental and moral fibre in Congress would become a party necessity. Party triumph would then be a matter of might in debate, not of supremacy in subterfuge.[26]

After graduating from Princeton, Wilson studied law at the University of Virginia for a year and a half before dropping out to complete his law studies on his own. He found the practice of law disappointing, however, and after a tough year in Atlanta he embarked upon doctoral studies at the Johns Hopkins University. Throughout this period he continued to write about "responsible" government, and by the time he was awarded his Ph.D. in June of 1886 he already had begun to establish a reputation as a promising young scholar of American politics and history.

While at Virginia, Wilson won election to the Jefferson Society and went on to become the society's president and the principal author of its new constitution. In orations and debates before the society, Wilson fashioned himself a practical speaker who appealed to reason rather than emotion. Following a debate with a future Pulitzer Prize winner and U.S. Senator, William Cabell Bruce, Wilson was disappointed when he was named best orator rather than best debater. For Wilson, "oratory" still had connotations of emotional and stylistic excess.[27] Wilson also reflected on oratory in a speech about John Bright delivered before the Jefferson Society at Virginia. Declaring the orator who maintained "complete sovereignty over his emotions . . . a thousandfold more powerful and impressive than he who 'saws the air' and 'tears a passion to tatters,'" Wilson defended Bright against charges of demagoguery, claiming that he actually possessed those "qualities of eloquence and single-minded devotion" that marked those great American statesmen, Webster and Calhoun. In describing Bright's virtues, Wilson emphasized how he never allowed his "passions" to "master him." His "marvelous powers of public speech" were grounded not in physical or emotional display but in praiseworthy principles and noble ideas:

No orator ever more signally illustrated the truth that eloquence is not of the lips alone. Eloquence is never begotten by empty pates. Groveling minds are never winged with high and noble thoughts. Eloquence consists not in sonorous sound or brilliant phrases. *Thought* is the fibre, thought is the *pith* of eloquence. Eloquence lies in the thought, not in the throat. . . . It is persuasion inspired by conviction.[28]

Wilson's distaste for passionate display reflected his faith in public opinion. In an unpublished essay on "Congressional Government" written during his first year at Virginia, he responded to fears that a cabinet government would be dominated by "artful dialecticians," producing a "reign of sophists rather than of wise men." These were "assuredly the objections of ignorance," Wilson argued, for "sophistry" could not walk "openly in the cloak of wisdom and truth unchallenged and undiscovered." As Wilson explained: "Subtle word-play, dialectic dexterity, rhetorical adroitness, passionate declamation cannot shield him from the searching scrutiny to which his principles and his plans will be subjected at every turn of the proceedings of the Houses. . . . A charlatan cannot long play the statesman successfully while the whole country is looking critically on." Few persons had any "just conception" of the "informing and unmasking disclosures of thorough debate," he argued, and he disagreed forcefully with those who believed that the masses could not be "brought to exercise intelligent discretion." From that opinion "I utterly dissent," Wilson declared; "I believe . . . the people's choice will be deliberate and wise."[29]

In December 1882, Wilson submitted a book-length polemic titled "Government by Debate" to Harper and Brothers. As Wilson described the book in a preliminary outline, "Government by Debate" addressed two essential questions: "Why have we no great *statesmen?*" And "Why have we no great political *orators?*" For Wilson, part of the answer was to be found in the lack of great moral and constitutional issues since the Civil War. We have no great orators, he argued, because "there is no inspiration—there are no *themes* to inspire—no *causes* to incite."[30] Yet the problems were also structural and institutional, and to address those problems Wilson proposed not only a cabinet government but also a host of other changes in the powers and terms of the president and members of Congress. Wilson's call for "sweeping constitutional changes" proved too "radical" for the publishers.[31] He subsequently conceived of a "different kind of book," a historical and descriptive study of the American system inspired by Walter Bagehot's classic comparison of the British and American systems.[32] The result was the work that served as Wilson's doctoral dissertation and, when published in 1885, immediately established his reputation as a political scientist: *Congressional Government: A Study in American Politics.* Although largely cannibalized from his earlier writings, this work remains the fullest explication of Wilson's early views on rhetoric and politics.

Divided into discussions of the House, the Senate, and the Executive, *Congressional Government* did not so directly advocate reform, but it explored at even greater depth the defects that Wilson sensed in the Founders' design. In his chapter on the House, for example, Wilson again lamented the lack of genuine debate in Congress, complaining that debates on the floor of the House had none of the "searching, critical, illuminating character of the highest order of parliamentary debate." Public opinion could not be "instructed or elevated" by congressional debate because Congress had become "divorced" from the "general mass of national sentiment." In his chapter on the Senate, Wilson emphasized another of his old complaints: the lack of great orator-statesmen. It was only "natural" that "orators should be the leaders of a self-governing people," he wrote, for representative government was, by definition, government by advocacy, discussion, and persuasion. Yet since the Civil War, the Senate had produced more "artful dialecticians" than genuine orators—men skilled at "tricks of phrase" and "rushing declamation," but lacking the character and instincts of great orators. "Men may be clever and engaging speakers," Wilson observed, but they could "scarcely be orators without that force of character, that readiness of resource, that clearness of vision, that grasp of intellect, that courage of conviction, that earnestness of purpose, and that instinct and capacity for leadership which are the eight horses that draw the triumphal chariot of every leader and ruler of free men." Recalling the great British orators, Wilson argued that in nations where oratory was valued, only the best men rose to leadership—as evidenced by Sir Robert Walpole, Chatham, Burke, William Pitt, and William Gladstone. This, then, was the surest protection against demagoguery, according to Wilson: a class of men educated to be "orator-statesmen," along with a public sufficiently informed and engaged to demand leadership by men of character and vision.[33]

In *Congressional Government,* Wilson had yet to recognize the potential of the presidency to provide the public leadership that he found lacking in a system dominated by Congress. At this point, he remained focused on the shortcomings of Congress and the implications of the lack of genuine debate for public opinion and representative democracy. "An effective representative body," Wilson wrote, "ought . . . not only to speak the will of the nation, . . . but also to lead it to its conclusions, to utter the voice of its opinions, and to serve as its eyes in superintending all matters of government,—which Congress does not do." Congress not only failed "to embody the wisdom and will of its constituents";

it also failed to seize "opportunities for informing and guiding public opinion." As a result, those tasks had fallen to the press, which spoke "entirely without authority" and privileged the "gossip of the street." The only hope was that men with "something very like genius"—men with that "extraordinary gift of eloquence"—might return to Congress and once again "captivate" the public. Unfortunately, that was not something that every generation could hope to see, Wilson lamented, as "genius and eloquence" were too "rare to be depended upon for the instruction and guidance of the masses."[34]

The publication of *Congressional Government* capped an eventful year in which Wilson married and also accepted his first faculty position at Bryn Mawr College. After an uninspiring three years at Bryn Mawr, Wilson moved to Wesleyan University in Connecticut, where he remained until his return to Princeton in 1890. At Princeton, Wilson's academic reputation soared as he developed a reputation as an outstanding classroom lecturer and published prolifically. Between 1893 and 1902, Wilson published nine books and thirty-five articles, beginning with a history of the Civil War, *Division and Reunion*, and ending with his five-volume *History of the American People*. These works lacked the scholarly merits of *Congressional Government*, but with their emphasis on broad themes and American heroes, they attracted a more popular readership and earned Wilson a national reputation.[35]

As a professor at Princeton, Wilson helped develop an undergraduate curriculum to prepare students for public service. He also earned a noteworthy reputation as a public lecturer. Wilson's papers from the 1890s are filled with reports of public lectures and addresses before alumni groups, historical and literary clubs, professional and community organizations, and churches on such topics as "Leaders of Men" and "Patriotism in Time of Peace." Wilson's triumphal moment came at Princeton's sesquicentennial celebration in 1896, when he delivered what the editors of the Wilson Papers have called "the outstanding speech of his academic career and one of the noblest of his lifetime": "Princeton in the Nation's Service."[36] Partly a celebration of the school's history and partly a statement of his own educational philosophy, the address recalled the long list of public men associated with Princeton and celebrated its "spirit of service." Yet beyond such platitudes, the address challenged the Progressive Era's faith in science and defended "the old drill, the old memory of times gone by, the old schooling in precedent and tradition." Imagining his "perfect place of learning," Wilson described "a free place" where "sagacious" and "hard-headed" men debated the "world's questions" and became accustomed to the "rough ways of democracy." It was a place of high ideals but "no fool's paradise." Wilson wanted students to "hear the truth about the past and hold debate about the affairs of the present," but they were to do so "with knowledge and without passion."[37] Echoing his schoolboy reflections on the ideal statesman, Wilson advocated combining an old-fashioned liberal arts education with the rough-and-tumble of political debate. It was, in some ways, a bold departure from prevailing pedagogical thought. But as the editors of the Wilson Papers have concluded, the sesquicentennial address made him one of the most "highly favored" professors at Princeton and eventually "echoed far beyond the Princeton campus."[38]

In 1902, the trustees of Princeton unanimously elected Wilson the thirteenth president of the college. By that time, he already had become well known as an educator and a scholar, and his views on oratory and statesmanship had been widely published. As Dayton David McKean noted in *A History and Criticism of American Public Address*, "Wilson never published any systematic statement of his views on the art of public speaking," but he did develop an implicit theory of rhetoric in his writings on history and politics. First, "content" was "fundamental to eloquence," for Wilson believed that eloquence could never be achieved in the absence of "high and noble thoughts." Second, he stressed the need to adapt to one's audiences, yet he most admired those orators who did so without compromising their principles and convictions. Third, he advocated emotional self-restraint, for an excess of passion could undermine even the best ideas and frighten more moderate and practical men. According to McKean, these principles were not only implicit in Wilson's scholarly writings, but they also guided his own oratorical practices, both as an academic and a politician.[39]

Yet Wilson's theory of rhetoric went well beyond such textbook principles of effective public speaking. Distinguishing the genuine orator-statesman from the artful dialectician, Wilson recognized that sophistry might win over an audience, but only the orator-statesman exhibited the true spirit of eloquence—a spirit rooted in broad, liberal learning, an understanding of the "character, spirit, and thought of the nation," and knowledge of "the history and leading conceptions" of the nation's political institutions. Wilson did not view such popular "spellbinders" as William Jennings Bryan or Robert La Follette as true orator-statesmen. To the contrary, he found it troubling that the likes of Bryan could compete for the White House with only "a good voice and a few ringing sentences." He complained more generally about the popularity of speakers who "disturb without instructing" and who "exaggerate, distort, [and] distract."[40] If one hoped to "catch some of the true spirit of oratory," if one hoped to "bring back to the ears and hearts of the American people some of the old strains of eloquence which used to delight them," there was only one way, according to Wilson: by studying and emulating the great orators of history, particularly Demosthenes and the "great English orators." Calling "the imitation of classical models" the "chief and best means of training the orator," Wilson used his editorials at Princeton to champion the oratorical pedagogy that he himself followed: "Only as the constant companions of Demosthenes, Cicero, Burke, Fox, Canning, and Webster can we hope to become orators."[41]

During the Progressive Era, Woodrow Wilson would continue to refine his views on oratory and political leadership. He also would put those theories to the test, first as president of Princeton, then as a rising young star of the Democratic Party. Consistent with his early writings, Wilson seized his "opportunities for informing and guiding public opinion."[42] Embodying his own ideals as an orator-statesman, he earned a reputation as a reformer with extraordinary oratorical talents. Yet Wilson also learned that there were limits to what one could accomplish through oratory—something he had recognized in his undergraduate writings. "In a free government founded on public opinion," Wilson observed in his biographical sketch of Chatham, the "great principles must be worked out cautiously, step by step." Public opinion "must not be outstripped," he observed, "but kept pace with."[43] In his zeal as a reformer, Wilson sometimes lost sight of that principle.

Rhetoric and Public Opinion in the Progressive Era

The Progressive Era was "a very different age," as Woodrow Wilson himself put it during the 1912 campaign. It was a "new social age," a "new era of human relationships."[44] In textbook accounts, the Progressive Era has been defined as a period of rapid social change as reformers restored government "to the hands of the people," then used that "popularly controlled government to regulate industry, finance, transportation, agriculture, and foreign policy in the interest of the many rather than the few." In the conventional view, journalistic "muckrakers" pointed the way during this period of democratization and social progress, and the reform impulse "reached a climax" under the leadership of Woodrow Wilson.[45]

Serious historical scholarship has long complicated this conventional wisdom. As early as 1955, Hofstadter described progressivism as "a rather vague and not altogether cohesive or consistent movement" that aimed at "some not very clearly specified self-reformation." Hofstadter was also among the first to sense "much that was retrograde and delusive" in the spirit of the progressivism—even "a little that was vicious."[46] In the 1960s, New Left revisionists went even further, arguing that "the period from approximately 1900 until the United States' intervention in the war"—the period "labeled the 'progressive' era by virtually all historians"—was "really an era of conservatism." According to Gabriel Kolko, for example, businessmen "defined the limits" of governmental intervention into economic affairs, and political capitalism "redirected the radical potential of mass grievances and aspirations" by channeling them into reform efforts that were "frequently designed by businessmen to serve the ends of business."[47]

Historians today generally recognize the Progressive Era as a complex mix of diverse and often contradictory impulses. As Ellen Fitzpatrick has argued, the "heterogeneity" of progressives across the nation has "discouraged historians who have sought to define a singular Progressive movement."[48] Moreover, historians now recognize that not "everything that happened in the period, or for that matter everything done under the banner of reform," represented "progress"—at least by "any modern definition" of the term.[49] At home, blacks suffered through the worst period in race relations since the Civil War during the Progressive Era, while abroad "progressive" America "warred ruthlessly on subject peoples, dominated weaker neighbors, and exerted its power over much of the world."[50] In race relations and foreign policy, what Hofstadter described as the "retrograde" impulses of the Progressive Era were especially obvious. For some historians, generalizations about "progressivism" are "meaningless and clear definition impossible."[51]

Yet to emphasize the diversity and ideological contradictions of the Progressive Era is to overlook important commonalities that, at the time, defined the essential spirit of the age. Most notably, "practically all self-described progressives" believed in a "national interest" or "public good" superior to "special interests and market outcomes."[52] And however else they may have differed, progressives believed that this "national" or "public" good was best revealed, not through philosophical or scientific investigation, but through public deliberation. For many progressives, the essential problem of the age was not poverty, nor corruption in government, nor even industrialization and the trusts, but rather what John Dewey would later call "the problem of the public": the need for improvements in "the methods and conditions of debate, discussion, and persuasion."[53] In an age of complex issues and unprecedented challenges, progressives worried that powerful special interests threatened to supplant the voice of the people, and they sought to revitalize and even reinvent government "by the people." Assuming that people were "basically rational," progressives believed that the "citizenry of America, if properly informed and empowered, would insist that government eschew special interests to pursue the common good." An educated and informed citizenry, they believed, would demand "justice" and do what was "morally right."[54]

Many Progressive Era reforms, from the movement to open schoolhouses to town meetings to the founding of many of today's civic and volunteer associations, reflected this faith in democratic deliberation. In their efforts to educate the public, promote public discussion, and give more organized and efficient expression to public opinion, progressives turned settlement houses into community forums, revived the Chautauqua movement, and appointed "civic secretaries" to organize public meetings and debates in local communities. They also invented school newspapers and university extension programs to bridge the gap between educational institutions and the communities they served. Yet progressives did not just invent new institutions and deliberative forums, they also looked to the past, nostalgically recalling a bygone era that was "more perfectly democratic, when power was wielded not by irresponsible political machines and mammoth corporations, but by platform giants whose only real hold was their capacity to convince their fellow citizens to lay aside selfish and parochial interests."[55] Progressives were thus both forward- and backward-looking. They invented new forums and new ways of talking about politics, yet they also longed for a return to the "golden age" of American oratory.

The result was what Robert Kraig has dubbed the "second oratorical renaissance"—an era in which oratory "that advanced issues and ideas became a more important part of the political landscape than it had been for a generation."[56] In political campaigns, on the lecture circuit, and in a variety of crusades led by "a new breed of reform politician," oratory again came to play a "determining role" in the political and social life of America. There were again "great debates" in Congress, and "in a development that would have significant repercussions for the rest of the century," the presidency became "a mighty platform for oratorical leadership."[57] All across America, ordinary citizens gathered in schools, in churches, and even in tents to listen to orators and to debate among themselves. By participating in such forums, ordinary Americans "learned the necessary skills of a democratic public: how to listen, how to argue, and how to deliberate."[58] The Progressive Era, in short, witnessed a remarkable renaissance of oratory and public deliberation; it was a most "rhetorical" of times.

Yet some of the key terms of Progressive Era ideology—organization, efficiency, rationality, expertise, and science—also contained the seeds of a very different view of democratic deliberation and public opinion. This view, rarely expressed early in the era but clearly manifested during World War I and in the postwar era, held that the "public good *could not* emerge from a democratic process that included everyone, because too many people lacked sufficient virtue and knowledge."[59] Advocates of this view favored a large, paternalistic government, guided by experts rather than the collective will, and some pushed for tougher voter registration rules and even literacy tests in the name of "good government"—that is, as "progressive" reforms. According to these advocates, it fell upon government, experts, and other elites to organize, direct, and articulate public opinion. In this view, public opinion did not rise up out of collective deliberation but rather was manufactured and manipulated "from above."[60]

This view of democracy and public opinion did not emerge out of a reactionary backlash against progressive reform. To the contrary, it was implicit in the writings of some of the leading progressive thinkers, including Herbert Croly and the young Walter Lippmann. In one of the most influential political treatises of the era, *The Promise of American Life,* Croly endorsed the "superior political wisdom" of Alexander Hamilton and concluded that the "national public interest" must be determined by experts and affirmed by a strong, charismatic national leader through "positive and aggressive action."[61] In his 1914 book *Drift and Mastery,* Lippmann likewise proclaimed the "scientific spirit" the "discipline of democracy" and argued for a strong central government guided by experts rather than public opinion.[62] Lippmann's antidemocratic skepticism reached full flower after the Great War, in *Public Opinion*—"the most damaging critique of public opinion and democracy yet written."[63] Yet the foundations of Lippmann's skepticism were laid a decade earlier by what David Danbom has called "scientific progressivism." Instead of the Christian principles that "fueled the initial thrust" of the progressive movement, scientific progressives had "faith in the expert rather than the goodness of the average citizen" and "yearned for an organized and efficient America rather than a morally regenerate one."[64]

Perhaps more than any other figure, Woodrow Wilson embodied

the tensions and contradictions of the Progressive Era. On the one hand, Wilson spent much of his scholarly life celebrating the classical oratorical tradition and advocating reforms to revitalize public debate and democratic deliberation. At every opportunity, he expressed his faith in public opinion and the wisdom of the "common man." On the other hand, he was the Princeton-educated intellectual who, as president, declared himself "the sole arbiter of the public interest" and demanded "acquiescence rather than real consensus."[65] As Hofstadter observed in *The American Political Tradition*, there was always "something insubstantial, . . . something forced" about Wilson's attitude toward the common folk. The "fact that he strove so consciously to be a democrat," in Hofstadter's view, was the "best evidence that by instinct he was not."[66]

The tensions in Wilson's political thought were clearly manifested in his most mature scholarly work, *Constitutional Government in the United States* (1908). Credited with inventing the modern rhetorical presidency, *Constitutional Government* reflected the Progressive Era's nostalgia for great orators and debates. In its emphasis on empowering the common people, it also reflected the era's faith in deliberative democracy and public opinion. At the same time, however, *Constitutional Government* stressed "the need for more energy in the political system,"[67] and it imagined a rhetorical presidency with enormous powers to lead and interpret public opinion. There is "but one national voice in the country," Wilson wrote in one of the most famous lines in the book, and "that is the voice of the President."[68]

In elaborating his vision of a president who spoke for the "whole people," Wilson recognized the potential for the president to dominate American politics. From "generation to generation," Wilson observed, "we have grown more and more inclined . . . to look to the President as the unifying force in our complex system." Elaborating on the sources of the president's power and authority, Wilson wrote:

The nation as a whole has chosen him, and is conscious that it has no other political spokesman. His is the only national voice in affairs. . . . His position takes the imagination of the country. He is the representative of no constituency, but of the whole people. When he speaks in his true character, he speaks for no special interest.[69]

If the president "rightly" interpreted "the national thought" and "boldly" insisted upon it, he could become politically "irresistible," for the country never felt "the zest of action so much as when its President is of such insight and calibre." The public had an "instinct . . . for unified action, and it craves a single leader," Wilson concluded. By discerning, articulating, and enacting the "real sentiment and purpose of the country," the president alone could satisfy the public's "instinct" for "unified action"—that craving for leadership that went unsatisfied in a government dominated by Congress.[70]

As Daniel Stid has argued, there can be "little doubt" that Wilson wrote *Constitutional Government* with Theodore Roosevelt in mind.[71] At times, Wilson seemed to comment directly on Roosevelt's leadership, and in his lectures during this same period he openly praised Roosevelt. "Whatever else we may think or say of Theodore Roosevelt," he told his undergraduates at Princeton, "we must admit that he is an aggressive leader. He led Congress—he was not driven by Congress."[72] At the same time, however, Wilson considered Roosevelt "brash and strident"—too much the "spellbinder"—and he "shared the widespread misgivings about the ex-president's supposed dictatorial tendencies."[73] Prone to vituperative harangues and leading too far in advance of public opinion, Roosevelt lacked the discernment and prudence—that is, he lacked the *character*—of Wilson's ideal statesman. He was an energetic and effective leader, but he was not of that "small class" of "wise and prudent" men Wilson imagined leading the country.[74]

In *Constitutional Government*, Wilson recognized that there were practical limits to what a president could accomplish by "going public." As Stid has argued, Wilson never suggested that appeals to public opinion should be "the sole, or even the primary, mode of leading Congress." He envisioned presidents using popular rhetoric "to focus the political debate in order to foster a consensus behind their national agendas," and when "feasible and appropriate" appealing "to the country for support." Yet appeals to public opinion were not always feasible or appropriate, and the president's leadership of public opinion had "to complement—it could not replace"—more "intimate communication" with Congress. Even under the best of circumstances "going public" provided only an "indirect form of control" over the actions of Congress. Indeed, going "over the heads" of Congress was sometimes not "a viable method" at all, as in the case of a president "trying to overcome opposition in the Senate."[75] The Senate, Wilson wrote, was "not so immediately sensitive to opinion" as the House and was "apt to grow, if anything, more stiff" if the president tried to pressure it with appeals to public opinion.[76]

Wilson's vision was thus more limited and constrained than today's rhetorical presidency. Wilson's rhetorical president did not routinely appeal to public opinion. Nor did he engage in partisan campaigns to force Congress into deferring to his agenda. As the spokesman for the "whole people," Wilson's ideal president transcended partisan divides, and he did not seek to manipulate public opinion but rather to engage the citizenry in "common counsel." He prevailed not by manipulating public opinion but by the force of his ideas and arguments in the "play of debate." Wilson's rhetorical president pursued bold policy initiatives, but he never led too far in advance of public opinion. Above all, Wilson's rhetorical president operated within the strict confines of an oratorical tradition that was, "at base," an "ethical tradition." Reflecting a "connection between eloquence and character" that has "atrophied" in our own day, he imagined a rhetorical presidency occupied by orator-statesmen who lived up to "an exalted code of conduct."[77]

As president of Princeton University from 1902 to 1910, Wilson both promoted and embodied his own theories of oratorical statesmanship. In his inaugural address at Princeton, he pledged to pursue the mission he had articulated six years earlier in his sesquicentennial address: the training of "efficient and enlightened men" for leadership and public service.[78] During the first few years of his presidency, he also used a "careful program of speeches and written statements" to win alumni and faculty support for curriculum reforms, fundraising efforts, and a "preceptorial," or British-style, tutorial system. The preceptorial system in particular put Princeton "on the map educationally" and made Wilson "something of an academic hero."[79] Yet toward the end of his presidency, Wilson lost two major reform battles with the Old Guard at Princeton: a dispute over Princeton's traditional "eating clubs," and another involving the location of a new graduate school. Championing democratic principles in both disputes, Wilson attracted national attention, but he also displayed his tendency to lead too far in advance of public opinion.

In the first of the two controversies, Wilson sought to replace the school's traditional eating clubs with a system of "quadrangles" with dormitories, eating halls, classrooms, and housing for some faculty. In Wilson's view, such an arrangement would eliminate "rivalries and cliques" among Princeton's students and create a sense of community, bringing "all four of the classes" together in "a sort of family life."[80] The idea provoked a storm of protest from faculty and alumni however, and after a prolonged debate the trustees voted to reject the proposal. Wilson appealed "over the heads" of the trustees to their common constituency—the alumni groups—but his public campaign proved too little too late. Historian John Morton Blum summarized Wilson's mistakes and how he ignored his own principles of rhetorical leadership:

> According to the principles of leadership he himself had formulated, he never should have raised it or pursued it as he did. Underestimating the force of tradition, which he ordinarily valued, he had neglected accurately to measure the opinion of his constituency or adequately to educate it. He had "pushed on" too soon, relied too much upon himself and his own insights and definitions, misinterpreted resistance as a selfish force which confirmed the merit of his own ideal. In varying degrees overconfidence and impatience spoiled his talents for perception and persuasion."[81]

Much the same might be said about Wilson's second major setback as president of Princeton: a bitter dispute with the graduate dean, Andrew West, over the location of a new graduate college. With Wilson demanding that the school be integrated into the university and West insisting that it remain "in lordly isolation away from the undergraduates,"[82] Wilson again took his case to the alumni in a series of well-publicized public speeches in 1910. With West in control of a sizeable bequest for the new college, Wilson again lost the debate, and historians have faulted him for missing opportunities to end the controversy, elevating minor issues to "the status of ideals," and displaying the "intolerance of a true believer."[83] Cooper has disputed comparisons between the graduate college controversy and the League debate, arguing that the differences were "more striking" than the similarities. Yet in both cases Wilson did try to "break a deadlock by appealing over the heads of his opponents to their common constituency." And in both cases the strategy failed.[84]

Nevertheless, Wilson's reform efforts at Princeton earned him a national reputation as a "crusader for democracy." In the "national political atmosphere created by the progressive movement," his struggle against the exclusive eating clubs was "readily interpreted as democracy against privilege," even though he consistently had argued that he had "no objection to the exclusivity of the clubs."[85] The controversy over the graduate school likewise contributed to Wilson's reputation as a champion of democracy, as Wilson himself cast the dispute as a contest between privilege and "the people." Speaking before an alumni group in Pittsburgh, Wilson sounded the high-minded refrain that Judge John W. Westcott would later quote as he nominated him for president: ". . . the great voice of America does not come from the seats of learning, but in a murmur from the hills and the woods and the farms and the factories and the mills, rolling on and gaining volume until it comes to us from the homes of the common men. Do these murmurs come into the corridors of the university? I have not heard them."[86]

During the presidential campaign of 1912, Wilson would build upon his reputation as democracy's champion. Defending government "of the people" against the alleged "paternalism" of Theodore Roosevelt, Wilson transformed his principles of oratorical leadership into campaign appeals, promising a revival of public deliberation and political renewal "from below." After the election, Wilson championed those same principles as he campaigned for his New Freedom legislation and, later, for military preparedness. Wilson's preparedness tour in particular reflected his principles of oratorical leadership. First he took his case to the people. Then he returned to negotiate with Congress as a "spokesman for the whole people." Wilson's success during his first term in office renders even more puzzling his self-defeating behavior during the League of Nations debate.

Enacting the Rhetorical Presidency

The campaign of 1912 proved a turning point for Woodrow Wilson, as his preference for old, traditional modes of oratorical leadership and public deliberation were challenged by new modes of political campaigning. As Ellis has noted, Wilson frowned upon the "emotionalism" of the "extended stumping tours" associated with Bryan and Roosevelt. Respectful of the "old-fashioned" proprieties, he insisted that people looked for "dignity in high office" and initially refused to mount a "demeaning 'rear-platform' campaign of the sort that William Howard Taft and Bryan had conducted in 1908."[87] Finally, however, Wilson gave in and "stumped" across the nation. Promoting the platform of progressive reforms that he would later dub "the New Freedom," he "lacked Theodore Roosevelt's animal heat" and his "capacity for arousing mass affection."[88] But with the Republican vote split he prevailed in "one of the great campaigns in American history"—a campaign that "crackled with excitement" yet also aired "questions that verged on political philosophy."[89]

Wilson's philosophical differences with Roosevelt not only reflected a central tension of the Progressive Era but also grew directly out of Wilson's academic writings. While Wilson agreed with Roosevelt on most issues, he claimed to differ with Roosevelt in his attitude toward leadership and popular governance, contrasting his own vision of political and spiritual renewal "from below" with Roosevelt's alleged "paternalism." Like Roosevelt, Wilson promised governmental action, but only after the great issues of the day had been thoroughly discussed and debated by the whole country. There was something "astir in the air of America," Wilson declared on the campaign trail, "an almost startling change in the temper of the people." In the past, political campaigns had been occasions for "whooping it up." But now there was a new spirit in America, a spirit of "frank discussion" and "common counsel." Citing the movement to open schoolhouse doors to town hall debates, Wilson concluded that Americans were longing to "get together" and "hear things of the deepest consequence discussed."[90]

As in his academic writings, Wilson lamented that Congress was no longer a site of great debates. He also worried about the lack of forums for ordinary citizens to discuss and debate the issues of the day. "For a long time," he observed, "this country of ours has lacked one of the institutions which freemen have always and everywhere held fundamental. For a long time there has been no sufficient opportunity of counsel among the people; no place and method of talk, of exchange of opinion, of parley." For Wilson, one of the great "needs of the hour" was "to restore the processes of common counsel" so that public opinion rather than "private arrangement" would determine governmental policy. Like many progressives, Wilson championed a revitalized public sphere as an end in itself—a reform to precede all other reforms. "We must learn . . . to meet, as our fathers did, somehow, somewhere, for consultation," Wilson declared on the stump. "There must be discussion and debate, in which all freely participate."[91]

For Wilson, the election of 1912 thus became a mandate for progressive reform and for a renewal of democratic deliberation. He agreed with Roosevelt on the need for a strong presidency. But for Wilson, the president's role was to facilitate debate and give voice to the "will of the people," not to impose elite opinion upon a docile and disinterested public. Invoking the public of classical democratic theory, Wilson insisted that a citizen was not "participating in public opinion at all" until he "laid his mind alongside the minds of his neighbors" in public discussion and debate. Contrary to Tulis's critique, Wilson did worry that some demagogue—"some man with eloquent tongue"—might come along and "put this whole country into a flame."[92] Yet he had faith in the ability of ordinary citizens to recognize and resist demagoguery. In the compilation of his campaign speeches published shortly after the election, *The New Freedom,* Wilson claimed to "feel nothing so much as the intensity of the common man." He also proclaimed his absolute faith in the ability of ordinary citizens to govern themselves:

> The men who have been ruling America must consent to let the majority into the game. We will no longer permit any system to go uncorrected which is based upon private understandings and expert testimony; we will not allow the few to continue to determine what the policy of the country is to be. It is a question of access to our own government. . . . It ought to be a matter of common counsel; a matter of united counsel; a matter of mutual comprehension.
>
> So, keep the air clear with constant discussion. Make every public servant feel that he is acting in the open and under scrutiny; and, above all things else, take these great fundamental questions of your lives with which political platforms concern themselves and search them through and through by every process of debate. . . .
>
> I am not afraid of the American people getting up and doing something. I am only afraid they will not; and when I hear a popular vote spoken of as mob government, I feel like telling the man who dares to so speak that he has no right to call himself an American. You cannot make a reckless, passionate force out of a body of sober people earning their living in a free country. . . . Do you see anything resembling a mob in that voting population of the countryside, men tramping over the mountains, men going to the general store up in the village, men moving in little talking groups to the corner grocery to cast their ballots, . . . Or is that your picture of a free, self-governing people? I am not afraid of the judgments so expressed, . . . because the deepest conviction and passion of my heart is that the common people . . . are to be absolutely trusted.[93]

Wilson generally remained true to his professed commitment to "common counsel" during his first term in office. Promoting his New Freedom legislation, he led public opinion "in a careful and constructive manner," occasionally appealing "over the heads" of Congress, but rarely resorting to the sort of dramatic personal appeals that Roosevelt made from the "bully pulpit." Moreover, Wilson "consistently combined his public, rhetorical efforts to sway Congress with a more informal and interactive mode of presidential-congressional relations."[94] Most importantly, Wilson appealed to pubic opinion with "discretion," blaming congressional resistance to his reform program on the "insidious" lobbyists rather than Congress itself and portraying himself as "merely the interlocutor and coordinator of Congress, not its dominating master."[95] Wilson neither criticized his congressional opponents publicly nor threatened to go "over their heads." Even when he dramatically broke one hundred years of precedent by appearing before Congress in person, he portrayed it merely as one "human being trying to co-operate with other human beings in common service."[96]

Wilson thus created at least the appearance of working with Congress on his New Freedom reforms. Even though he eventually would address the House or Senate twenty-seven times, making the address to Congress "a major weapon in his oratorical arsenal," he did so in a spirit of "common counsel," limiting those addresses to "basic principles" and leaving "leeway for the adjustments and compromises" that became "the hallmark" of his presidency.[97] The result, as Cooper has written, was a "spectacular, possibly unmatched, record of legislative and party leadership." As Cooper concluded, only FDR's New Deal and Lyndon Johnson's Great Society "rival Wilson's accomplishments with the New Freedom between 1913 and 1916."[98]

At first glance, Wilson proved less successful promoting preparedness. Taking his case to the people in January and February 1916, Wilson "failed to reach any significant number outside of those who shared already his new point of view," according to Blum.[99] Arthur S. Link agreed, arguing that Wilson was "deluded" by the "friendly editors and cheering throngs" into "thinking he had changed the Midwestern mind," a mind tradition-bound by America's isolationist history.[100] Yet the case can be made that Wilson accomplished precisely what he set out to accomplish with his "swing around the circle." Staking out a rhetorical middle ground between "the pacifists on one side and the militarists on the other," he portrayed the tour as part of his "duty . . . to hold frank counsel with the people themselves."[101] Then casting himself as a spokesman for the "whole people," he returned to Washington to broker a compromise that effectively "eliminated preparedness as a party issue in 1916."[102]

Wilson had embraced preparedness only reluctantly after the sinking of the *Lusitania,* and even then he did so partly for political reasons: to keep Theodore Roosevelt and the preparedness movement under "prudent control."[103] Still committed to neutrality in the European war, Wilson proposed only a moderate military build-up during his first term in office. Yet that buildup did not go far enough for the interventionists, while it went too far for many of his fellow Democrats in Congress. William Jennings Bryan, who had resigned from Wilson's cabinet in protest of the administration's stern warnings to Germany, even took to the hustings to argue against the president's plan. Wilson, however, positioned himself above the political fray. Describing his preparedness tour as an exercise in "common counsel," he professed an interest only in clarifying an issue that had been "deeply clouded by passion and prejudice."[104] More importantly, he claimed to embrace the principles animating both sides in the debate. In his speech before eight thousand people in Milwaukee on January 31, for example, the president pledged to protect both the peace and the honor of the nation. However, he concluded, the choice was out of his hands: "In the first place, I know that you are depending upon me to keep this nation out of the war. So far I have done so. And I pledge you my word that, God helping me, I will if it is possible. But you have laid another duty upon me. You have bidden me see to it that nothing stains or impairs the honor of the United States. And that is a matter not within my control. That depends upon what others do, not upon what the Government of the United States does."[105]

In so defining the issue, Wilson cast himself as the "spokesman for the whole people." He had heard the "unmistakable voice" of "the great body of this nation," he said, and the message was clear: "We depend upon you to keep us out of war. . . . But we depend upon you to maintain unsullied and unquestioned the honor and integrity of the United States."[106] Claiming to speak as "the trustee of the nation," he explained in Chicago that he had been "called upon" to express the "sober judgments" of the whole nation, not any "individual opinions," and the next day in Des Moines he claimed to express "the spirit of America" more truly than his critics.[107] In Topeka he insisted that he had come "not to plead a cause" but only to "sweep away" untruths that might "cloud the issue." As president, he concluded, it was his duty to "subordinate everything to the conscientious attempt to interpret and express . . . the genuine spirit of my fellow citizens." And according to Wilson, that "spirit" was clear. The American people cherished peace and wanted to avoid war, but they also "stood ready to do their duty in the hour of need."[108]

Wilson reinforced his persona as a spokesman for the "whole people" by disavowing any particular plan for building up the military. "I am not a partisan of any one plan," he declared in the first speech of the tour. "I have had too much experience to think that it is right to say that the plan that I propose is the only plan that will work, because I have a shrewd suspicion that there may be other plans which will work." Two days later in Pittsburgh, Wilson confessed that he did, in fact, have a plan, but he again insisted that "the details do not make an difference" and concluded: "I believe in one plan; others may think that an equally good plan can be substituted, and I hope my mind is open to be convinced that it can." In St. Louis on February 3, he expressed more directly his willingness, even eagerness, to negotiate and compromise with Congress. "I am not jealous . . . of the details," Wilson told the crowd of twelve thousand in the St. Louis Coliseum. "No man ought to be confident that his judgment is correct about the details. No man out to say to any legislative body, 'You must take my plan or none at all'—that is arrogance and stupidity."[109]

During his preparedness tour, Wilson occasionally lapsed into questioning the motives or tactics of his political opponents. In New York, Wilson feigned surprise that some had allowed "partisan feeling or personal ambition" to "creep into the discussion" of preparedness, and in Cleveland he lamented that the issue had arisen in an election year. He then instructed: "The man who brings partisan feelings into these matters and seeks partisan advantage by means of them is unworthy of your confidence."[110] In Des Moines, he accused *some* of his "fellow citizens" of "seeking to darken counsel on this great matter," and—without naming names—he criticized advocates on both sides for stirring up a "heat of passion" and making "our air tense." Our "first loyalty," Wilson reminded his listeners, must be to America. Before an audience of some four thousand at Soldiers' Memorial Hall in Pittsburgh, Wilson admonished those whose "counsel is passion" and called for calm deliberation and "cool judgment": "It is not wise, it is not possible, to guide national policy under the impulse of passion. I would be ashamed of the passion of fear, and I would try to put the passion of aggression entirely aside in advising my fellow citizens what they should do at any great crisis of their national life. . . . I know it is not easy. When the world is running red with blood, it is hard to keep the judgment cool. . . . But, while I can understand the excitements of the mind which circumstances have generated, I would tremble to see them guide the decisions of the country."[111]

Wilson's call for "cool judgment" reflected the neoclassical ideals of his writings on oratory. The role he enacted during the debate, however, reflected his new conception of a rhetorical president—one who both led and interpreted public opinion. Claiming to understand the "temper of the people" better than others, Wilson deciphered public opinion from the "crowds at the stations" and the "multitudes" who packed great halls to hear his speeches. He even sensed the true "spirit of the nation" in the "ardent display" of the Stars and Stripes during his tour. Embarking upon his "errand from Washington," he had expected only to meet "quiet audiences and explain to them the issues of the day." Instead, he had been met by large and enthusiastic crowds that declared, "in one fashion or another," that they loved their country and "stood ready to do their duty in the hour of need."[112] Like today's rhetorical presidents, Wilson urged his supporters to make their voices heard.[113] Yet he presented such pleas not as attempts to rally public opinion but as reminders of the responsibilities of citizenship. According to Wilson, citizens had a duty to speak out and become part of public opinion. Donning his professor's hat in Kansas City, he reflected on why the participation of ordinary citizens was necessary if democratic deliberations were to produce sound collective judgments: "We are all of us fit to be judges about what is none of our business, and that is the way that great bodies of men come to the most cool-headed judgments. Their passions are not involved, their special interests are not involved; they are looking at the thing with a certain remove, with a certain aloofness of judgment."[114]

During this tour, Wilson thus reaffirmed his faith that public opinion served as an effective check on the distortions and excesses of the demagogue. "We can control irresponsible talkers amidst ourselves," he observed in Milwaukee. "All we have got to do is to encourage them to hire a hall, and their folly will be abundantly advertised by themselves."[115] In the last major address of the tour, in St. Louis, he again encouraged a vigorous and open debate, expressing his confidence that the public would see through the deceptions of his critics. Echoing *Constitutional Government,* he concluded: "They have a right to talk, but they have no right to affect our conduct. Indeed, if I were in your place, I would encourage them to talk. Nothing chills folly like exposure to the air, and these gentlemen ought to be encouraged to hire large halls. And the more people they can get to hear them, the safer the country would be."[116] During his preparedness tour, Wilson may not have changed many minds. But from "the standpoint of politics," as Thomas J. Knock has observed, he "met the challenge masterfully."[117] Creating at least the appearance of public support for preparedness, he built a bipartisan congressional majority behind the administration's program and robbed the Republicans of their most powerful issue in the 1916 campaign.

In his second term, of course, war would test the limits of Wilson's patience with "common counsel" and "cool" deliberation. In declaring war, as Hofstadter observed, Wilson was forced to "turn his back upon his deepest values,"[118] including his commitment to "government by debate." Hinting at things to come, Wilson declared in his "War Address" of April 2, 1917, that "disloyalty" would be met with the "firm hand of stern repression," and in a Flag Day address that same year he sounded an even more ominous warning: "Woe be to the man or group of men

[57]

that seeks to stand in our way in this day of high resolution when every principle we hold dearest is to be vindicated and made secure for the salvation of the nations."[119] War had changed everything. The most obvious manifestation of that, of course, was the Committee on Public Information (CPI).

The story of the CPI's unprecedented campaign to silence dissent and forge a consensus behind the administration's war policies has been told many times, and the details need not detain us here. Suffice it to say that the CPI represented the antithesis of Wilson's vision of an informed and freely deliberating democratic polity. Headed by progressive journalist George Creel, the CPI distributed an estimated 75 million pamphlets, plastered stirring prowar posters on walls across the nation, and mobilized 75,000 so-called Four Minute Men to give speeches to tens of millions of Americans—all singing the praises of "Americanism" and discrediting "all things German."[120] Manipulating news coverage and strongly discouraging dissent, the CPI encouraged not "common counsel" but "hysteria, hatred, [and] an atmosphere of intolerance."[121] In the climate of patriotic conformity promoted by the CPI, there was little room for the "play of debate."

The CPI not only betrayed Wilson's vision of "government by debate," but it also signaled the beginning of a new era of scientific propaganda and public relations. In this new era, public opinion would no longer be viewed as an oracle to be obeyed, but rather as a political resource to be manipulated or even manufactured. As he began his postwar crusade for the League of Nations, Wilson stood in the middle of this historic transformation of America's political culture. The second oratorical renaissance was giving way to the Age of Propaganda.

Conclusion

Woodrow Wilson did not alone invent the rhetorical presidency. Nor did he envision today's rhetorical presidency—the presidency of slogans, sound bites, and the "permanent campaign." The rhetorical presidency evolved over time, and Wilson's contributions reflected both progressive ideals and the era's nostalgia for the "golden age" of oratory. As perhaps nobody else, as Kraig has argued, Wilson embodied the "conflicting oratorical standards" of the Progressive Era. Combining the "élan of the old oratory" with an understanding of the "necessities of modern mass communication," he was a "near perfect synthesis" of the "old and new," somehow managing, "not unlike Lincoln before him," to seem "both modern and classical" at the same time.[122]

In dismissing Wilson's views on demagoguery as "strained" and "inadequate,"[123] Tulis has failed to grasp the significance of the larger, quintessentially progressive conception of rhetoric that undergirded both Wilson's political theory and his public speaking. Wilson did not deny the threat posed by demagoguery. To the contrary, he frequently criticized the spellbinders of his own day, and he devoted much of his scholarly work to describing the character and requirements of responsible rhetorical leadership. Like most progressives, Wilson had faith in the ability of ordinary people to govern themselves. Yet he also shared the progressive view that ordinary citizens needed to be educated in the ways of democratic deliberation and provided more forums for expressing their views. Like most progressive reformers, Wilson was both optimistic and concerned about the prospects for an enlightened democratic public. The people were capable of recognizing and resisting the deceptions of demagogues, he believed, but only if educated to distinguish between the true "orator-statesman" and the charlatan.

Unfortunately, as Clements has argued, Wilson sometimes "mistook" his own ability to "move and inspire an audience" for evidence that he had an "instinctive understanding of their wishes." His "power over an audience and seeming rapport with its members" sometimes gave him the "illusion" that he was speaking for the people.[124] Peter Levine has gone even further, arguing that Wilson advocated "calm, national discussion aimed at consensus" but really sought political conformity. "Wilson's fault was to declare himself the sole arbiter of the public interest and to demand acquiescence rather than real consensus," Levine concluded. He assumed "that his own beliefs and values epitomized the national interest."[125]

In this respect, Wilson might be counted among the "scientific" progressives described by Danbom.[126] He professed faith in democracy, but he also saw the need to "educate" the public, lest they come to the wrong conclusions. As he left on his "swing around the circle" in September of 1919, Wilson complained that the opposition had misrepresented the treaty, and he described his tour as an exercise in setting the record straight. Before long, however, it would be Wilson who was distracting and misleading the public in the League of Nations debate. Pledging to educate and empower public opinion, he ultimately defied public opinion himself.

CHAPTER 2

The Rhetoric of "Common Counsel"

I have not come to paint pictures of fancy.
SPOKANE, WASHINGTON, SEPTEMBER 12, 1919

"I have not come here tonight to indulge in any kind of oratory," Woodrow Wilson told a crowd of 10,000 people in the St. Louis Coliseum on September 5, 1919—just the second day of his Western tour.[1] And again the next day, at the Convention Hall in Kansas City, Wilson declared that "this great subject is not a subject for oratory," but rather "a subject for examination and discussion," an opportunity for the president to "report" to his "fellow citizens" on the results of the peace conference, and to "remind" them of "some of the things that we have long desired and which are at last accomplished in this treaty."[2] Wilson's claim that he was touring merely to "report," "expound," or "discuss" the treaty—but not to engage in "oratory" or "debate"—reflected a distinction that was crucial to Wilson but has been lost on historians and students of the modern rhetorical presidency. In Wilson's vision of the rhetorical presidency, the responsible leader did not go "over the heads" of Congress with appeals to the people. Rather, he deliberated *with* the people, articulating their shared principles and values and giving voice to their political judgments.

According to conventional wisdom, Wilson got off to a slow start on his Western tour. "As in his previous campaigns," historian John

Milton Cooper Jr. has written, "Wilson took a little time to hit his stride," and his speeches during the second week of the tour—in the upper Midwest—were especially ineffective. When he spoke in Bismarck, in Cooper's view, "he rambled, as he did again the next day at Billings. That evening at Helena he gave his longest and most disjointed speech on the tour, as he meandered on about Article X, reservations, Shantung, and the Monroe Doctrine."[3] Similarly, Robert C. Hilderbrand has argued that it "should not be supposed" that the "large audiences" the president attracted in the Midwest reflected his "effectiveness on the stump." At most of his early stops, according to Hilderbrand, Wilson received "a warm but not hysterical welcome," and he responded with "addresses clearly lacking in effectiveness."[4]

Some have attributed this slow start to a lack of preparation, claiming that Wilson had "prepared nothing" before leaving Washington.[5] Yet Wilson typically spoke extemporaneously, and many of the best speeches of his career had been delivered with little or no advance preparation. Moreover, Wilson had been delivering speeches about the treaty and the League of Nations for the better part of a year, including two major addresses since his return from Europe in July. Finally, it simply was not true that Wilson "prepared nothing" before leaving on the tour. Well before he left Washington, as Robert Saunders has noted, Wilson typed up twenty-one "themes," highlighting the "cardinal ideas he would extemporaneously elaborate on" in his tour speeches. He also prepared detailed notes on the "real character and full scope of the treaty," the provisions of the League Covenant (including a list of the twenty-six articles by number and subject), and the "radical change of circumstances" that dictated a "Change of Policy."[6] As the tour progressed, Wilson could be seen "hunched over his portable typewriter, laboring on his next speech" as the presidential special sped toward its next stop.[7] He even spoke from notes on occasion during the tour—a rarity in his career. If anything, he was more prepared for his Western tour than he had been for his previous speaking campaigns.

Others have cited Wilson's deteriorating physical condition as an explanation for his shaky start. Yet if the thin, dry air of the West and the "accumulated effects of fatigue" took their toll on Wilson's speeches, as

Cooper has suggested, then his performances should have deteriorated over time. Instead, Wilson seemed to get stronger as the tour progressed, with the "rhetorical and emotional apogee" of the tour coming during the third week—in California. Like most historians, Cooper also ranks Wilson's final speech of the tour, in Pueblo, Colorado, among the "best performances" of the tour, even though Wilson's headaches had become so bad by that time that he "could hardly see."[8]

The whole debate over why Wilson got off to a slow start reflects a curious tendency among historians to celebrate the more passionate, even demagogic speeches of the Western tour. Treating the size and enthusiasm of his audiences as the measure of eloquence, historians have reserved their highest praise for the rousing, often combative speeches that Wilson delivered late in the tour, particularly in California. They seem to assume that, by arousing public opinion, these speeches served Wilson's purpose of putting pressure on the Senate. Yet as Cooper has recognized, Wilson never said his goal was to rally public pressure against the Senate. Indeed, he "never said that he was trying to achieve any particular result" by going to the people. Perhaps he believed that he could "foment so much pressure from public opinion" that the Senate would "come to heel." But he also talked of the tour as "simply a good thing," as something that he just "wanted to do."[9]

There were many reasons why Wilson's Midwestern speeches might have inspired less public enthusiasm than his later speeches: widespread pro-German sentiment in the Midwest, the "rock-ribbed" isolationism of the region, and a preoccupation with economic concerns, to name just a few.[10] Yet despite these obstacles, Wilson did generate surprising enthusiasm at most of his early stops, and his speeches were widely covered and reprinted in newspapers across the nation, often with complete texts. True to his word, Wilson generally "discussed" rather than "debated" the treaty while touring the Midwest, and he rarely attacked his critics or waved the bloody shirt of war sentimentality. Embodying his ideal of a president who both led and interpreted public opinion, he sought to educate his audiences about the treaty and to share his vision of a new world order.

To the extent that Wilson's early speeches failed, they failed not as speeches but as media events. In a new age of professional journalism, newspaper reporters took it upon themselves to assess public opinion, and with polling still a decade and a half away that meant measuring the success of Wilson's tour by crowd reactions. When Wilson failed to attract large and enthusiastic crowds, reporters judged his speeches weak and ineffective. When the crowds grew larger and more boisterous, reporters praised the president's eloquence and more positively assessed his chances of "winning" the debate. That journalistic dynamic helps to account for the prevailing view that Wilson did not hit his rhetorical stride until he reached California, where he drew large and enthusiastic crowds. It also helps to explain the legendary status of his final speech in Pueblo, Colorado—a speech that was greeted by a long ovation and reportedly left many in tears.

This chapter begins by recalling some of the strategic planning that went into Wilson's Western tour. While Wilson himself may have had some rather old-fashioned ideas about the "orator-statesman," his closest adviser, Joseph Tumulty, took a decidedly modern approach to planning his "swing around the circle." Like today's presidential press secretaries, Tumulty emphasized "news management" in every aspect of his planning. He approached the Western tour as a "media event," not as an exercise in "common counsel." Hoping to wield public opinion as a political weapon, Tumulty strove to create at least the appearance of "grass-roots" support for the League of Nations. Intent on putting pressure on the Senate, Tumulty pioneered the sort of media-centered tour characteristic of the modern rhetorical presidency.

In the second part of the chapter, I reconstruct the first three days of Wilson's Western tour, illustrating how the tension between Wilson's rhetoric of "common counsel" and the new journalism was evident from the outset. Speaking in Columbus and Indianapolis on the very first day, the president for the most part lived up to his pledge to "report" on the treaty and "expound" upon its provisions. Yet more interested in political drama than ideas, the reporters traveling with the president focused on perhaps the most uncharacteristic statement of his first three days on the road: his challenge to his critics to "put up or shut up." On Saturday, September 6, Wilson delivered perhaps the most thoughtful and magnanimous address of the entire tour—a speech in Des Moines, Iowa, in which he acknowledged his critics' legitimate concerns and emphasized their shared principles and common hopes for a world without war. Yet highlighting the president's "fighting spirit," the newspapers instead reported his more combative remarks, largely ignoring the positive and constructive tone of his speech in Des Moines. Like today's political journalists, reporters in Wilson's day looked for political drama.

During his second week on the road, Wilson delivered some of the longest and most detailed speeches of the entire tour. Yet upstaged by events back east (including a violent police strike in Boston and damaging testimony by a former aide), Wilson's words received less and less newspaper coverage as the tour progressed. With reporters writing "briefer and briefer reports" and paying more attention "to local receptions and events,"[11] readers across the nation learned more about the radical politics of the upper Midwest than about Wilson's case for the treaty. Meanwhile, the Senate moved forward with efforts to attach reservations to the agreement. By Wilson's own standards, these early speeches were among the best of the tour. Yet they have been largely forgotten, perhaps because they were already "old news" to the reporters traveling with the president at the time.

According to contemporary accounts, all was going well on the tour as Wilson reached the Pacific Coast on Saturday, September 13. The president had "steadily advanced his cause," the newspapers reported, and the public generally supported ratification "without delay."[12] Yet just beneath the surface, Wilson's own advisers worried about his health and also about the failure of his speeches to quiet talk of reservations back in Washington. Tumulty urged a change in Wilson's speech-making strategy. Recommending a new emphasis on the costs of the Great War and the threat of another, even more destructive war, Tumulty persuaded the president to embrace the passionate, even combative rhetorical style of the spellbinders of the day. In taking Tumulty's advice, Wilson not only abandoned his own principles of oratorical statesmanship but also alienated many senators. In the final analysis, his drift toward demagoguery may have cost him the debate.

The Old Rhetoric and the New Journalism

It was, as Arthur S. Link observed in *Wilson the Diplomatist*, "one of the most fateful decisions of his career": Woodrow Wilson's decision, as he put it, to "go to the people and purify the wells of public opinion that had been poisoned by the isolationists and opponents of unreserved ratification" of the Versailles treaty.[13] According to most historians, it was a misguided decision at best, and at worst a reflection of Wilson's deteriorating mental health. Wilson had "nothing to gain by going to the country," historian John Morton Blum has argued, "for public opinion, even if he could arouse it, would not affect the Senators."[14] Even before he began the tour, it already had become "perfectly obvious" that he could obtain ratification of the treaty "only by accepting the procedure demanded by the so-called mild reservationists." According to the editors of the Wilson Papers, Wilson's "decision to go to the country" was simply "irrational."[15]

At the time, however, few considered Wilson's decision "irrational." As Robert Kraig has noted, most of the "leading newspapers of the country believed Wilson's rhetoric had the capacity to influence the outcome of his contest with the Senate."[16] In addition, Wilson's own advisers assured him that a "swing around the circle" could prove decisive. Joseph Tumulty, not surprisingly, "considered Wilson the most effective spokesman of his own cause," and he had little doubt that the president could "create such overwhelming sentiment for the League" that the mild reservationists, "moved by the weight of public opinion," would be forced to support his position.[17] In a letter to Wilson in mid-July, Treasury Secretary William McAdoo also urged the president to take his case to the people, noting that a "good many" of his "best friends" were "very eager" to have him tour. McAdoo predicted that, with his "irresistible style," Wilson would simply "rout the opposition."[18]

On Capitol Hill, few seemed to doubt that a presidential tour could be decisive. Congressional Democrats begged Wilson to tour, according to Tumulty, insisting that "nothing could win the fight for the League of Nations except a direct appeal to the country by the President in person."[19] Meanwhile, Wilson's Republican critics revealed their respect for Wilson's oratorical powers by launching a counter tour featuring two of their most effective orators, William Borah and Hiram Johnson. Republican congressmen even introduced resolutions aimed at blocking Wilson from touring altogether or, failing that, to provide federal funding for anti-League speakers.[20] Wilson and his advisers were hardly alone in imagining that Wilson might go out and arouse such a popular storm as to force the Senate to heel. As the *New York Times* editorialized, the "hearts of the Republicans sink into their boots at the prospect of Mr. Wilson's advocacy among the people of the ratification of the Treaty of Peace, undisfigured, undenatured."[21]

Yet to suggest that Wilson toured solely to pressure the Senate is to ignore both his view of presidential leadership and his comments at the time. As Cooper has argued, Wilson "probably would have made some kind of tour even if he had encountered less opposition and criticism on Capitol Hill." For him, "contact with the people" was important in itself—a motivation that "sprang from his deepest convictions about democratic government" and a "near mystical faith in the efficacy of informed public opinion." Long before he entered politics, Wilson described the "education of the public" as the essential task of democratic leadership, and he viewed that leadership as "a two-way process in which the leader both instructed and learned from the led."[22] Brushing off warnings that the tour might injure his health, Wilson declared it his "duty" to tour, not because it might win the debate, but because he owed it to the people. As for his health, Wilson seemed unconcerned. As he reportedly told Secretary of the Navy Josephus Daniels: "It will be no strain on me—on the contrary, it will be a relief to me to meet the people. No, the speeches will not tax me. The truth is, I am saturated with the subject and spoiling to tell the people about the Treaty. I will enjoy it."[23]

Wilson's Western tour, then, was not the product of an angry, spur-of-the-moment decision. To the contrary, it was perfectly consistent with Wilson's views of presidential leadership and his past behaviors. Moreover, the tour had been in the works for months. As early as January, Tumulty began pushing for a speaking tour, and rumors of the tour appeared in the newspapers as early as February. More than two months before returning from Paris, the president had stated that he expected to tour the country upon his return.[24] By the end of June, Tumulty had even drafted a tentative plan: a major speech in New York immediately upon his return from Europe, followed by a speech presenting the treaty to Congress, and finally an extended tour of the country covering some 10,000 miles and stopping in more than two dozen cities. When Wilson returned from Europe on July 8, the first part of the plan went smoothly. Landing in Hoboken, New Jersey, Wilson "motored through crowded streets to New York's Carnegie Hall," where he delivered a major speech to "4,000 electrified admirers." Two days later, however, the speech to the Senate was "a dud," as Wilson botched the delivery and failed to address the major concerns of those skeptical about the treaty.[25] Ignoring Tumulty's advice that he give a hard-hitting speech emphasizing the threat of war and radicalism should the treaty be rejected, he instead spoke in vague generalities and melodramatic clichés: "Dare we reject it and break the heart of the world? . . . The stage is set, the destiny disclosed. . . . We cannot turn back. We can only go forward, with lifted eyes and freshened spirit, to follow the vision."[26]

After the failed Senate speech, the tour was put on hold for nearly two months as Wilson negotiated with senators and grappled with pressing domestic problems. By late August, however, Wilson and his advisers sensed that the "tide of public opinion was setting against the League," so Tumulty "hastily completed" the plans he had drawn up earlier and the tour was publicly announced on August 27.[27] The tour would focus on the Midwest and Far West, altogether avoiding the Democratic South and the Republican East. Illinois would be skipped entirely because of the vociferous opposition of its leading newspaper, its senators, and various ethnic groups, while California would be targeted with nine major speeches. There were to be about forty formal speeches, "in places ranging from tents and stadia to opera houses and tabernacles," along with various "unscheduled appearances on the rear of the train."[28] The tour would begin at Columbus, Ohio, on September 4, cover some 10,000 miles in twenty-seven days, and conclude on September 29 in Louisville, Kentucky.

Tumulty's planning for the trip extended well beyond the general itinerary. Taking a modern approach, Tumulty invited twenty-one newspaper reporters to accompany the president on his trip, along with wire service reporters and motion picture photographers.[29] The journalists on board included Charles H. Grasty of the *New York Times,* Philip Kinsley of the *Chicago Daily Tribune,* and Robert T. Small, a southerner whose dispatches appeared in both the *Atlanta Constitution* and the *Washington Post.*[30] Also onboard the train were reporters from the *Baltimore Sun,* the Louisville *Courier Journal,* and the Cleveland *Plain Dealer,* along with several wire service correspondents. Whenever the train stopped, local reporters and photographers would join the press entourage, while between stops Tumulty would circulate among the reporters. Occasionally, Wilson himself would come forward to the club car to chat informally with the press.[31]

Tumulty relied on advance agents and pro-League citizens to plan the president's day in each city, with detailed schedules, called maneuver sheets, outlining the arrangements for accommodations, intra-urban transportation, and appointments with local politicians and dignitaries. These maneuver sheets, which were distributed to the traveling reporters twenty-four hours in advance of each stop, covered "every minute from the President's arrival to his departure," often allowing "little time for privacy or relaxation."[32] Tumulty also made sure that the tour stopped in enough major news distribution centers to allow the reporters to file their dispatches, and he supplied local reporters with publicity materials on the president's peace aims.[33] Meanwhile, Wilson's stenographer, Charles Swem, produced official transcripts of Wilson's speeches, which were then "immediately mimeographed and distributed." Tumulty and the League to Enforce Peace also supplied texts of Wilson's speeches, "printed in readily usable formats," to 1,400 small daily newspapers around the country.[34]

At the start of the tour, Tumulty's planning paid off, as major newspapers devoted banner headlines to Wilson's departure and reported in great detail on the itinerary and goals of the trip. This tour would be "the most arduous ever undertaken by a president," the *Atlanta Constitution* reported, covering almost as much distance as the president's trip to

France. Indeed, it would be even "more strenuous" than his European tour because of "its continuity and the long rides through the west." The president, the *Constitution* reported, was "prepared to make now the fight of his political life ... for the peace treaty."[35]

Wilson's aides actually tried to lower expectations of high eloquence on the tour by telling reporters that the "pressure of work at the White House during the past few days" had given the president "no opportunity to prepare any of his speeches in advance." He would deliver all of his speeches extemporaneously, the *Washington Post* reported, speaking "chiefly from notes made during the trip."[36] The White House also enlisted the ranking Democrat on the Senate Foreign Relations Committee, Senator Gilbert M. Hitchcock of Nebraska, to help shape expectations in advance of the tour. Speaking to the *Atlanta Constitution*, Hitchcock reported that the president was "determined to devote his addresses ... almost entirely to the subject of the treaty of peace and the league of nations." His "main purpose" would be to "analyze the treaty in detail," to explain the "workings of the league of nations to the people," and to describe the consequences should the United States fail to join the "other, great powers" in this effort "to make another world war impossible." The president might have something to say about "the opposition to the treaty," Hitchcock commented, but he planned no "personal attacks" on senators opposing the treaty.[37]

Wilson's critics also tried to massage press expectations. As the president prepared to depart, Senate Republican leaders told the *Atlanta Constitution* that strong and mild reservationists already had reached agreement on three reservations: one upholding America's rights to interpret the Monroe Doctrine, another insisting upon the right to decide all domestic questions without interference from the League, and a third asserting the nation's right to withdraw from the League for any reason. They also told reporters that they were close to agreement on a fourth, more controversial change: a reservation to Article X reasserting the authority of Congress to commit troops overseas. Most importantly, they told the paper that they would be "unmoved" by any public pressure for ratification without reservations, and that Wilson was "nourishing a false hope" if he thought he could "arouse public opinion to such a point" that they would be forced to retreat from their position."[38] Publicly, Wilson already had gone on record against amendments or reservations, but secretly he had provided Hitchcock with four "interpretive reservations" that he thought might be acceptable.[39] At the time, most observers simply assumed that some compromise would be found.

In retrospect, historians agree that Wilson was nursing a "fantasy" if he thought that he could "dominate the Senate through management of public opinion."[40] From the outset, they suggest, Wilson understood that he would have to compromise. Over the first ten days of the tour, however, Wilson seemed relatively unconcerned with the Senate debate. Celebrating his escape from Washington and expounding upon general principles rather than answering his critics, he played the orator-statesman, educating the public about the general provisions of the treaty and saying little about the proposed reservations. If Wilson was concerned about his critics in the Senate, there was little evidence of that in his early speeches.

A "Fighting Spirit"

To the reporter for the *New York Times*, Wilson "appeared to be in excellent health" as he boarded his special railroad car, the *Mayflower*, to begin his Western tour on the evening of September 3. Dressed in a blue coat, white trousers, white shoes, and a straw hat, Wilson arrived at Union Station about fifteen minutes before the scheduled departure. A crowd gathered in the concourse and cheered. After escorting Mrs. Wilson to their private car, Wilson returned to the platform and laughed and joked with friends until it came time to depart. Accompanied by Mrs. Wilson, his physician Cary T. Grayson, Charles L. Swem, his personal stenographer, and of course Joseph Tumulty, Wilson's entourage also included a small group of secret service men and the large contingent of newspaper correspondents. The unprecedented coverage of the tour was, in itself, big news. As the *Times* noted, there were more newspapermen accompanying Wilson than had ever before "made a Presidential tour."[41]

Departing at 7 P.M., the Presidential Special set out for its first stop, Columbus, Ohio. Ohio had helped to reelect Wilson in 1916, but reporter David Lawrence sensed in Wilson's reception in Columbus a noticeable letdown from the wildly enthusiastic crowds that had greeted the president in Europe. To anybody who had witnessed "the cheering throngs on the Champs Élysées," Lawrence later recalled, "the reception at Columbus was a painful anti-climax." There was "nothing triumphal or heroic about the President's journey down the streets of Columbus," Lawrence recalled; he had attracted "more attention in that very city seven years before as a relatively unknown candidate for President."[42] Even Tumulty, who later proclaimed the tour "a veritable triumph," conceded that "the first meeting at Columbus" had been a "disappointment as to attendance."[43]

Still, Tumulty sensed "no weariness or brain-fag" in Wilson's speech that day before a packed Memorial Hall. "To those of us who sat on the platform," he recalled, "this speech with its beautiful phrasing and its effective delivery seemed to have been carefully prepared."[44] In his diary, Grayson characterized the speech as an effective, hard-hitting response to the treaty's critics. "When he arrived at the hall," Grayson wrote, Wilson "lost no time in getting right after the opponents of the Treaty," particularly those who had complained that the terms of the Treaty of Versailles were "unjust" and "too severe upon Germany." According to Grayson, Wilson "made a great hit with the crowd" as he excoriated the German government for its disregard of "all forms of international law and all forms of decency in warfare."[45]

Yet from the outset of his speech in Columbus, Wilson actually seemed to distance himself from the debate in Washington. Declaring his "very profound pleasure" at finally finding himself "face-to-face" with his fellow citizens, he began the speech, not by responding to his critics, but by explaining that he had come to "report" to his "fellow countrymen" and engage them in "common counsel." "I have for a long time chafed at the confinement of Washington," he declared, and he insisted that he had not come to Columbus to debate the opposition. "The only people I owe any report to are you and the other citizens of the United States," he told his listeners in Columbus, and he had come to explain "just what this treaty contains and what it seeks to do."[46]

Wilson devoted the first section of his address in Columbus to the terms of peace settlement. Defending the settlement in principle, he explained why harsh punishment of Germany was necessary to prevent future wars. "The terms of the treaty are severe," Wilson acknowledged, "but they are not unjust." They punished "one of the greatest wrongs ever done in history," but they were not designed to "overwhelm" or to "humiliate" the German people. The men at the peace table had a "vivid sense" of Germany's crimes, including "the utter disregard which she had shown for human rights—for the rights of women and children and those who were helpless." They had "seen their lands devastated by an enemy that devoted itself not only to the effort of victory, but to the effort of terror—seeking to terrify the people whom they fought." Considering all that, the negotiators actually had "exercised restraint in the terms of this treaty." They demanded "no indemnity," but "merely reparation, merely paying for the destruction done," and even that would not be "pressed beyond the point which Germany can pay." There was "no national triumph" reflected in the treaty, "no glory" for any of the victorious nations, Wilson concluded. Putting aside their personal agendas, the negotiators thought only of "their people, of the suffering that they had gone through, of the losses they had incurred." And they sent "notice" that "mankind" would never again allow such aggression.[47]

Wilson did "get after" his critics on several occasions. "I am astonished at some of the statements I see made about this treaty," he declared at one point. Such statements could only be made "by persons who have not read the treaty," or "who, if they have read it, have not comprehended its meaning." Moments later Wilson again criticized the treaty's opponents by suggesting that they had forgotten the nation's "promises" upon entering the war: "I wonder if some of the opponents of the League of Nations have forgotten the promises we made our people before we went to that peace table. We had taken by process of law the flower of our youth from every countryside, from every household, and we told those mothers and fathers and sisters and wives and sweethearts that we were taking those men to fight a war which would end business of that sort." In declaring that America would be "unfaithful" to the "loving hearts who suffered in this war" if it rejected the treaty, Wilson saddled his critics with responsibility for redeeming that promise.[48] Yet at no point did Wilson answer specific objections to the treaty or refer to any of the treaty's critics by name.

Instead, Wilson devoted the bulk of his address in Columbus to what reporter David Lawrence later described as a "comprehensive survey" of the treaty.[49] "Now, look what else is in the treaty," he began. The peace settlement would end the historical practice of holding together "by military force" peoples "who did not want to live together" and were "constantly chafing at the bands that held them together." By upholding the principle that "people have a right to live . . . under the governments which they themselves choose to set up," the peace treaty would reunite "pitiful Poland," free Bohemia from Austro-Hungarian domination, and recognize the nationality of the "Slavic peoples to the south, running down into the great Balkan Peninsula." "The old alliances, the old balances of power," Wilson explained, "were meant to see to it that no little nation asserted its rights." Under the new world order, a different principle would prevail, an idea that Wilson labeled an "American principle": that people had the right to live under a government of their own choosing. It was simply a matter of "giving people what belonged to them."[50]

Wilson touted the treaty as unique in history, as never before had a "congress of nations" considered "the rights of those who could not enforce their rights." Never before had "the rights of people" prevailed over "the rights of government." The "heart" of the treaty was not that it punished Germany; that, Wilson said, was a "temporary thing." Rather, the treaty rectified "the age-long wrongs which characterized the history of Europe." It was a "big job," and the treaty did not right every injustice in the world, Wilson conceded. But "so far as the scope of our treaty went," it "rectified the wrongs" that had been the "fertile source of war in Europe."[51]

Like a schoolteacher, Wilson lectured the people of Columbus on the lessons of the war. "Have you ever reflected, my fellow countrymen, on the real sources of revolutions?" he asked. "Do you remember what Thomas Carlyle said about the French Revolution?" Wilson answered his own questions with a long philosophical reflection on the history of political conflict in Europe:

> Men don't start revolutions in a sudden passion. . . . The French people had been deeply and consistently wronged by their government . . . and the slow agony of those hundreds of years had after a while gathered into a hot anger that could not be suppressed.
>
> Revolutions don't spring up overnight. Revolutions gather through the ages; revolutions come from the long suppression of the human spirit. Revolutions come because men know that they have rights and that they are disregarded.

In trying to "right the history of Europe," Wilson concluded, the treaty negotiators had to take into account the long-simmering anger of "great peoples" long suppressed. But ultimately they were guided by principle: they redrew the map of Europe based on "the American principle of the choice of the governed."[52]

Finally, Wilson returned to what he characterized as "the central idea of this treaty": "that nations do not consist of their government but consist of their people!" That principle, according to Wilson, underlay every provision of the treaty, from its prohibitions against colonial exploitation to its provisions for a League of Nations. By providing both checks against evil and encouragement for good works, the treaty promised to "draw the hearts of the world into league, draw the noble impulses of the world together and make a poem of them." With literary flourish, Wilson spoke of the treaty as "a mirror of the fine passions of the world, of its philanthropic passions, of its passion of pity, of its passion of human sympathy, of its passion of human friendliness and helpfulness—for there is such a passion." This, then, was the treaty that had provoked so much controversy. "Did you ever hear of it before?" Wilson asked. "Did you ever know before what was in this treaty? Did anybody before ever tell you what the treaty was intended to do?"[53]

Wilson's speech in Columbus was a principled, even eloquent defense of the peace settlement and the League of Nations. Insisting that the negotiators were in complete agreement on "principles," he claimed that all had come to the negotiating table "under instructions" from their people and "did not dare come home without fulfilling those instructions." Wilson himself "never would have come back" had he failed to fulfill the people's demands, for that would have made him an "unfaithful servant." This was not just an "American treaty," Wilson declared, but one expressing "the heart of the peoples," all of the "great peoples" who were "associated in the war against Germany." Hence, he had "not come to debate the treaty." "It speaks for itself, if you will let it," he insisted. Those who opposed it had a "radical misunderstanding" of the "instrument itself," and he urged his audience to ignore them: "Don't let them pull it down. Don't let them misrepresent it. Don't let them lead this nation away from the high purposes with which this war was inaugurated and fought." He then concluded on a sentimental note, insisting that he had upheld his end of his bargain: "As I came through that line of youngsters in khaki a few minutes ago, I felt that I could salute it because I had done the job in the way I promised them I would do it. And when this treaty is accepted, men in khaki will not have to cross the seas again."[54]

To some observers, Wilson's speech at Columbus was most note-worthy for what it failed to address: the objections to the League Covenant itself, and Wilson's resistance to the proposed reservations. Quoting Thomas Carlyle on the French Revolution and reflecting at length on the territorial dispute over High Selesia, Wilson said almost nothing about Article X, the Monroe Doctrine, or America's right to withdraw from the League. "Some gentlemen have feared with regard to the League of Nations that we will be obligated to do things we don't want to do," Wilson said in the only apparent reference to Article X. But Wilson did not "debate" those "gentleman," nor did he explain why he objected to their efforts to clarify America's rights and obligations. Claiming to know "the heart of this great people" better than "some other men I hear talk," Wilson essentially dismissed his critics as out of touch with public opinion.[55]

Indeed, Wilson had nothing at all to say to those who objected to the treaty's silence on the Irish question or its controversial provision granting Shantung to Japan.[56] According to the *New York Times*, some thought they might have heard a reference to the Irish situation in Wilson's reference to "aged-long wrongs" that he hoped would one day be rectified. But nobody heard any reference to the Shantung question, and at the end of the speech, the *Times* reported, a "Chinaman in the gallery jumped to his feet" to "heckle" the president for that omission: "Mr. President, how about Shantung?" Asked later about the incident, the president claimed not to have heard the question.[57]

According to Tumulty, the "newspaper group" accompanying the tour shared his enthusiasm for the Columbus speech.[58] Yet in a memoir published several years later, reporter David Lawrence recalled the fifty-minute speech as warmly received yet unresponsive to criticisms of the treaty. "If interruptions of applause mean anything," Lawrence wrote, "then Mr. Wilson's audience in Columbus not only seemed to accept his doctrines but to exhibit faith in the man who was exhorting them anew to follow his leadership." Lawrence recalled the "deafening roar" when the president promised that "men in khaki" would "never have to cross the seas again." Yet Wilson's "constant exaltation of American ideals and principles" and his talk of the "promise made to the lads who died," while sounding a "sentimental note," failed to address the real issues. The president's strategy had been "simply to explain the Treaty and to discuss only incidentally the objections which had been raised against it." "Again and again," Lawrence concluded, "the President failed to explain why the people should accept his view rather than the view of the Treaty opponents. . . . It was the familiar appeal—asking the people to have faith."[59]

Lawrence's recollections reflected a journalistic perspective even more evident in coverage of Wilson's speech later that same day in Indianapolis—an address to between 16,000 and 20,000 people jammed into an auditorium usually reserved for the "display of prize produce." After a shaky start in a building "not intended for speech-making," Wilson again delivered a speech that, for the most part, focused on the principles underlying the peace settlement and the promise of the League of Nations.[60] Yet in Indianapolis, Wilson responded more directly to criticisms of the treaty, and in a brief flash of anger he lashed out against his critics. Not surprisingly, the reporters had found their headline. Wilson had delivered two long speeches, but his first day on the road would be remembered for just five words: "Put Up or Shut Up."

As in Columbus, Wilson began his address in Indianapolis by declaring that he had not come "to make a speech in the ordinary sense of that term." Instead, he had come on a "very sober errand": to "report" on the work of the treaty negotiators and to explain how, as "your servants," they had fulfilled their "duty." Complaining that his critics had focused on just three of the twenty-six articles of the Covenant, he insisted that they ignored the "heart" of the agreement: the pledge not to go to war without first taking disputes to the League of Nations. Had such a mechanism been in place, Germany never would had gone to war, and it "never would have dared" to violate the territorial integrity of its neighbors. When we "sent those boys in khaki across the sea," Wilson intoned, "we promised them, we promised the world, that we would not conclude this conflict with a mere treaty of peace." America had gone to war so that "wars like this could not again occur."[61]

Wilson again defended harsh punishment for Germany, recalling how that nation had dismissed treaties as "mere scraps of paper" and had "laid in ruins" the "little kingdom" of Belgium. Yet he devoted most of his speech in Indianapolis to explaining how the League would prevent future wars by effecting an "absolute" boycott of aggressor nations. Employing a personal analogy, Wilson also suggested how the moral force of world opinion could be more powerful than military force:

> If I had done wrong, I would a great deal rather have a man shoot at me than stand me up for the judgment of my fellow men. I would a great deal rather see the muzzle of a gun than the look in their eyes. I would a great deal rather be put out of the world than live in a world boycotted and deserted. The most terrible thing is outlawry. The most formidable thing is to be absolutely isolated. And that is the kernel of this engagement. War is on the outskirts. War is a remote and secondary threat. War is a last resort.

Wilson conceded that the League was not "certain to stop war." Yet insisting that it would make war "violently improbable," he described it as the "first treaty in the history of civilization" to bring the great powers together in the cause of peace and emphasized the moral principles embodied in its Covenant—principles that the United States had always embraced. Wilson explained: "We do not stand off and see murder done. We do not profess to be the champions of liberty and then consent to see liberty destroyed. We are not the friends and advocates of free government and yet willing to stand by and see free government die before our eyes."[62]

Wilson was noticeably more responsive to his critics in Indianapolis. Responding directly to concerns that Article X might force the United States into war, he proclaimed that provision "the conscience of the world" and declared that it went to the "heart of this whole bad business" because it pledged all members of the League "to respect and to preserve against all external aggression the territorial integrity and political independence of the nations concerned." While critics might be right that it "robbed" the United States of "some degree of our sovereign independence," it did so only insofar as "every man" who made a "choice to respect the rights of his neighbors" gave up some measure of "absolute sovereignty." That did not mean, however, that the United States could be forced, against its will, to go to war. The Council of the League of Nations could only "advise" the United States to fight, and there would be "no compulsion upon us to take that advice except the compulsion of our good conscience and judgment." Moreover, there could be no "advice" without a "unanimous vote" that would "include our own." So "if we accepted the advice" of the League, Wilson concluded, we would be "accepting our own advice." As such, there was "not one note of surrender of the independent judgment of the government of the United States" in the treaty.[63]

Wilson also responded, at least indirectly, to complaints that the treaty failed to resolve the Irish question. In obvious reference to the matter, he recalled how a "good many delegations" had visited Paris with "real causes to present," and he expressed regret that the conference could not solve all of those problems. Unfortunately, the conference had "to turn away from questions that ought to some day be discussed and settled" by the "opinion of mankind," Wilson explained. Turning that unfinished business into an argument for the League, however, Wilson spoke of his "favorite article in the treaty," Article XI, which provided that any nation could bring to the attention of the League "anything that is likely to affect the peace of the world or the good understanding between nations." At present, Wilson explained, "we have to mind our own business." Under the League, however, we could "mind other peoples' business," and anything that affected the peace of the world could be "brought to the attention of mankind." Extending his faith in public deliberation to the world stage, Wilson declared that "publicity and discussion" was the one thing that wrongdoers most dreaded, for "if you are challenged to give a reason why you are doing a wrong thing it has to be an exceedingly good reason." If you gave a "bad reason," the "opinion of mankind" would turn against you.[64]

Finally, Wilson responded to critics of the Shantung provision, addressing the controversy as "one of a number of difficulties" that the Paris negotiators had faced. As Wilson explained it, the Shantung concession was the product of an unfortunate remnant of the old world order: a secret treaty between Japan, France, and Great Britain. Given that the war had been fought, in part, to uphold the "sacredness of treaties," the conference could not demand the abrogation of that treaty. Wilson also claimed that the United States had secured from Japan a "promise" to eventually return Shantung to China "without qualification." In the future, Wilson noted, no such "secret treaty shall have any validity." So, again, the League of Nations was not the problem but the solution. If it accomplished "little more than the abolition of private arrangements between great powers," Wilson argued, it would go far toward "stabilizing the peace of the world" and eliminating unjust "secret agreements."[65]

Wilson's speech in Indianapolis was a curious combination of calls for nonpartisanship and sharp attacks on his Republican critics. On the one hand, Wilson urged his listeners to "forget what party I belong to" and to judge the treaty on its merits. He was making this journey as a "democrat," Wilson said, "spelling it with a little 'd,'" and he declared that his partisan concerns were "absolutely negligible." On the other hand, he lashed out at those opposed to the treaty as "absolutely ignorant." "If they do read the English language," he said at one point, "they do not understand the English language as I understand it. If they have really read this treaty and this Covenant, they only amaze me by their inability to understand what is plainly expressed." In concluding the speech, Wilson again declared himself perfectly at ease with his own conscience because he had kept his promises to the "men in khaki." He could "look all the mothers of this country in the face . . . and say, 'The boys will not have to do this again.'" The critics of the treaty were quick to complain but had nothing better to offer. "It is a case of 'put up or shut up,'" Wilson concluded. "Opposition is not going to save the world. Negations are not going to construct the policies of mankind. A great plan is the only thing that can defeat a great plan."[66]

"Put up or shut up"—it was a line that surprised many people. It certainly was not in character for Wilson to use such a "common" expression, and it overshadowed everything else Wilson said that first day of the tour.[67] On September 5, the *Chicago Daily Tribune* trumpeted Wilson's challenge in a banner headline across all eight columns of its front page: "'Put Up or Shut Up,' Wilson to Treaty Foes." Other papers also emphasized Wilson's challenge, with some suggesting that the president was simply giving his audiences what they wanted.[68] Reporting from onboard the president's train, for example, Philip Kinsley reported that the president had "opened fire on his league of nations opponents" and noted that he "stirred the crowd to cheers" when he called his critics "absolutely ignorant." According to Kinsley, Wilson's audience in Indianapolis signaled its approval of the president's confrontational tone by cheering and shouting back: "Give it to 'em! Hit 'em again!"[69]

Departing Indianapolis at 10 P.M., Wilson's train headed west toward St. Louis, where he was to deliver two major addresses the following day: one to a luncheon for 1,500 businessmen at the Hotel Statler, and the other to a larger rally at the coliseum where he had been nominated for president three years earlier. From there he would travel to Kansas City and Des Moines for major addresses on Saturday, September 6, staying overnight in Des Moines and enjoying a day of rest on Sunday. As Wilson was speaking in Indianapolis, however, the Senate Foreign Relations Committee voted to recommend four reservations: one asserting the right of Congress to determine when troops would be deployed under Article X; another insisting upon America's right to withdraw from the League unconditionally; a third declaring America's right to determine when issues such as tariffs or immigration might be considered by the League; and the fourth proclaiming the United States the "sole interpreter" of the Monroe Doctrine.[70] According to the *Washington Post*, the committee's action made it "practically certain" that "drastic reservations" would pass by an "overwhelming majority." With Wilson barely started on his tour, the *Post* thus declared the debate over reservations "to all intents and purposes over."[71]

Wilson responded angrily to this news out of Washington. In the first of his two speeches in St. Louis, Wilson touched on the economic implications of the treaty, as one might expect in a speech to the Chamber of Commerce. Yet he devoted most of the speech to lambasting his critics, complaining that they had shrouded the whole subject in "mists . . . difficult to penetrate." Noting that some who opposed the treaty had professed "fine purposes when we went into the war," Wilson complained that they now focused on just "three or four clauses"—"mere details"—in the "great human document." The United States could not now just withdraw from world affairs and "mind our own business," Wilson insisted; the age of isolationism was "gone and all but forgotten." Finally, he accused his critics of betraying those who had fought and died in the war. Living in a "past age" and "incapable of altruistic purposes," those who refused to "see the game through," he concluded, were "absolutely contemptible quitters."[72]

Wilson went even further in his address later that evening before 12,000 wildly enthusiastic supporters in the St. Louis Coliseum. Complaining about the "amazing ignorance" of his critics, the president rejected from the outset any changes to the treaty and insisted that the "only alternative" to ratification without reservations was to "reject the peace" and to "stand alone in the world." Appealing to "selfish interests," Wilson promised that, should the treaty be ratified, the United States would be the "senior partner" in a new world order. "The financial leadership will be ours," he proclaimed; "The industrial primacy will be ours. The commercial advantage will be ours." Yet if the United States were to reject the treaty, American businessmen would become the "hostile rivals of the rest of the world" and the nation would be forced to maintain "a great standing army." Indeed, rejection of the treaty would mean "a concentrated, militaristic organization of government" and the end of "free debate" and "public counsel." It was, Wilson conceded, a "very ugly picture" that he painted, and he placed responsibility for the choice squarely on the treaty's critics. "I wonder if some of the gentlemen who are commenting upon this treaty ever read it," he declared in the home state of Senator James A. Reed, one of his most vociferous critics. "If anybody will tell me which of them hasn't, I will send him a copy," he said to laughter and a chorus of shouts: "Reed! Reed!" Toward the end of the speech, Wilson again provoked loud applause as he complained that the "real voices" of the people had become "faint and distant" in that "strange city" of Washington, D.C. He then vented his frustration with the debate: "You hear politics until you wish that both parties were smothered in their own gas."[73]

According to reporter Robert T. Small, the president had taken the people of St. Louis "into his confidence." "Under the influence" of his "very friendly crowd," he had "officially recorded his opinion" of the senators opposing him as follows:

> They are gentlemen incapable of altruistic purposes and therefore suspicious of others who have high motives.
>
> They are "absolute, contemptible quitters if they do not see the game through."
>
> They joined in the President's expressions of high purposes when we went into the war, but would now betray the men who fought by emasculating the league of nations.
>
> They are dreaming and living in a forgotten age.
>
> They would make us despised and distrusted among the nations of the world.

Wilson's "pent-up bitterness" had already "burst forth," Small reported on just the second day of the tour, and there was "no telling" what he might say about his critics by the time he reached the Pacific Coast.[74]

Small did not have to wait that long. Declaring himself in a "fighting spirit," the president went after his critics again the next day in Kansas City, repeating his challenge to "put up or shut up" and questioning their motives. Some of the critics, Wilson began, might "conscientiously" but "ignorantly" oppose the treaty, but others had some "private purpose of their own" and opposed the treaty "with passion, with private passion, with party passion." At one point, he even drew a vague and puzzling comparison between his critics and the Russian Bolsheviks:

> Negation will not save the world. Opposition constructs nothing. Opposition is the specialty of those who are Bolshevistically inclined. . . . I am not comparing any of my respected colleagues to Bolsheviki; but I am merely pointing out that the Bolshevistic spirit lacks every element of constructive opposition. They have destroyed everything, and they have proposed nothing. And, while there is a common abhorrence for political Bolshevism, I hope there won't be any such a thing growing up in our country as international Bolshevism, the Bolshevism that destroys the constructive work of men who have conscientiously tried to cement the good feeling of the great peoples of the world."[75]

According to historian Kendrick Clements, no one could fail to grasp Wilson's reference to Bolshevism in the "autumn of the Red Scare."[76] At the time, however, reporters seemed unsure what to make of the comment. Was he accusing treaty opponents of being like Bolsheviks? Or did he mean to suggest that they were encouraging the spread of Bolshevism by delaying the treaty?[77] However they interpreted the remark, the reporters again had their headline. The president again had attacked his critics, calling them "Bolshevistically inclined" and predicting that history's verdict would be harsh: "When at last, in the annals of mankind they are gibbeted, they will regret that the gibbet is so high."[78]

Wilson's speech in Kansas City stood in sharp contrast to his final speech on this initial leg of the tour—a speech later that same day in Des Moines, Iowa. Speaking just hours after his combative, even mean-spirited address in Kansas City, Wilson told the people of Des Moines that he had come "not to fight anybody" but simply to "report" on the treaty, and he lived up to that pledge by delivering one of the most magnanimous speeches of the entire tour.[79] Focusing on the great principles embodied in the treaty and the bright promise of the League of Nations, Wilson's speech in Des Moines was a philosophical address that, perhaps more than any other speech of the tour, reflected his scholarly ideals of oratorical statesmanship. As perhaps no other speech on the tour, it illustrated what Wilson meant when he talked about engaging his fellow citizens in "common counsel."

Wilson began his speech in Des Moines in the role of the school-master, lecturing on the historical and philosophical roots of the Russian revolution. He noted how the people of Russia had been deceived by a "little group of men just as selfish, just as ruthless, just as pitiless" as the czar himself, and he warned that the "poison" of disorder and chaos was spreading. Wilson thus clarified the relevance of Bolshevism to the debate, observing that in a time of political anarchy and revolution, the world looked to America for leadership. According to Wilson, the "spirit of America" demanded that the nation assume that responsibility; the "processes of history" dictated the end of American isolationism. He also presented one of the most detailed explanations yet of the principles and major provisions of the peace treaty. After reviewing the territorial settlements and the conditions imposed upon Germany, he first addressed the Shantung settlement, frankly conceding that he did not like that particular provision "any better than you do." Discussing the "famous Article X," he then urged his audience not to "let anybody persuade you" that "you can take that article out and have a peaceful world," for that provision cut at the taproot of war by saying to all nations: "Keep on our own territory. Mind your own business." Finally, Wilson observed that the League of Nations would be established "whether we are in it or not." If the United States chose to join the League, it would become "the determining factor in the development of civilization." If it rejected that opportunity, however, it would have to "watch every other nation with suspicion"—and it would in turn be "watched with suspicion."[80]

Wilson's speech in Des Moines appealed to pathos, but it was the pathos of American idealism, not hatred for Germany or the fear of radicalism. Recalling "beautiful stories" about American troops in Europe, Wilson told of how the dispirited Allies "got their morale back the minute they saw the eyes of those boys." Those eyes, Wilson intoned, were "American eyes. They were eyes that had seen visions." Because those soldiers reflected the idealism of the United States, Wilson professed no doubt about the people's judgment of the treaty. Yet worried about the delay caused by a "handful of men," he feigned bewilderment over how anybody could still object to the treaty. There were "no lurking monsters" in the document, "no sinister purposes" hidden behind its language; everything was "said in the frankest way." If they would just read the treaty, they would recognize it as "an un-paralleled achievement of thoughtful civilization." Wilson concluded on a poetic note:

> To my dying day, I shall esteem it the crowning privilege of my life to have been permitted to put my name to a document like that; ... when passion is cooled and men take a sober, second thought, they are going to feel that the supreme thing that America did was to help bring this about and then put her shoulder to the great chariot of justice and of peace which was going to lead men along in that slow and toilsome march—toilsome and full of the kind of agony that brings bloody sweat—but nevertheless going up a slow toilsome incline to those distant heights upon which will shine at last the serene light of justice, suffusing a whole world in blissful peace.[81]

In Des Moines, Wilson thus returned to the principled, high-minded rhetoric that defined his ideal orator-statesman. He did not pander to popular prejudices, nor did he try to scare his audience into supporting the treaty. Instead, he defended the treaty in principle and showed charity toward his opponents, emphasizing not the dangers of rejecting the treaty, but rather the bright promise of the League of Nations. He made his case not by calling his critics names, but by admitting the treaty's imperfections and stressing "the value of discussion." Writing in 1962, rhetorical scholar Mary G. McEdwards sensed in the Des Moines speech the "tone and style of stump oratory," a style that was "long familiar to politicians" but "formerly . . . abhorrent" to Wilson.[82] Yet more than any other speech on the tour, Wilson's speech in Des Moines actually eschewed the passionate histrionics of the spellbinders of the day. Striking a balance between reason and emotion, Wilson highlighted the fundamental principles at stake and invoked the noble sentiments behind America's decision to go to war. In the "center of the isolationist Midwest," as the Des Moines *Register* commented, Wilson presented the League of Nations as the "climax of human progress."[83]

As his last speech in the first leg of his tour, Wilson's speech in Des Moines might have figured prominently in the newspapers' Sunday editions. The president had been greeted by "cheering thousands" in the streets of Des Moines, and the 10,000 people who "crowded the Coliseum to its very rafters" had responded warmly to his address.[84] Yet more interested in his "fighting words" in Kansas City, reporters instead emphasized his criticism of the "Bolshevistically inclined." Under the headline "Wilson's Fight Talk Wins in the West," Small reported that the "one unmistakable fact" to come out of the first few days of the tour was that people liked to hear the president "lambast the senators." The people would listen "attentively enough" to his explanations of the treaty and the League, but it was not until he talked about the "amazing ignorance" of his opponents that the crowds warmed up. The "harder he hits," Small concluded, "the greater the delight of his hearers."[85]

In retrospect, however, historians deemed Wilson's attacks on his critics "most ill advised." As historian Thomas Bailey argued in his classic study of the treaty debate, Wilson's comment that he wished politicians from both parties would be "smothered in their own gas" was neither a "graceful expression, nor a tactful one," for the president needed the support of senators from both parties. And why would Wilson first apologize for challenging treaty opponents to "put up or shut up," then repeat the exact same words in Kansas City? Not only did the vernacular "not become Wilson," but also his attacks on those who opposed him only gave more ammunition to his critics. Nobody was a "quitter" and nobody would "shut up," one senator protested, while *Harvey's Weekly* cited the president's confrontational language as evidence of his growing desperation: "Yet he rushed about the country like a howling dervish, shrieking 'Put up or shut up, you contemptible quitters, before you are hanged on a gibbet!'" To many, Bailey concluded, it looked as if the president were "publicly airing a private quarrel."[86]

Yet if Wilson seemed desperate to some, others sensed that he was inspired by his reception. Everywhere he went—with the possible exception of Columbus—the president was greeted by large and enthusiastic crowds, and his speeches invariably met with long ovations and shouts of approval.[87] In Indianapolis, the *Atlanta Constitution* reported, "thousands of persons . . . crowded the streets and cheered lustily as the president passed," and the 16,000-seat auditorium was "filled to overflowing" with cheering supporters.[88] Wilson also received "an unexpectedly enthusiastic reception" in St. Louis—"the warmest since his return from Paris"—while in Kansas City another "eager crowd" of some 15,000 packed the convention hall "to the rafters" and showed their support for the president with a "mass flag salute."[89] Some 8,000 people "swarmed" around his train as it stopped briefly in St. Joseph, Missouri, and when the president arrived in Des Moines he was greeted by a "surging mass" of people in "the most enthusiastic welcome" yet.[90] Reflecting on his reception in an interview with Small, Wilson proclaimed himself "well satisfied" with the crowds and "convinced more than ever" that the "people of the country" were "with him."[91]

Reporters covering the tour painted a more complex portrait of public opinion. According to the *New York Times*, it was "generally admitted" that the president's call for a League of Nations was a "winning proposition." The "situation as a whole" was "favorable to his cause," the *Times* reported, as the public was "very largely in favor" of a League in which the United States would "play a leading part." Furthermore, there was a "distinct feeling in many quarters" that the opposition was simply trying to "embarrass the President," with the public especially disapproving of efforts by "radical elements in the Senate" to kill the treaty altogether. At the same time, however, the *Times* reported that the public remained open to "arguments for reservations" and that a great many people could be classified as "mild reservationists."[92] Never imagining that the president might refuse to compromise on that issue, the *Times,* in effect, declared the debate over:

> Judging from the events of yesterday and today, it is generally admitted, even by opponents of the League of Nations, that if the President will accept a program providing for some reservations he will have the support of the vast majority of the people in the sections through which he has passed. To that extent, according to prevailing opinion, the President has won his fight already. [93]

In the week to come, Wilson would enter hostile territory—Republican states with large German American populations and strong isolationist traditions. In Nebraska, he would confront the loyal following of irreconcilable Senator George W. Norris; in Montana he would face crowds of radical miners; and by the end of the week he would be speaking in the home state of one of his most vociferous critics, Senator William Borah of Idaho. As the *New York Times* reported, Wilson already had failed to keep himself "in check" on occasion, and the temptation to lash out at his critics would only increase in the week to come.[94] As it turned out, Wilson did manage to control himself, and in fact he delivered some of the longest and most thoughtful speeches of the entire tour during this second leg of his journey. Yet slighted by reporters at the time, these addresses have received little attention from Wilson biographers and historians of the treaty debate. They are the "forgotten speeches" of Wilson's Western tour.

The Forgotten Speeches

It was 9:00 A.M. on Monday morning when Woodrow Wilson began the second leg of his Western tour with a parade through Omaha, Nebraska. Reporters covering the tour found the crowds in Omaha "depressingly small," but Grayson claimed that the presidential party was "amazed" to find the streets "lined for blocks" and the windows of the buildings "filled with people anxious to see the President and cheer him." "It had not been expected that there would be much of a turn-out," Grayson recalled, and there would have been "little disappointment" if there had been "only a few people on the streets."[95] When the president arrived at the auditorium, he found it "crowded to the roof" with some 7,500 people, many of whom had "gone without beds for the night to see him."[96] In a strongly Republican state where irreconcilable Senator George W. Norris had a "loyal following," the presidential party claimed to be well pleased with the welcome.[97]

Wilson met with similar receptions the rest of the week. In Sioux Falls, the streets were crowded despite rainy weather. His audience in Sioux Falls "taxed the capacity of the Coliseum," which held about 7,000 persons.[98] In the Twin Cities, a "great crowd" greeted the president's train, and his reception at the Minneapolis Armory was "the most enthusiastic and largest up to date." That evening Wilson addressed a crowd of some 15,000 at the St. Paul Auditorium—again "one of the most enthusiastic" meetings that the president had "ever addressed anywhere," in Grayson's assessment.[99] The next day at Bismarck, Wilson's "first audience of farmers" filled the 1,500-seat city auditorium and "cheered when the President spoke of American ideals."[100] In Billings on September 11, nearly 9,000 people (including a "large number of Indians") filled another big auditorium, and in Helena later that day the crowd proved "extremely friendly to the President," despite the presence of a "large number of radicals." Only in Coeur d'Alene, Idaho, did the crowd disappoint, as fewer than 2,000 turned out to hear Wilson speak in a circus tent that could have held many more. Later that same day, however, nearly 5,000 people filled the National Guard Armory in Spokane, and the crowd was "demonstrative and apparently well pleased" with the president's speech.[101]

Yet nothing prepared Wilson and his entourage for their reception upon arriving at the Pacific Coast. At Tacoma, and particularly at Seattle, the reception was "so overwhelming and unrestrained as to recall Wilson's triumphal Italian tour." Greeted by some 25,000 flag-waving citizens at the Tacoma Stadium, Wilson delivered a few brief remarks before motoring to the Armory for an address before an audience of some 5,000 people. Along the parade route the crowds were so large and rowdy that Secret Service agents had to "hurl people back from the presidential automobile."[102] In Seattle, the spirit of the crowd seemed "akin to fanaticism," the *New York Times* reported, as "throngs" of people greeted the president in "a continuous and riotous uproar." The patriotic fervor peaked as Wilson reviewed the Pacific fleet, standing "bareheaded" on the forward turret of the historic battleship *Oregon* as dreadnoughts and destroyers passed in review.[103] Wilson concluded his day with a public dinner and a major address to a standing-room-only crowd of 6,300 people at the Seattle Arena. Thousands more were locked out of the packed arena and "kept up such a roar of cheering" that Wilson had to interrupt his speech to acknowledge the "welcome but inopportune" demonstration.[104]

Events, however, conspired against Wilson. The week began with Senator Hitchcock reporting to Wilson on his desperate attempts to stem the tide of a Democratic revolt against the president's uncompromising position on reservations. As of September 8, the *Chicago Daily Tribune* reported, seven Democrats had come out in favor of reservations, leaving only forty of forty-seven Democrats still with the president and perhaps no more than twenty-seven senators "dependable" in their commitment.[105] Meanwhile, the opposition tour, featuring senators Borah and Johnson, was drawing huge and enthusiastic crowds in some of the same cities where Wilson had spoken.[106] Then, on September 12, William C. Bullitt, a former member of the American peace delegation in Paris, testified before the Senate Foreign Relations Committee that even Secretary of State Lansing had called parts of the treaty "thoroughly bad" and the League of Nations "entirely useless." Near the end of his sensational testimony, Bullitt recalled a conversation in which Lansing reportedly said, "I believe that if the Senate could only understand what this treaty means, and if the American people could really understand, it would unquestionably be defeated, but I wonder if they will ever understand what it lets them in for."[107]

Appearing unaffected by these events, Wilson delivered a dozen major addresses over the next six days in Nebraska, the Dakotas, Minnesota, Montana, Idaho, and Washington. In general, as August Heckscher has noted, Wilson's speeches during this leg of the tour were "remarkable for their cogency and force," as he "continued to expound . . . the mixture of idealism, hard-headed economics, and controlled polemics which had already won him respectful hearings."[108] In Helena he wandered off topic to express his "shame as an American citizen" over race riots in some cities and to denounce a police strike in Boston as a "crime against civilization."[109] In one or two other addresses Wilson also took shots at his critics. For the most part, however, he continued to "expound" upon the treaty, avoiding criticism of particular senators and ignoring the advice of friends that "he 'warm up a bit,' pull out all the stops, and give the audiences some 'sob stuff.'"[110]

Wilson began the week with what historian Cooper has called one of the "most effective" speeches in "this segment of the tour": his address at the Auditorium in Omaha on Monday, September 8.[111] With a copy of the treaty in hand, Wilson reviewed the territorial settlements and the labor provisions of the treaty. In a state with a large German American population, he also reiterated his argument that the treaty was not too harsh on Germany. Germany had committed a "criminal act against mankind," Wilson explained, and it would have to "undergo the punishment." "Not more than it can endure," he insisted, but enough to pay "for the wrong that it has done." Turning to the League, Wilson lamented that critics had portrayed it as "an arrangement for war," and he reviewed, for the first time, each of the four reservations that had been proposed by the Foreign Relations Committee. Arguing that the reservations would "change the language of the treaty without changing its meaning," he explained his opposition: "A reservation is an assent with a 'but' to it. We agree—but." Such changes, he insisted, would force him to "go back to Paris and say, 'I am much obliged to you, but we don't like the language used.'" The United States could not now "rewrite this treaty," Wilson concluded; "We must take it or leave it."[112]

Wilson delivered a very different speech later that same day in Sioux Falls, South Dakota. Touching only briefly on the proposed reservations, he instead delivered a more philosophical and emotional address, reflecting on the causes of war and articulating his own vision of a new world order. Recalling what Europeans "saw in the eyes of the American boys" who went overseas, Wilson argued that the United States had gone to war not merely to defeat Germany but to defeat "everything that Germany's actions represented." For generations, Germany had prepared for this war, Wilson explained, and had manifested precisely the attitude of those now opposed to the League: they wanted to go it alone, armed to the teeth and refusing to cooperate with other nations. That was the "fundamental choice" now facing the nation: "You have either got to have the old system, of which Germany was the perfect flower, or you have got to have a new system." If, on the one hand, America chose the "old system," it would mean a "great standing army," higher taxes, and a "military government in spirit if not in form." If, on the other hand, America joined the League, it would bring about "an absolute reversal of history, an absolute revolution in the way in which international affairs are treated." The choice, then, was between "the League of Nations and Germanism," and Wilson claimed to be "speaking the voice of America" when he championed the League.[113]

Over the next five days Wilson would deliver ten more major addresses and several briefer speeches. In the first of three addresses in the Twin Cities, he warned a special session of the Minnesota State Legislature that delays in ratification of the treaty could encourage labor unrest and exacerbate the nation's economic problems. Lamenting the "downright ignorance" of the treaty's opponents, Wilson concluded, "The facts are marching, and God is marching with them." The United States had to either welcome those facts or "subsequently, with humiliation, surrender to them." "It is welcome or surrender," Wilson concluded. "It is acceptance of great world conditions and great world duties or scuttle now and come back afterwards."[114]

Later that day at the Minneapolis Armory, Wilson again emphasized the "revolution" that had taken place in world affairs, contrasting the "old order of things" with the new world order. In the old order, international policies were based on power rather than the "general moral judgment of mankind." That order was gone, for the "mass of men" were now "awake" to their rights and would not allow the world to "sink back into that old slough of misused authority again." America thus faced a "great choice," according to Wilson. Either join the "mass of mankind" and "take part in guiding and steadying the world," or look forward to another "generation of doubt and of disorder." Reading from notes, Wilson concluded the speech by summarizing the goals and provisions of the League charter. Once again he presented the choice in stark, either-or terms: "Our choice . . . is only this: shall we go in and assist as trusted partners or shall we stay out and act as suspected rivals. We have got to do one or the other. We have got to be either provincials or statesmen. We have got to be either ostriches or eagles."[115]

Generally, Wilson resisted the temptation to "tap base and unattractive sentiments," and Cooper proclaims it "remarkable and creditable" to Wilson that he so "sparingly" resorted to "anti-German appeals."[116] An anti-German reference in Sioux Falls dominated the headlines for that day,[117] however, and in his final address in the Twin Cities he denounced "German intrigue" and launched what one reporter called a "terrific attack" on "hyphenated Americans."[118] Speaking before a large and enthusiastic crowd at the St. Paul auditorium, Wilson not only declared a hyphen "the most un-American thing in the world," but also accused some German Americans of dreaming of a day when the United States and their fatherland would "unite to dominate the world." The "hyphen which looked to us like a snake" had "reared its head again," he warned, and the "his-s-s" of its purpose was to keep the United States out of the "concert of nations." Yet despite these "old intrigues," Wilson expressed his "most unbounded confidence" that the treaty would be ratified. "All that is needed is that you should be vocal and audible," Wilson exhorted. "I know what you want. Say it and get it."[119]

Wilson continued to present the choice facing the nation in stark, uncompromising terms as he headed west across the upper Great Plains. In Bismarck on September 10, Wilson announced that the nation had a choice between "this treaty with this Covenant or a disturbed world and certain war." In an area of strong isolationist sentiment, Wilson also lectured his audience on how the "processes of civilization" had left isolationism behind, declaring: "You cannot disentangle the United States from the rest of the world." At the same time, he tried to assuage concerns that Article X would drag the United States into war, and he again denounced the Bolsheviks and warned that "the world is in disorder." Overall, however, Wilson remained positive, upbeat, and optimistic. Expressing complete confidence that the treaty would be ratified, he rejoiced in the prospect of America fulfilling her "destiny" and concluded, "It is a noble purpose. It is a noble principle." The United States would join the League, and "with the blood of every great people in our veins" the United States would turn to the rest of the world and say, "We still stand ready to redeem our promise. We still believe in liberty."[120]

Wilson continued in the same vein in Billings on September 11. The president began the speech like many others, defending the treaty against charges that it was too harsh on Germany and emphasizing how it was based upon an American principle: that people had "a right to determine their . . . own form of government." Wilson quickly turned to the larger meaning of the war, however, posing a rhetorical question with special meaning for those who had lost boys in the "blistering Argonne" and had come long distances to "get what comfort they could from their President":[121] "Thousands of our gallant youth lie buried in France. Buried for what?" Wilson answered his own question by insisting that the war had been fought for the "salvation of mankind everywhere." In a region "pervaded with . . . radicalism," as the president himself observed, he again spoke of the "chaotic spirit" infecting the world and of the lesson to be learned from "pitiful Russia." "There are disciples of Lenin in our own midst,"

Wilson declared, and the only way to counter radicalism was to "deprive it of food." Marveling at how the "human heart" remained hopeful despite "all the unspeakable terrors and injustices" in the world, he then concluded with an anecdote that he would repeat several times over the course of the tour:

> A woman came up to me the other day and grasped my hand and said, "God bless you, Mr. President!" and then turned away in tears. I asked a neighbor, "What is the matter?" and he said, "She intended to say something to you, Sir, but she lost a son in France." That woman did not take my hand with a feeling that her son ought not to have been sent to France. I sent her son to France and she took my hand and blessed me. . . . Down deep in it was the love of her boy, the feeling of what he had done, the justice and the dignity and the majesty of it, and then the hope that through such a poor instrumentality as men like myself could offer, no other woman's son would ever be called upon to lay his life down for the same thing.[122]

Despite a recurrence of his headaches and the onset of what Grayson described as "asthmatic attacks," Wilson delivered the longest speech of the entire tour later that day in Helena, Montana.[123] The "question," he began, was "nothing more nor less than this: shall the great sacrifice that we made in this war be in vain, or shall it not?" Noting that the prevailing mood, particularly in the West, had been to stay out of the war, Wilson recalled that he had once shared that view—until the people demanded that he respond to Germany's "challenge." Now the question was not whether America should have entered that war, but rather what could be done to prevent another world war—a war that would be the "final war" for "civilization itself." Wilson's answer, of course, was the League of Nations, for the "experience of mankind" proved that if people simply talked things over it became "more difficult to fight." By simply requiring nations to talk before deciding to fight, Wilson promised that the League would provide "better than 95 per cent insurance against war."[124]

Wilson's speech in Helena also included one of his most comprehensive responses to the reservations endorsed by the Senate Foreign
Relations Committee. There was "nothing in the Covenant" to prevent
the United States from withdrawing "whenever we please," he insisted,
nor could the United States be forced to go to war under Article X of
the Covenant. The League could only "advise," not "direct," the United
States to take military action, he noted. Likewise, there was nothing at
all in the document that could be "taken as invalidating the Monroe
Doctrine," and the Covenant "distinctly" said that the League would
"take no action . . . and make no report" concerning "exclusively domestic" questions. In short, not a single one of the proposed reservations
was necessary, yet the treaty's opponents could talk of nothing else.
"I have not heard them talk about anything else," Wilson complained;
"It is a very wonderful document, and you would think there were
only four things in it."[125]

Wilson's speech in Helena also introduced perhaps the most enduring image of the Western tour: the scene at the American cemetery in
Suresnes, France, where Wilson had spoken on Memorial Day. Focusing
the debate on the larger meaning of the war, Wilson began and ended
his speech in Helena with that image—an image more famously associated with his final speech in Pueblo. In Helena, he began:

> As I think upon this theme, there is a picture very distinctly in my
> mind. On last Memorial Day I stood in an American cemetery in
> France, just outside Paris, on the slopes of Suresnes. The hills slope
> steeply to a little plain. And when I went out there all the slope of
> the hill was covered with men in the American uniform, standing,
> but rising tier on tier as if in a great witness stand. Then below,
> over a little level space, were simple crosses that marked the resting
> place of the American dead.
>
> And just by the stand where I spoke was a group of French
> women who had lost their own sons, but, just because they had
> lost their own sons and because their hearts went out in thought
> and sympathy to the mothers on this side of the sea, they had made
> themselves, so to say, mothers of those graves, and every day had

gone to take care of them, every day had strewn them with flowers. And they stood there, their cheeks wetted with tears, while I spoke, not of the French dead, but of the American boys who had died in the common cause.

In closing, Wilson returned to that "scene"—"that slope at Suresnes, those voiceless graves, those weeping women"—and concluded on a sentimental note: "My fellow citizens, the pledge that speaks from those graves is demanded of us. We must see to it that those boys did not die in vain. We must fulfill the great mission upon which they crossed the sea."[126]

In Coeur d'Alene, on Friday, September 12, Wilson continued to warn of the "poison" of radicalism and to describe the League of Nations as "insurance" against war. In Idaho, home of irreconcilable Senator William Borah, he claimed to be "amazed" that "men in responsible positions" could still oppose the treaty outright—a reference to Borah that reportedly met with "complete silence."[127] In Spokane, he again complained that the treaty's opponents had misrepresented "exactly what this great Covenant does."

Yet it was Wilson himself who most confused the treaty debate by sending mixed signals on the question of reservations. In Coeur d'Alene, he expressed no "moral objection" to Congress clarifying its interpretation of the treaty, so long as reservations were not made a "condition to our ratification of it."[128] In other words, he seemed open to "interpretive" reservations. Later that same day in Spokane, however, he returned to his hard-line position, insisting that reservations would merely "say over again" what the Covenant already said "in plain language." Devoting much of his speech in Spokane to the proposed reservations, he declared flatly that "not one" of them was "justified" and disputed the need for each, "one by one." If the treaty's critics were "more frank and honest," he concluded, they would admit that reservations would "make it necessary that we should go back to Paris and discuss in new language the things which . . . are already in the document."[129]

Clearly, the League of Nations debate hinged on Wilson's attitude toward reservations. Yet the reporters covering the tour said little about that issue in their dispatches of September 12. Instead, they emphasized Wilson's complaint about the "element of personal bitterness" in the debate and a rare reference to the upcoming presidential election. "I leave the verdict with you . . . my Republican fellow citizens," Wilson had said in Spokane, "that you will not allow yourselves for one moment, as I do not allow myself for one moment, as God knows my conscience, to think of 1920 when thinking about the redemption of the world."[130]

"For a moment," Small reported, "we fairly held our breath and thought the time of positive declaration had arrived." With "a few well chosen words," the president might have eliminated the "personal element" from the debate by announcing that he would not seek re-election. Had he done that, Small speculated, he would have won such overwhelming public approval that the Senate would have been forced to ratify the treaty "without reservation or qualification of any sort."[131] Yet Wilson chose not to make that pledge, and he mentioned the 1920 election just once more during the tour. Perhaps he feared that withdrawing from the race would backfire, freeing still more Democrats to support reservations. Or perhaps he thought Republicans might make good on their threat to delay voting on the treaty until a new president assumed office. Whatever his thinking, Wilson failed Small's "acid test" of political sincerity. He had missed his chance to prove to the public his "absolute sincerity" and "disinterestedness in personal exaltation."[132]

A Change in Strategy

In retrospect, September 12 marked an important turning point in the Western tour, not because of Wilson's reference to the 1920 election but because Joseph Tumulty penned two important memos that day. Urging a change in strategy, Tumulty called for a more aggressive approach, recommending that the president talk more about the costs of the Great War and the threat of another, even more destructive war. He also urged the president to respond more directly to his critics, pointing out that Republicans had originated the idea of a League of Nations in the first place. As a scholar, of course, Wilson had criticized speakers who "sawed the air" with emotional appeals, and early in the tour he had resisted the temptation to "debate" his critics. Yet confronted with reports that the tour was having "no effect" on the Senate (except, perhaps, to "stiffen opposition"), Wilson now seemed prepared to take the offensive.[133]

Tumulty wrote his memos en route to Tacoma. In the first of the two memos, he urged Wilson to focus his speeches more on the costs of the war, reminding his audiences of both the money spent and the number of men killed and injured. Tumulty even supplied statistics, noting that the war had cost the United States some "one million dollars an hour for two years" and that "battle deaths" had ranged from 50,300 for the United States to 1.7 million for Russia. The "battle deaths in this war alone," Tumulty wrote, "exceeded those of the previous hundred years by one and a half million." In the second memo, Tumulty suggested that Wilson quote from his own War Address to remind Americans of why they went to war in the first place. He also urged the president to emphasize how leading Republicans, including Taft and Roosevelt, first came up with the idea of a League of Nations. Finally, he urged Wilson to present ratification of the treaty as a choice between "peace or war" and to emphasize the costs of war in human terms. He even drafted a long passage illustrating how the sacrifices of war might be communicated in a more "eloquent way":

These figures are cold but it is the tragedy that lies behind those figures which calls forth our emotion and our interest and even our pity. They speak of broken hearts, desolated homes and ravaged fields. They speak of mothers bereft of their sons whom they freely gave to the Nation to vindicate the splendid conceptions of liberty and freedom which the genius of America typifies. They speak of wives in despair and of sweethearts whose tender hopes were cut asunder. They speak of the flower of European and American youth going out to die that the world may be free. Do not these figures carry home a lesson to you all? What do you think these boys died for? What do you think these mothers who freely gave up their sons wished for down in the depths of their very hearts and souls? These boys died like crusaders that men might be free, that their children might be free. No mother ever gave up her son to war who did not in her heart of hearts pray that statesmen might develop some instrumentality which might make these horrible things forever impossible. No man who visited Europe and who witnessed the wreck and ruin wrought by this monster of war did not pray God that out of this maelstrom of blood and tears might come a League of Nations that might make this thing of war impossible in the future.[134]

Wilson had done some of what Tumulty suggested all along, of course. The next day in Tacoma, however, he followed his secretary's script to the letter, beginning with the line from his own War Address: "We shall fight . . . for the things which we have always carried nearest to our hearts,—for democracy, for the right of those who submit to authority to have a voice in their own governments, for the rights and liberties of small nations, for a universal dominion of right by such a concert of free peoples as shall bring peace and safety to all nations and make the world itself at last free." He then talked about the costs of the war, twice repeating Tumulty's statistics on U.S. expenditures: "The expenditures of the United States were at the rate of $1,000,000 an hour for two years. $1,000,000 an hour, including the nighttime, for two years." Finally, he turned to "battle deaths," citing figures for each belligerent nation before quoting Tumulty's memo almost verbatim: "The total of all battle deaths in all the wars of the world from the year 1793 to 1914 were something under 6,000,000; . . . in all the wars of the world for more than 100 years, fewer men died than have been killed upon the field of battle in the last five years."[135]

Wondering aloud whether the nation had "forgotten," Wilson credited the "leading figures" of the Republican Party with the "great idea" of a League of Nations. He then took Tumulty's advice again, translating the statistics on battle deaths into more human and emotional terms. The treaty debate was not just about the cost of the war, he noted, but also about the "aching hearts" of those who lost loved ones in the Great War. His voice reportedly shaking, Wilson prayed to God that the little children who waved flags as his train passed would "never have to carry those flags into battle." He concluded by reminding his critics of all that the treaty had accomplished:

> It has liberated great populations. It has set up the standards of right and of liberty for the first time, . . . and then has placed back of them this splendid power of the nations combined.
>   . . . Let them catch this vision; . . . let them take counsel of weeping mothers; let them take counsel of bereaved fathers who . . . are now alone; let them take counsel of the lonely farms where there used to be a boy to help the old man . . . ; let them realize that the world is hungry, that the world is naked, that the world is suffering, and that none of these things can be remedied until the minds of men are reassured."[136]

Perhaps exhausted by a long day of parades and ceremonies and "not feeling very well," Wilson delivered a less passionate speech before a packed house at the Seattle arena that evening.[137] Blaming the "partisans of Germany" for prolonging the debate, Wilson recited his well-worn summaries of the League's provisions for international arbitration, boycotts of rogue nations, and mutual defense. As he had many times before, he also assured his audience in Seattle that there would be "no sacrifice" of American sovereignty under Article X, and he reiterated his openness to reservations that did not "change the treaty." "If all that you desire is to say what you understand the treaty to mean," he said, "no harm could be done by saying it." But if reservations "altered" the meaning of the treaty, it would be necessary to take it "back to the conference table." And according to Wilson, the world was in no "temper to discuss this treaty over again." More "profoundly disturbed" than ever before, the world demanded "some sort of settlement."[138]

Wilson was no doubt inspired by his reception in the Pacific Northwest. The *New York Times* compared the president's welcome in Seattle to his triumphal postwar parades and also observed that "no such scenes" had taken place at "any other city on this tour." Indeed, no more remarkable demonstration of support had ever been witnessed in the "history . . . of recent political campaigns," the *Times* reported.[139] Twenty-five years later, historian Thomas Bailey also would compare Wilson's reception to his "triumphal Italian tour," describing the crowds in Tacoma and Seattle as "overwhelming" and "unrestrained."[140] Wilson's welcome in the Northwest not only seemed to confirm that he had the people behind him but also renewed his spirit. As if "struck by the light of the Pacific," biographer Heckscher wrote, Wilson "found a new mood" when he reached the West Coast, and that mood would carry over into the next week as he toured California.[141]

As Wilson paused for his second day of rest on Sunday, September 14, the reporters traveling with the president took stock of what he had accomplished. In a special to the *New York Times*, for example, Grasty reflected on the "spirit" of the people and summarized public opinion as "generally favorable" toward the treaty. Those who had heard the president's "persuasive exposition of the subject" had become "more positive in their desire for prompt affirmative action," Grasty reported, although he remained skeptical that "popular interest" in the treaty had been deepened by the "public discussion pro and con." The people were "not excited about it," he reported, "but they would like to see early ratification." At the same time, Grasty sensed sympathy for the Senate's efforts to clarify American rights—as long as those efforts did not force a "re-submission to the signatories."[142]

The *New York Times* published an even more detailed analysis of public opinion the following day. "The opinion is generally held that the President has steadily advanced his cause since he started on this nation-wide tour," the *Times* reported, "at least to the extent of winning support for the big principles he advocates." According to the *Times*, the public believed that "the Treaty of Peace should be ratified without delay"; most believed that a League of Nations could prove helpful in preventing war and "in stabilizing the world."

Yet based on conversations with "hundreds" of "men and women in all walks of life," the *Times* also reported that the public expected some sort of compromise between the president and the Senate reservationists—a middle ground that would "prove acceptable" to both sides. In summarizing the prospects for ratification, the *Times* concluded:

> The President everywhere has received a most generous reception and a very attentive hearing. His addresses for the most part have not been framed with the purpose of evoking the plaudits of his hearers, but his audiences have been enthusiastic and wholly friendly. There have been spots where local conditions, such as pro-German activities, have tended to keep down the street crowds, but these instances have not been more than two or three in number. On the whole, the tour thus far has been satisfactory from the President's viewpoint. . . .
>
> During the past week the President has campaigned in six States, Missouri, Nebraska, North Dakota, South Dakota, Idaho and Washington. In each of these, when he left, it was seen to be the case that the majority of the people were for quick ratification of the Peace Treaty with the League of Nations Covenant. The people also, it would appear, are not ready to condemn utterly a program of reservations which would not destroy, and would be well satisfied if Mr. Wilson and the opposition Senators would come speedily to an agreement.[143]

The newspapers thus credited Wilson with winning over the public. At the same time, however, most assumed that he eventually would compromise on the question of reservations. At the time, nobody imagined that he would resist reservations to the point of scuttling the whole treaty. Yet apparently emboldened by the demonstrations of public support, Wilson would become even more defiant as he toured California. Before long he would even threaten to kill the treaty himself rather than accept any changes.

Conclusion

Speaking in Indianapolis on the very first day of his Western tour, Woodrow Wilson declared that he had no intention of "arguing this thing with you, my fellow citizens," and he drew cheers when he expressed no doubt about the "verdict of the American people."[144] He was not on a "political errand, even in the broad sense of that term," he insisted again five days later in St. Paul, Minnesota,[145] and for the most part his early tour speeches seemed consistent with that view of his mission. "Expounding" upon the treaty, Wilson rarely attacked particular critics and instead emphasized his positive vision of a new world order. "Everywhere he went," as Link observed, he "pleaded in good temper, not as a partisan, but as a leader who stood above party strife and advantage."[146] Historian Bailey offered a similar assessment: "The addresses were pitched . . . on an extremely optimistic key. Wilson made it clear that he was not arguing or fighting with any one. He was traveling to find out what the people were thinking and saying, he wanted the pleasure of seeking fresh 'inspiration' from them. He was merely explaining the treaty and making a report to the people. He never for one moment doubted that the treaty would be ratified; the only thing that concerned him, he said, was the delay."[147]

Yet other historians have blamed that very attitude for Wilson's "slow start" on the tour. According to Cooper, for example, Wilson spent too much time "explaining provisions" of the treaty instead of "pleading his case and rallying support." Cooper stated, the "need to explain his program to an ignorant and apparently misled public" placed Wilson "too much on the defensive," with the president forced to play the role of "Professor" Wilson, the "schoolmaster" of politics.[148] In Cooper's view, Wilson's speeches also proved ineffective because he "failed to reach out to senators or suggest possible areas of compromise."[149] Other historians likewise have faulted Wilson for refusing to negotiate in public. Rather than "seeking accommodation," Lloyd Ambrosius has argued, Wilson ignored or criticized the very senators he needed to persuade, and that goes a long way toward explaining why the tour "produced no favorable results back in Washington."[150]

Joseph Tumulty, of course, had little interest in compromising with the Senate. Convinced that the Senate could be brought to heel by arousing public opinion, he urged a more aggressive and confrontational approach—one that foreshadowed the modern rhetorical presidency. As Wilson toured California and turned back toward the east on the last leg of his journey, he increasingly took Tumulty's advice, delivering passionate and defiant speeches and urging his supporters to demand ratification. In the long run, however, the strategy backfired. With his new approach, the president stirred up impressive demonstrations by the crowds who came out to see him. Yet his drift toward demagoguery also undermined the possibilities for compromise with the Senate and, in the final analysis, defied the public's support for compromise and quick ratification of the treaty.

CHAPTER 3

The Drift toward Demagoguery

My fellow citizens, we must realize that a great and final
choice is upon the people. Either we are going to guarantee
civilization or we are going to abandon it.
SALT LAKE CITY, UTAH, SEPTEMBER 23, 1919

The chaos in Seattle had been "mild in comparison," Philip Kinsley reported on Wednesday, September 17. When the president first stepped up to deliver his speech at the San Francisco auditorium, he was greeted by the longest demonstration of the entire tour, followed by "a series of shorter yells in the back rows, a demonstration that appeared to be a studied effort to break up the meeting." For fifteen or twenty minutes the president could not speak at all and stood "quietly, composedly, a slip of paper in his hand, his smile changing to a frown." For the first time on his Western tour, the president had been heckled. A "noisy, rebellious minority"—identified in newspaper accounts as elements of the Irish radical group Sinn Fein—had tried to "make things difficult for the president." And by all accounts "they succeeded."[1]

Wilson had arrived in California, where large numbers of Chinese and Irish Americans objected to the treaty's Shantung provision and its silence on Irish independence. Beginning the third week of his tour, which he would spend mostly in California, Wilson faced "the most challenging and taxing days of the tour": the "invasion" of irreconcilable

Senator Hiram Johnson's home turf, where a "volatile and uncertain public" had been "deeply stirred" by various "passions."[2] Wilson's advisors were worried. Not only did the president face unpredictable crowds in the Golden State, but also back in Washington it now appeared certain that the Senate would vote for reservations. Meanwhile, California's own Senator Johnson was shadowing the president, speaking to enthusiastic audiences in many of the same cities Wilson had just visited.

More worrisome still was the president's health. Writing in his diary after the president spoke to a predominantly female audience of 3,000 at the Palace Hotel in San Francisco, Dr. Cary Grayson observed that the president was "not feeling well." He had suffered from a "splitting headache" all morning, and for a time it appeared doubtful that he would be able to make his address at all. Grayson did "everything possible to relieve his pain," and the president ended up making a "splendid address." But the busy schedule was taking its toll, despite the fact that Grayson was doing "everything possible to prevent a breakdown." As he left California, Grayson noted that the president was "suffering very serious fatigue as a result of his exertions," along with "constantly recurring headaches" and "irritation in his throat." The trip had been "far too strenuous" and had exhausted "every possible bit of vitality" the president had left, and Grayson was growing "more and more apprehensive" of the results.[3]

As it turned out, Wilson not only survived California but also left triumphant. Expecting to find hostile audiences, he instead met with "unprecedented ovations," and he even managed to allay some of the "peculiar apprehensions of the people of the Golden State."[4] After just his first day in the state the newspapers were already reporting that he had "overcome the opposition" in the Bay Area. Sentiment in Northern California was now "unquestionably for acceptance of the agreement," the *New York Times* reported on September 19, with the understanding that the United States shall exert its influence in the League to see that the wrongs done to China are righted." By the end of his visit, the newspapers were reporting that the president had won over the entire state. By a margin of "at least two to one," the *New York Times* reported on September 22, Californians now supported "the President's program without drastic reservations." Reporter Charles H. Grasty proclaimed, "This is Woodrow Wilson country now." Crediting Wilson with changing the "temper of the public," the *Los Angeles Times* predicted that no Republican would now "dare fight to postpone action."[5]

Given the results, it comes as little surprise that historians have praised Wilson's California speeches as "the best of the tour"—indeed, among "the finest of his life."[6] Blending "predictions of another war with facts and figures about the death and destruction of this war," Wilson stirred up a "potent rhetorical concoction" in California, historian John Milton Cooper Jr. has written, not only answering the states' special concerns but also putting his critics on the defensive.[7] In Oakland, Wilson made his "most stirring emotional appeal" yet, according to Cooper, and his speech in San Diego—delivered via an electronic "voice phone" to a crowd approaching 50,000—was "the finest of the whole tour." Despite persistent headaches and the accumulating strain of the tour, Wilson rose to the challenge, and Californians responded with a great "outpouring of support" that seemed to have a "tonic effect" on the physically ailing president.[8]

By his own oratorical standards, however, Wilson's California speeches bordered on demagoguery. No longer did he "expound" upon the principles and provisions of the treaty, engaging his fellow citizens in "common counsel." Instead, he lashed out at his critics, questioning their motives and even their loyalty to the nation. Following Joseph Tumulty's advice, Wilson also wallowed in emotion, recalling the horrors of the war just ended and exploiting fears of another, even more terrible war. Losing patience with the slow processes of democratic deliberation, the president left California claiming victory and declaring the debate over. Yet Wilson did not sound like a man confident of victory. To the contrary, his rhetoric became increasingly shrill and combative over the final week of the tour.

Wilson's drift toward demagoguery culminated in a speech "filled with defiance and highlighted by flashes of anger" in Salt Lake City. Warning the people of Utah that "the specter of Bolshevism" hung over the treaty debate, he blamed opposition to the treaty on "pro-German influences" and implied that even the mild reservationists had betrayed their country. It was, as Cooper has noted, the "worst outburst" of "inflammatory statements" of the entire tour,[9] and it reflected Wilson's growing frustration with his critics back in Washington. More importantly, it may have destroyed any remaining chance for compromise with the Senate.

This chapter charts Wilson's drift toward demagoguery on the West Coast leg of his tour. Beginning with his two speeches in Portland on September 15, I show how Wilson arrived in California with the political momentum and deftly handled the hecklers in San Francisco. He also effectively responded to the state's special concerns over the Irish and Shantung issues. In Southern California, Wilson's impassioned denunciations of his critics electrified his huge and enthusiastic crowds, and as he left the state and turned back toward the East, the newspapers concluded that he had public opinion behind him. In Utah, however, Wilson seemed to come unraveled, lashing out at the mild reservationists and questioning their motives. Waving the bloody shirt and refusing to compromise, the president not only betrayed his own principles of oratorical statesmanship but also sabotaged his dream of a new world order.

Confronting the Opposition

Despite the remarkable scene just two days earlier in Seattle, President Wilson confessed to being "somewhat depressed" as he began a brief, impromptu address before an enthusiastic crowd of two hundred professional and business men in Portland on Monday, September 15. Earlier in the day, an automobile accident had claimed the life of the Cleveland *Plain Dealer*'s Washington correspondent, Ben F. Allen, along with that of a seventy-three-year-old local man who had volunteered to drive in the presidential motorcade. Two other reporters, Robert T. Small of the Philadelphia *Public Ledger* and Stanley Reynolds of the *Baltimore Sun*, were injured in the crash on the scenic Columbia highway. "It was the first accident of serious nature to occur during the President's tour of the country," the *Los Angeles Times* reported, and according to the *Washington Post* it "cast a pall" over the entire presidential party.[10]

The accident did nothing to dampen the enthusiasm of the crowds that greeted the president in Portland, however. From the moment his train arrived, "the President and Mrs. Wilson were followed by cheering crowds," and while those crowds were "almost as large" as those in Seattle they were of a "different spirit," according to the *New York Times*: "It was real enthusiasm, and not the mob spirit found in Seattle."[11] At the train station the crowd started "a roar of welcome" that continued "all the way along an automobile ride through Portland's principal streets," and when Wilson traveled from his hotel to the auditorium later that evening he again rode through "densely crowded streets" and was "cheered all the way."[12] "The State of Oregon is apparently sound League of Nations territory," the *New York Times* reported, with Republicans and Democrats joining together to give the president "one of the big ovations of the tour." Notwithstanding the arrest of two ship workers for "cursing" the president, Portland's enthusiasm for the president seemed "genuine and sustained."[13]

Wilson nevertheless seemed subdued as he began his brief address before a businessmen's luncheon in Portland. Greeted by a standing ovation, he began by reflecting philosophically upon the progress of civilization. Whether "you will or not," he declared at one point, "our fortunes are tied in with the rest of the world." The choice now facing the nation was not between isolationism and international involvement but between leading the world or being left behind. In an analogy quoted widely in the papers, Wilson asked rhetorically, "What are you going to be? Boys running around the circus tent and peeping under the canvas?" Wilson professed no "disrespect to anybody," yet he drew applause when he characterized any man who opposed his vision of a "new partnership" among nations as a "quitter." As a "Covenanter," Wilson was no "quitter." He was determined to overcome the "influences of evil" and "see this job through," for the treaty was nothing less than the "culmination of American hope and history."[14]

Wilson warmed to his task that evening before 7,000 cheering supporters in the Portland Auditorium. Quoting Senator Lodge's endorsement of a League of Nations in 1915, Wilson for the first time mentioned his chief antagonist by name. He also prompted laughter and cheers when he declared that he did not have "any respect at all" for some of the treaty's opponents. Reflecting on the fate of the "little children" who crowded around his train, he proclaimed it his mission not only to honor those who had died but also to save the next generation from war. There was "only one means" to "fulfill the promise" that had been made to those who had sacrificed their lives, "only one conceivable way" to prevent the "unspeakable" from happening again: ratify the treaty without delay or reservations. Later in the address, Wilson repeated his charge that "pro-German propaganda" had contributed to "paralysis" and "fear," and he again accused those who were "delaying this thing" of having "forgotten what this war meant." Forget the details, Wilson urged his listeners, and instead reflect on the heroism of those who died. He then repeated a story he had first told in Billings:

I wonder if [the critics of the treaty] have had mothers who lost their sons take them by the hand, as they have taken mine, and looked things that their hearts were too full to speak, praying me to do all in my power to save the sons of other mothers from this terrible thing. And I have had some fine women come to me and say . . . "I had the honor to lose a son in the war." How fine that is— "I had the honor to sacrifice a son for the redemption of mankind!" And yet there is a sob back of the statement, there is a tear brushed hastily away from the cheek.

A woman came up to the train the other day and seized my hand and was about to say something but turned away in a flood of tears. And I asked a stander-by what was the matter, and he said, "Why, Sir, she lost a son in France." Now, mind you, she didn't turn away first. I ordered her son overseas. I advised the Congress of the United States to sacrifice that son. . . . She had nothing in her heart except the hope that I could save other sons, . . . And, God help me, I will save other sons.[15]

As the president left Portland on Monday, September 15, reporters covering the tour generally agreed that the people of Oregon had fallen in line with the rest of the nation: they supported Wilson, but they also agreed with the mild reservationists. "The sentiment in Oregon," Kinsley wrote in the *Chicago Daily Tribune,* was "generally in favor of the league," although people were "interested in reservations and inclined to think that some ought to be adopted." Like people in the rest of the country, Oregonians wanted assurances that American interests would be protected, but nobody favored reservations that might "kill or seriously impair" the treaty.[16] On September 16, the *New York Times* likewise reported that only a "small minority" of Oregonians supported the irreconcilable senators, but many did favor reservations. Most people opposed "any course" that might "cripple the treaty of peace or make it necessary to send it back to the Peace Conference," the *Times* concluded. Oregonians did not have a "deep interest" in the treaty, but there was a "distinct feeling" among people "in all walks of life" that the debate had dragged on too long and ought to be "ended without delay."[17]

California, however, was a different story. With large populations of Chinese and Irish Americans, there was intense interest in the treaty. Moreover, it was expected that, for the first time, Wilson would face hostile audiences, for California was the home state of Senator Hiram Johnson, a leading voice of the irreconcilables. As Wilson's train wound through the Siskiyou Mountains on its thirty-four-hour run to California, the president had plenty of time to contemplate the upcoming challenge. The trip was a "beautiful one," Grayson observed, and "two deer and a large quantity of fruit of all kinds" were put onboard the train at stops along the way.[18] Yet as the train crossed into California shortly after 2:00 P.M. on Tuesday, September 16, everybody on board sensed that the next few days could prove decisive.

The president arrived in Oakland at 8:00 A.M. on Wednesday, September 17, and the presidential party traversed the bay in a "gaily decorated" ferryboat, landing in San Francisco at 9:30 A.M. Proceeding in an open car up Market Street, the president and Mrs. Wilson were escorted by cavalry, marines, and sailors as they received an "uproarious welcome" from "cheering throngs" on both sides of the street. At the end of the parade a flag-waving crowd of schoolchildren "cheered lustily" for the president and Mrs. Wilson. Afterward, the first couple retired to their quarters at the St. Francis Hotel. Following a brief rest, the president proceeded by car to the Palace Hotel, where he was scheduled to speak at 1:00 P.M. to a luncheon sponsored by the Associated Women's Clubs of San Francisco.[19]

Wilson's address to the women's luncheon was "one of the best of the entire trip," in Grayson's view, and it "fairly electrified" the crowd.[20] Responding to Senator Johnson's chief complaint, Wilson addressed concerns that the British Empire would have six votes in the General Assembly of the proposed League of Nations while the United States would have but one. He also discussed three of the four issues at the center of the debate over reservations: Article X, the Monroe Doctrine, and the right of withdrawal. Directly confronting concerns over the Shantung provision, Wilson candidly declared that he, too, was "not satisfied with this settlement," and he provided a lengthy explanation of how it came about and why it was "irrational" to think that defeating the treaty would somehow help China. Yet toward the end of the speech, Wilson seemed to lose patience with his critics. "That settles that matter," he declared after arguing that the alleged British voting advantage was no advantage at all. He then turned on his critics, proclaiming the hyphenated American "no comrade of mine" and refusing to "argue anything with a hyphen." German "propaganda" had again "boldly raised its head," Wilson insisted, and whatever their motives the treaty's critics were aiding Germany's cause. Calling himself a "very patient man," Wilson nevertheless declared that the debate had dragged on long enough. Not only was the delay encouraging the enemies of America, but also there was no longer any doubt about the outcome: "I haven't the slightest doubt as to what the result is going to be. I have felt the temper and high purpose of this great people as I have crossed this wonderful land of ours."[21]

Wilson had planned to "clear the table" of all remaining objections to the treaty in his address that evening before some 12,000 persons at the San Francisco Civic Auditorium.[22] "It was my purpose," he told the noisy crowd early in the speech, "to analyze the objections which are made to this great League." Yet delayed from beginning the speech on time and interrupted by heckling from a "pro-Irish element,"[23] Wilson only briefly discussed the proposed reservations, and he also said less than planned about California's special concerns: the Shantung provision, the Irish question, and Senator Johnson's complaint about the six British votes. As the crowd gradually settled down, the president managed to address several of these issues, assuring his audience that the Shantung and Irish controversies could best be resolved through the League of Nations. Yet toward the end of the speech, Wilson again seemed to lose his patience, claiming that the "hope of Germany" had been "revived" by the delay. He also took more shots at his critics, accusing them of "encouraging the pro-German propaganda." At one point he even quoted a German official praising Senator Lodge as the "soul of the opposition." Finally, he retreated to Tumulty's themes, talking about the bereaved widows who had blessed him on the tour. If by "evil counsel or unhappy mischance" the treaty were defeated, he said, those widows would be betrayed and the "great battle" would have to be "fought over again." "The world is profoundly stirred," Wilson warned in closing, and progress could not be made "amidst chaos, disorder, and strife." Peace would come only when men "agreed to be calm, agreed to be just, agreed to be conciliatory, agreed that the right of the weak is as majestic as the right of the strong." And that, Wilson concluded, was the promise of the League of Nations.[24]

When the president awoke the next morning, his headache was "still with him," but he was "very much cheered over the warmth of his reception in the home stamping ground of Senator Johnson."[25] Appearing at another luncheon at the Palace Hotel at noon—this one involving about 1,500 members of the Associated Business Men's Clubs of San Francisco—the president and Mrs. Wilson were cheered as they entered the room, and the audience interrupted the president "many times" during his speech. According to the Associated Press, the make-up of the audience inspired the president to present ratification as "a good business proposition," but he concluded by reflecting at some length on the cost of the war, citing Tumulty's statistics on the expenditures and the number of battle deaths for each country.[26] About a million and a half more men were killed in this war "than in all the wars of something more than 100 preceding years," Wilson noted in echoing Tumulty's memo of September 12. War, he concluded, inevitably destroyed "the flower of the manhood" of the nations involved.[27]

Later, in a brief, ten-minute appearance before an estimated 10,000 faculty and students at the University of California at Berkeley, Wilson delivered a very different sort of speech—an impromptu address that said almost nothing about the treaty or the League of Nations, but rather vented the president's growing frustration. Confessing to "impatience with the debate," Wilson accused both the treaty's opponents and "some of the newspapers" of "misleading the opinion of the United States." They had not told the public "what was in the treaty," he complained, and they had misrepresented it as "containing little traps for the United States." "I admit that there are debatable things," Wilson stated to the assembled faculty and students, "but I do not admit that they need to be debated so long. Not only that, but I do insist that they should be debated more fairly."[28] With his trip barely half over, the president seemed to have lost his enthusiasm for the "play" of debate. Now he seemed intent on silencing his critics.

Wilson continued to insist that the public had been "singularly and, I sometimes fear, deliberately, misled" in his speech that evening at the Oakland Municipal Auditorium. Rather than discuss the "incidental features" of the treaty, he chose to focus on what he saw as its most "salient and outstanding characteristics": the basic principles it embodied, its historic "firsts," and its promise as "insurance" against war. According to Wilson, the treaty would indeed punish Germany "for the crime she attempted to commit." Yet it began not with that but with the League of Nations—a "permanent partnership" among the "free self-governing peoples of the world." It was the "first treaty ever" defined in terms of the "rights of human beings" rather than the interests of nations—the "first people's treaty in the history of international dealings." More than that, it was the first treaty to give "liberty to peoples who never could have won it for themselves," and the first to establish relations among nations on a "cooperative" rather than a "competitive" basis. In addition, the treaty contained a "great charter of liberty" for laborers, and it coordinated "all the great humane endeavors of the world," including efforts to combat drug trafficking and various humanitarian efforts. In short, the treaty was nothing less than "an organization of liberty and mercy" for the entire world. Still, a "small, small group of our fellow citizens" worried about how the United States could "get out of the League." Wilson answered those who quibbled over such details with a pair of rhetorical questions: "Why . . . do we hesitate to redeem the destiny of America? . . . Why do we debate details when the heart of the thing is sound?"[29]

Wilson's visit to the Bay Area may have brought out the hecklers, but the consensus among reporters was that the president had "gone far" to "break down the opposition" to the treaty. Wilson had "materially advanced the cause for which he came out to fight," the *New York Times* opined, and the paper pronounced his visit to the Bay Area yet another "turning point" in the tour. Dismissing the hecklers as a small, noisy minority, the *Times* predicted that the majority of people would now "turn in resentment" against anyone who opposed the treaty. Wilson's reception in the Bay Area "added to the cumulative evidence" that the "mass of the American people" wanted the treaty passed "without unnecessary delay," possibly with reservations that would safeguard American interests, but "without changes of a sort that sort that would nullify the work of the Peace Conference."[30]

As Wilson left the Bay Area, he thus had every reason to be optimistic. He had invaded hostile territory and emerged victorious, making a "strong impression" with his responses to the Shantung and Irish questions and convincing people that the treaty should be ratified without delay. Writing from his bed while recovering from his auto accident, reporter Small marveled at how even San Francisco's hostile newspapers had fallen under Wilson's spell. Quoting from "Mr. Hearst's San Francisco Examiner," Small provided a fascinating glimpse into how reporters of that day viewed Wilson as a speaker, particularly in comparison to his nemesis from California, the "spellbinder" Hiram Johnson:

In oratory, Wilson is exacting, but a "rabble rouser" he is not, or an inspirational orator. He does not get his hearers to their feet shouting hysterically.

Hiram Johnson has it all over him in that quality. . . . Hiram, going at full steam could rouse a crowd to making ten times as much noise as the president evoked last night. And, Johnson would get out just as big a throng, but if the president lacks the dramatic quality, he certainly is pleasing in his declamation, and just as certainly he argues logically from his point of view. Too many generalities complained some, as we elbowed our way out. But I must say I considered the address a masterly presentation of his side of the big debate.[31]

Ironically, Wilson would drift further and further away from this "pleasing" and logically compelling style as the tour progressed. In San Diego, he would respond impetuously to his critics, ignoring the great principles that he had emphasized earlier and complaining about the length of the debate. In Los Angeles, he again seemed to lose his patience, tossing out accusations of conspiracy and questioning the patriotism of his critics. As Wilson left California, the reporters covering the tour remained convinced that he had the public behind him. Yet nobody imagined that Wilson would prove so stubborn on the question of reservations. Nor could anyone have predicted that he would escalate his attacks on those he most needed to persuade: the nineteen or twenty mild reservationists who held the balance of power in the Senate.

Triumphant in Southern California

Traveling south from Oakland, the president's train entered the beautiful San Fernando Valley on the morning of September 19, then stopped briefly in Los Angeles where the president disembarked for a "brisk walk" through the rail yard. Those who expected to see a president "aged" by "weighty affairs," the *Los Angeles Times* reported, would have been "surprised" by his "elastic step" as he strolled through the railroad yard.[32] Switching from the Southern Pacific to the Sante Fe line, the president's train next passed through the "rich orange groves" and "stately palms" south of Los Angeles before hugging the Pacific coast en route to San Diego. As usual, cheering crowds gathered at the stations along the way, but Wilson strictly adhered to his doctor's order that he refrain from rear-platform speeches. The president's health was "said to be excellent," according to a dispatch published in newspapers across the country, but sixteen days of travel and speeches had been "very fatiguing" and the president had developed a "slight cold."[33]

Arriving in San Diego at 3:27 P.M., the president was driven to the hotel for a public reception, then to the big stadium where he was to participate in a historic event: the first real test of the "magnivox," or "voice phone," as Grayson called it—an "electrical device" designed to broadcast the human voice across vast distances.[34] As Wilson circled inside the stadium in his car, a crowd of between 40,000 and 50,000 cheered and waved American flags. Hundreds of young girls in white dresses spelled out "Welcome" in the back rows of the stadium.[35] Arriving at the stage, Wilson stood in a "glass cage" some twenty feet square and open in the front, speaking into megaphones that carried his voice through electrical wires to resonators scattered throughout the stadium. Reports on the success of the experiment differed. According to Grayson, all but a small portion of the crowd could hear "every word," but the AP reported that only part of the crowd could hear the president and that there were "many empty seats" by the time he finished.[36] Whatever the actual success of the experiment, it was, as the New York Times reported, a "remarkable spectacle," one "seldom equaled in this country." As the president addressed the vast crowd, applause from the far ends of the stadium came back "like a booming echo," and the cheering passed "in waves down one side of the crowd, along the rear of the stadium, and then back on its way toward the platform where the president was speaking." The president did not "relish this experience," Grayson recalled; afterward he called it the "most difficult speech he had ever tried to deliver in his life." But he was thrilled by the reception, as each city tried to "outdo" the others "in greeting the president."[37]

Picking up where he had left off in Oakland, Wilson began his

speech in San Diego by complaining that people had "not been informed as to the real character and scope" of the treaty. Accusing his
critics of emphasizing issues that were "incidental, and not central,"
he promised to focus instead on the "larger purposes" for which
America had gone to war: the principle that "every great territory in
the world belongs to the people who are living on it." The "heart of
humanity beats in this document," Wilson declared, yet the public had
not gotten "the slightest hint" of its "great features." "They never tell
you what is really in this treaty," Wilson complained. "If they did, your
enthusiasm would sweep them off their feet." Denying any "personal
ambition," Wilson quoted at length from a speech by Senator Lodge in
which he endorsed an alliance of "civilized nations" to prevent wars.
He also quoted from an editorial by Theodore Roosevelt endorsing
a "league for peace." Ironically, Wilson ended up devoting much of
the speech to those issues he earlier had deemed "incidental": the alleged British voting advantage, and the so-called Lodge reservations.
Insisting that "certain reservations" amounted to an unwillingness
to assume the same obligations as other nations, Wilson proclaimed
such an attitude "unworthy of the honor of the United States" and
concluded: "I will not join in claiming . . . an unjust position of
privilege for the country which I love and honor. . . . Neither am I
afraid of responsibility. Neither will I scuttle. Neither will I be a little
American."[38]

Wilson's speech in San Diego reflected not only Tumulty's advice
but also the influence of his critics. Mentioning Senator Lodge by
name not once but twice, Wilson found himself debating his critics
rather than expounding upon his own vision of a new world order.
As he discussed the proposed reservations, some even noted "some
bitterness in his tone." Toward the end of the speech, that bitterness
exploded in an angry warning that rejecting the treaty would mean a
"death warrant" for the nation's children. Those children would have to
fight the "final war," and in that war "there would not be merely seven
and a half million men slain," Wilson warned. The "very existence of
civilization" would be threatened.[39]

Cooper has called Wilson's speech in San Diego the "finest of the whole tour," yet in some ways it was among the most demagogic.[40] Substituting ad hominem and emotional appeals for an explication of the principles and provisions of the treaty, the speech did not provide a comprehensive overview of the treaty, as most of his earlier speeches had done. Nor did it engage the opposition in debate over the treaty's virtues and drawbacks. Instead, it reflected Wilson's frustration with the debate and his growing irritation with his critics. No longer did Wilson engage his audiences in "common counsel." Now he tried to scare and shame people into supporting his uncompromising position.

Wilson conceded as much later that same day in a brief after-dinner speech. Admitting that he had become "disturbed" by the debate, Wilson again lashed out at his opponents, accusing them of "assisting Germany, whether they want to do so or not." Because the debate had dragged on so long, it was "heartening the representatives of Germany," he argued, for they hoped to accomplish through the debate "what they were not able to do by arms": separate the United States from its European allies. In addition, the prolonged debate—perhaps "coincidentally"—coincided with a "revival of pro-German propaganda all over the United States." According to Wilson, the debate had gone on long enough and the time had come for a decision. "We have no choice except between these alternatives," he told his dinner audience in San Diego, "we must go forward with this concert of nations, or we must go back to the old arrangement, because the guarantees of peace will not be sufficient without the United States."[41] Wilson simply refused to acknowledge the middle ground that many Americans reportedly favored: ratification of the treaty with mild reservations.

If San Diego marked a historic first, Los Angeles signaled Wilson's ultimate triumph, as he took the city by storm and appeared to erase all remaining doubts that he had the people behind him. Arriving in the city at 9:00 A.M. on Saturday, September 20, the president rested in his rail car for an hour and ten minutes before proceeding to the Alexandria Hotel, where the presidential party occupied forty-three rooms. Around noon, he went back to the station, then paraded by car through the city back to his hotel. "A mighty cheer, a great surge of sound . . . rolled along forty-five blocks of the city's streets," according to the *Los Angeles Times,* as an estimated 200,000 people gave Wilson "a genuine, heartfelt and spontaneous" welcome. Standing in a car beautifully decorated with a bronze eagle, American flags, and "roses, carnations, and other California flowers," Wilson smiled, bowed, and waved his hat to the "dense lines of waving, shouting humanity." It was "the largest crowd that ever witnessed a parade in this city," according to a police captain quoted in the papers, and it was the most impressive reception of the entire tour.[42] "From my observation today," one unusually talkative Secret Service agent told a reporter for the *Los Angeles Times,* "I would say that it was the greatest reception so far given the President."[43]

Following the parade, Wilson enjoyed an elegant luncheon in his hotel suite, and Grayson announced that the president planned a "quiet afternoon" with no visitors.[44] Tumulty was busy, however, penning two more memos urging the president to answer his critics on Shantung and the alleged British voting advantage. Tumulty also wanted Wilson to respond more directly to the widespread isolationist sentiment in the region. In the "matter of isolation," Tumulty wrote, "I understand there is a feeling here that we should keep separate and apart from European embroilments." Tumulty enclosed both a speech by Senator Johnson and two editorials from West Coast papers that expressed such views. In suggesting a response, Tumulty urged the president to invoke a speech that President McKinley delivered the day he was assassinated—an address in which the Republican president proclaimed the "age of isolation" over. He also urged the president to "impress the fact upon the people" that "provincialism" meant "playing the game alone," and that, in turn, meant "increased taxation and a nation at arms." Tumulty also wanted the president, like McKinley, to stress how technology had rendered isolationism obsolete by creating the possibility of "aerial attacks" on America.[45]

At 6:00 P.M., the president entered the banquet room at the Alexandria through an arch of grape vines illuminated like "glow-worms in a garden." He was greeted by a demonstration that drowned out the orchestra playing for the 515 diners. To one reporter for the *Los Angeles Times,* it was a great start to the "fall social season," as the flower-strewn hall, the "fountain centerpiece surrounded by banks of California fruits," and the beautiful gowns of the women all seemed to overshadow the president's "brief address."[46]

Wilson's address, however, was anything but sociable. Commenting on the "one thing that has troubled me in this affair," he complained that much of the opposition's argument was "not based on reason." When he returned from Paris, he had expected only a "negligible percentage of our people" to oppose the treaty, but "then something intervened." Once again, German propaganda "lifted its hideous head," and opposition to the treaty caught on in those "quarters of the country" where pro-German sentiment had been strongest during the war. "I hear the hiss of it on every side," Wilson commented, warning that "Germany would be the only nation in the world to profit" if America retreated. Then, in closing, Wilson reflected on McKinley's declaration that the age of isolationism was over, and he even invoked the holy grail of the isolationists, Washington's "Farewell Address." Creatively reinterpreting that text, Wilson claimed that what Washington really "had in mind" when he warned against "entangling alliances" was what opponents of the League hoped to "lead us back to"—the "day of alliances," the "day of balances of power." The League of Nations, he insisted, actually represented "a process of *disentanglement*."[47]

Wilson continued his critique of isolationism later that evening at what the *Los Angeles Times* described as a "monster mass meeting" at the Shriners' Auditorium.[48] Following Tumulty's advice, Wilson devoted the bulk of his address to the three issues most often raised by Californians: the Shantung provision, Great Britain's alleged voting advantage, and isolationism. On the first two issues Wilson played the schoolmaster, lecturing the crowd on the history of the Shantung controversy and explaining how voting worked in the Assembly and the Council of the proposed League. "All this nonsense about six votes and one vote can be dismissed, and you can sleep with perfect quiet," Wilson concluded. On the "policy of isolation," Wilson became more philosophical, proclaiming it "impossible and selfish" for the United States to "play a lone hand" in the world. "You can no more separate this [nation] from the rest of the world than you can take all the tender roots of a great tree out of the earth and expect that tree to live," he declared. "All the tendrils of our life—economic, social, and every other kind—are interlaced in and are inextricable with similar tendrils of mankind." According to Wilson, the question was not whether the United States would be engaged with the rest of the world but rather whether she would lead or follow. "That is the only question you can ask," he concluded. "As I put it the other night, you have got this choice: you have got to be either provincials—little Americans—or big Americans—statesmen. You either have to be ostriches with your heads in the sand or eagles."[49]

Wilson's speech in Los Angeles was, at one level, one of the more upbeat of the tour. Prompting laughter with his digs at the opposition, Wilson displayed little of the bitterness of his remarks in Berkeley, for example, and he generally emphasized the "great ideal purposes" behind the treaty rather than the threats of radicalism and war. At another level, however, the speech assumed an even more threatening attitude toward his critics, as the president not only accused them of misleading the public but also of putting personal ambition and partisanship above loyalty to their country. "It is a matter of unaffected amazement on my part," he told his listeners early in the speech, "that there should be men in high station to oppose its adoption." Accusing treaty opponents of scrutinizing "certain details" while forgetting the larger "majesty of the plan," he recalled how their misrepresentations had "made it necessary" for him to tour in the first place. Late in the speech, he even suggested that the treaty's critics lacked both patriotism and sympathy for those who had sacrificed during the war. When we reached "the borders of the United States," he argued, we were "neither Republicans nor Democrats," and it became our "duty" to subordinate our political differences and become "a united family." More than that, there was a "tender side" to this "great subject," a side that Wilson highlighted with a series of rhetorical questions: "Have these gentlemen no hearts? Do they forget the sons that are dead in France? Do they forget the great sacrifice this nation has made?" To oppose the League of Nations, Wilson implied, was to betray those who died as "champions of right and of liberty."[50]

According to newspaper accounts, Wilson's speech electrified the

6,000–7,000 people lucky enough to get into the auditorium after waiting in line all day.[51] The crowd proved "one of the most eager, enthusiastic and attentive audiences" of the entire tour, jumping to their feet and cheering for four minutes when the president first stepped to podium, then continuing to cheer, shout, and wave flags throughout the speech. When Wilson expressed amazement that anybody in high office could oppose the treaty, people in the crowd shouted "Shame on them!" More cheers erupted moments later as the president declared the Covenant a "people's treaty." When the president posed the choice between acting like ostriches or eagles, the crowd responded with cries of "Eagles! Eagles!" And the crowd "stood up and shouted its approval again" when the president proclaimed that "America is no quitter." In its headline on Sunday, September 21, the *Chicago Sunday Tribune* suggested that Wilson had not merely rallied his supporters but won over the entire city: "President Wins Los Angeles to His League Plan: Shouts Approval of Pact at a Tremendous Meeting."[52]

As reporters paused to assess Wilson's progress in their Sunday editions, most declared his California visit an unqualified success. In the *Los Angeles Times,* for example, Robert B. Armstrong declared that Wilson had "crystallized public opinion" against further delay and that the "obstructionists" were in disarray and retreat. While the opposition tour had attracted only "curiosity seekers," the president's reception in California was a clear "repudiation" of the treaty opponents in the home state of their "chief propagandist," Senator Johnson. According to Armstrong, there was now "no doubt" that the treaty would be ratified—probably with four mild reservations—no later than October 15, perhaps as early as October 1. For all practical purposes, the debate was over. The "barnstorming Senators" had retreated to Washington, and the opposition was "breaking up and fussing among themselves."[53]

Similarly, *New York Times* reporter Grasty proclaimed Wilson's reception in Los Angeles "the climax of the whole tour" and concluded that he was "now getting the cumulative effect of his missionary work." Wilson's welcome in California was "not merely a welcome," but "an enlistment in the cause which he represents," Grasty reported. Californians liked Wilson's "broad ideas," and the "sentiment for ratification" was "simply overwhelming." Quoting Harry Chandler, the publisher of the *Los Angeles Times,* Grasty concluded that Chandler "spoke the mind" of the whole city when he denounced the "contentious attitude" of Senator Johnson and proclaimed the League not merely "our politics . . . but our religion." In Grasty's report, Chandler even spoke of "polls" in California showing a "6 to 1 majority" in favor of the treaty.[54]

In constructing this protreaty portrait of public opinion, journalists called attention to some profound changes in the American political landscape. For one, women had played an important role in the debate, especially in Southern California where they had full suffrage and constituted "at least 50 per cent of the voting strength." As the *New York Times* reported, the women of Southern California were "practically all in favor of a League," and many had been doing "effective missionary work" on its behalf. The women were "not opposed to reservations," according to the *Times,* and in fact many supported reservations protecting the "legitimate interests" of the United States—so long as those reservations did not "destroy the large things at stake." In general, however, the women stood behind Wilson. The *Times* left it to "one of their leaders" to summarize their attitude: "They feel that the League of Nations may at least be effective in postponing war and that there is a good chance that it will spell the end of war. Therefore, they are in favor of giving it a chance to operate."[55]

The protreaty portrait of public opinion also implied that Wilson had overcome both partisanship and the strong isolationist sentiment in the West. Claiming to speak for "the people" of Southern California, the *Los Angeles Times* praised Wilson for transcending "party platforms" and representing all of the people: "He comes to us, not as a Democratic President, but as OUR COUNTRY'S PRESIDENT."[56] Even more significantly, the historically isolationist West had responded enthusiastically to Wilson's call to international leadership, sounding almost eager to take on the world. "There is no 'little Americanism' here," Grasty reported in the *New York Times.* "These people have no fear whatever of foreign entanglement. They want to get in the game and see what they can do. This is a community of winners and fear does not enter into their composition."[57]

While most reporters agreed that the president's explanations of the treaty had "proven effective," a few remained cautious.[58] Writing for the *Chicago Sunday Tribune*, Kinsley reported that there was still a "real debate" in California, with local newspapers and party leaders still divided over the treaty. The sentiment in Los Angeles was "said to be" sufficiently pro-League "to offset the antagonism in San Francisco and the north," but the president failed to arouse his "great San Diego audience" to any "perceptible enthusiasm for his view of America's destiny."[59] Similarly, Small reported that "nonpartisan" sources had confirmed that "80 per cent" of Southern Californians supported the treaty and that the "overwhelming sentiment" in all of the states the president had visited was for "the quickest possible ratification of the treaty." Yet while Wilson was now "having his innings," it remained to be seen whether the great crowds that greeted Wilson reflected anything more than "natural curiosity." More importantly, of course, the question of reservations remained to be settled. Arguing that Wilson's "salvation" had been the support of Republican newspapers, Small noted that most of those papers were still "anxious that the mild reservations should be accepted by the President." In one of the few reports that anticipated Wilson's later difficulties, Small concluded that Wilson had yet to make a "convincing" argument "that the proposed mild reservations to the covenant . . . would constitute a real menace to it."[60]

As Wilson left California, the question of reservations seemed but a minor detail still to be worked out. For all practical purposes, most observers agreed that the debate was over. Wilson had gone into hostile territory and emerged a conquering hero. The president now seemed poised to return to Washington and negotiate a settlement with the mild reservationists. Yet as Wilson wrapped up his Western tour with visits to Nevada, Utah, Wyoming, and Colorado, he did not sound at all like a man prepared to strike a bargain. To the contrary, he sounded defensive, even desperate, as he "declared war" on his critics and became even more defiant in his resistance to changes in the treaty.

A Sore Winner

Grayson urged Wilson to stay in bed and rest on Sunday morning, September 21, but the president insisted on going to church with Mrs. Wilson. Afterward, the president met with representatives of the local chapters of the League to Enforce Peace (LEP). Wilson's answers to seven questions put to him by the LEP representatives so impressed these "former followers" of Hiram Johnson that they sent telegrams to the senator urging him to cease his opposition to the League of Nations. Following these meetings, Wilson left Los Angeles at 7:00 P.M., "cheered" by what Grayson called "one of the warmest demonstrations in the city's history."[61]

Wilson made one last stop in California on Monday, speaking briefly in Sacramento, Senator Johnson's hometown. According to the *New York Times*, Wilson's reception in Sacramento was "most cordial," although Kinsley reported that many people in Sacramento still supported Johnson and were "not ready to desert him, even on this issue."[62] As Wilson entered the city, people lined the tracks for more than two miles, and they formed "a great sea of faces" as his train came to a stop at the station. The president had not been scheduled to speak, but he finally gave in to the "urgent entreaties" of the city's businessmen and delivered a five-minute address from the rear platform of the *Mayflower*. In that speech Wilson thanked the crowd of some 15,000 for the "extraordinary and delightful" welcome and their "great outpouring" of support for his "great cause." Twice declaring that the world could not "go back" to the old ways, he also warned that the nation could "not much longer hesitate," lest the world "sink back into that slough of despond" that caused the Great War.[63]

After a difficult trip across the Sierras, with smoke from forest fires and changes in altitude adding to his discomfort, Wilson arrived in Reno shortly after 8:00 P.M. to deliver his only major address of the day. The Sagebrush State had given Wilson resounding victories in 1912 and 1916, and its entire congressional delegation was made up of Democrats. People from across the state traveled to Reno for the occasion, and as the presidential party disembarked from the *May-*

flower red flares shot into the air from downtown rooftops while a brass band struck up a tune. According to Thomas Bailey, "nothing noteworthy happened at thinly populated Reno."[64] Yet Wilson was "at his rhetorical best" in Reno, according to historian Loren B. Chan, as he alternately "coaxed and cajoled" his audience in language both "plain and precise."[65]

Speaking via an electrical hook-up to audiences in three other theaters,[66] Wilson began his speech in the 1,900-seat Rialto theater by flattering his audience, praising their "frontier community" for its "spirit of adventure." He then took a shot at his critics, describing them as men who had their "eyes over their shoulders," always "looking backward." Donning his professor's hat, Wilson then lectured the people of Reno on the Vienna Conference, the American and French Revolutions, and the origins of the Monroe Doctrine and its status under the proposed League of Nations. Next discussing "one or two details" about which the public had been "diligently misinformed," he returned to the issue of Great Britain's six votes in the Assembly and, finally, to the Shantung provision. Toward the end of the speech, he ridiculed those worried about the right to withdraw from the League, accusing them of "cowardice." Proving that the accusation was no slip of the tongue, Wilson then went on to explain "how much better it feels" to embrace the "impulse of courage":

> Your blood is at least warm and comfortable, and the red corpuscles are in command when you have got some spunk in you. But when you have not, when you are afraid somebody is going to put over something on you, you are furtive and go about looking out for things, and your blood is cold, and you shiver when you turn a dark corner. That is not a picture of the United States. When I think of these great frontier communities, I fancy that I can hear the confident tread, tread, tread of the great hosts that crossed this continent. They were not afraid of what they were going to find in the next canyon. They were not looking over their shoulders to see if the trail was clear behind them. They were making a trail in front of them, and they had not the least notion of going back.[67]

Wilson was frequently interrupted by applause in Reno, particularly as he recalled how America had entered the first world war as the "chief champion and spokesman of liberty." The real meaning of the treaty, he claimed, was forged not at Paris but "at Château-Thierry and in Belleau Wood and in the Argonne." Reflecting Tumulty's advice, Wilson emphasized the sacrifices of those who died and the betrayal that would result from failing to ratify the treaty. "Our men did not fight over there for the purpose of coming back and letting the same thing happen again," Wilson told his audience. "They went over there expecting that the business would be finished. And it shall be finished."[68]

The next day the presidential special sped across the desert, greeted by the "entire populations" of some small towns and even by "Indian squaws with papooses on their backs." In Montello, Nevada, a crowd of schoolchildren gathered to serenade the president with "My Country, 'Tis of Thee," but the president slept late and missed the performance.[69] Passing the Great Salt Lake, the president and Mrs. Wilson spent time on the rear platform "enjoying the salt breeze," and after arriving at Ogden at about 2:30 P.M. the presidential party took an automobile ride through cheering crowds in the business district. The president also issued a short written greeting to the people of Utah, and after a crowd gathered at the station and "clamored for a speech," he delivered a brief address from the rear platform of the *Mayflower*.[70]

Wilson's address in Ogden, while brief, was enormously revealing. Under the constraints of a rear-platform speech, Wilson stripped his remarks bare of substantive arguments and instead lashed out at those "men in public life" who failed to recognize that the "heart" of the people throbbed "deep and strong for this great enterprise of humanity." Having crossed the continent, Wilson could now report that "80 percent" of the people supported the treaty, and he called upon the public to "assist the judgment" of those public men who failed to see the light. He did not mean to "coerce the judgment" of those men, but he did try to shame them. Recalling the "disloyalty" of some Americans before the war, Wilson accused his critics of serving "Germany's purpose" and betraying those who died in the war. "I, for my part, am in to see this thing through," he concluded, "because these men who fought the battles on the fields of France are not now going to be betrayed by the rest of us."[71]

Wilson's remarks in Ogden "caused much comment," according to the *New York Times,* with reporters attributing the president's bitter tone to news from Washington that Senator Henry Ashurst of Arizona and seven other Democratic senators had defected to the reservationist camp. That news came as "somewhat of a surprise," the *Times* reported, given the president's "splendid reception" in California.[72] The president's health also may have contributed to his cranky mood, as the irritation in his throat and "coughing spells" had "interfered greatly with his rest," according to Grayson. Nevertheless, the president participated in the "usual automobile parade" after arriving in Salt Lake City at 4:30 P.M. He then rested in his hotel until 7:30, when he left to address an audience that "filled every corner" of the Mormon Tabernacle.[73]

Conditions at the Tabernacle could not have been worse for the ailing president. Inside the hot, unventilated building some 12,000 people had been waiting since 6:00 P.M.[74] The "fetid air" was "unlike anything I have ever experienced," the First Lady recalled in her memoir, and the "heat and human odours" were even worse up on the stage. Noticing that Mrs. Wilson had turned a "deathly white," her maid passed her a bottle of smelling salts, which the First Lady gratefully inhaled before pouring some on a handkerchief and passing it up to the president. By the time Wilson finished speaking, Mrs. Wilson recalled, even his coat was "soaked through with perspiration."[75]

Wilson began his speech in Salt Lake City as he had many others: by flattering his audience and announcing that the nation faced the "most critical decision" in its history. As he was nearing the end of his tour, he could now "render testimony" to the fact that an "overwhelming majority" of Americans supported the treaty. "One by one," he argued, the objections had "melted away." "One by one," it had become evident that all of the critics' objections were "without sufficient foundation." So why did the Senate still hesitate? Why did the "forces of objection," having been "driven out of one post after another," now center their fire on the "heart of the League itself"? The answer was simple, according to Wilson: they really sought to kill the treaty altogether. Going public with reports that Lodge and the mild reservationists had agreed on a reservation to Article X, Wilson read the language of the proposed reservation: "The United States assumes no obligation under . . . Article X to preserve the territorial integrity or political independence of any other country . . . unless, in any particular case, Congress . . . shall by act or joint resolution so declare."[76] Confused by Wilson's reading, the audience applauded. The president then lashed out in anger: "You want to applaud that? Wait until you understand the meaning of it, and if you have a knife in your hands with which you intend to cut out the heart of this Covenant, applaud. But, if you want this Covenant to have a heart in it, . . . withhold your applause."[77]

Wilson's attitude had hardened. "Reservations are to all intents and purposes equivalent to amendments," he insisted, and the proposed reservation to Article X would constitute an "absolute refusal" on the part of the United States to carry the "same responsibility" as other League members. In other words, the proposed reservation would constitute a "rejection of the Covenant." Some who advocated reservations were "high-minded, patriotic Americans," but according to Wilson they had "not looked into the matter" sufficiently. In Wilson's view, the "only popular clamor" for the "various reservations"—indeed, the "only popular clamor" behind rejecting "any part of this treaty"—came from "exactly the same source" as the "pro-German propaganda" of the war years. By aligning with those propagandists, even the "honorable and enlightened men" who advocated reservations were serving "the purposes of Germany." More than that, they were undermining all that the boys in khaki had accomplished "on the field of France."[78]

In the words of the editors of the Wilson Papers, the president had "declared war" on the mild reservationists.[79] In Salt Lake City, Wilson had reiterated his usual themes: the principles of self-determination and arbitration embodied in the treaty, the right of any member of the League to gain a hearing, and the promise of a restoration of the Shantung Province to China, to name just a few. Yet there was now something different about his tone—a new defiance, even a noticeable anger, that manifested itself in a stubborn refusal to budge on the question of reservations. In Coeur d'Alene less than two weeks earlier, Wilson had declared himself open to interpretive reservations. Now he equated any such reservation with rejection of the treaty. The "great and final choice" was now "upon the people," Wilson concluded: "Either we are going to guarantee civilization or we are going to a abandon it." And should the United States chose the latter course, radicals with "antagonism towards our process of government" stood ready to exploit the situation: "We feel the evil influence on this side of the Atlantic, and on the other side . . . every public man knows that it is knocking at the door of his government."[80]

Journalists at the time observed that the president had spoken with "unusual force and deliberation" in Salt Lake City.[81] Decades later, historian Arthur S. Link likewise would conclude that Wilson "summarized all his pleading" for the treaty with "unrivaled feeling at the Mormon capital."[82] Yet the first signs of "real trouble" with Wilson's health also appeared in Salt Lake City, as the president "faltered in his speech" and did not seem to have his "usual command over words."[83] Moreover, the speech itself was unusually combative and also misleading, even deceptive. As historian Cooper had argued, Wilson was simply wrong to charge that reservations were "to all intents and purposes equivalent to amendments." And he compounded that error by maintaining that all the signatories, including Germany, would have to approve any reservations passed by the Senate. Combined with his blunder in stirring up applause for the proposed reservation to Article X, Wilson's speech in Salt Lake City was, in Cooper's judgment, "unquestionably the worst of the whole tour."[84]

Even the loyal Joseph Tumulty recognized that Wilson had missed his mark in Salt Lake City. "Frankly," Tumulty told the president, "your 'punch' did not land last night. . . . As a newspaperman put it this morning, you simply pushed the ball; there was no snap in your stroke." Neither the press nor his audience "really caught the point" of why reservations were unacceptable, nor did they grasp why Wilson considered Article X the "heart" of the treaty. Again urging Wilson to focus on the sacrifice of war, Tumulty drafted yet another passage that he thought might supply the missing "punch." Tumulty's language cast both ratification of the treaty and rejection of the proposed reservations as matters of national honor:

> My experience during the last three weeks has convinced me that the heart of America is in this great enterprise. . . . With this conviction in mind . . . I shall resist with all my heart and soul any attempt to dishonor or besmirch the integrity of the United States. The men at Château-Thierry and Belleau Wood went into this great enterprise without reservation; they did not come out until they had provided us with a way to accomplish the ultimate and greatest result for which they fought—the establishment of a permanent peace. This is the most solemn hour in the life of America. A mistake now would be irreparable. . . . It is your duty as much as it is my duty to impress upon the Senate of the United States the danger of repudiating the principles of permanent peace and failing to ratify this treaty as it was written at Paris. . . . The honor, good faith, and integrity of this nation in this great matter must not be betrayed.[85]

Tumulty's advice, along with Wilson's deteriorating health, would write the storyline for the last chapter of Wilson's Western tour: the dramatic tale of his final speech in Pueblo, Colorado. In Cheyenne and Denver, Wilson would become still more defiant, threatening to kill the treaty himself if the Senate insisted upon reservations. Then, in Pueblo, he would pull out all the stops, repeating his threat to kill the treaty and exploiting fears of another, even more destructive world war. By the time he left Pueblo, Wilson had left little room for compromise, even with the mildest of the reservationists. Perhaps he thought he could mend fences once he returned to Washington. Or perhaps he thought that public opinion would simply overwhelm those who still stood in the way of ratification. Whatever his thinking, it proved a terrible miscalculation. He already had angered many in the Senate, and he would only make things worse in the final two days of the tour.

Conclusion

From "Columbus to San Francisco," Grasty reported after the president's first day in California, public opinion was now "in varying degrees" favorable to ratification. "Nine men out of ten" supported the League of Nations, while rejection "in toto" did not "find any favor whatever." Wilson was no "popular hero;" the "mass of people" were not "particularly keen on the President's scoring a great personal triumph," Grasty observed. Indeed, most people "wouldn't mind a bit" if the Senate put its mark on the treaty by voting for reservations. Yet public opinion was "overwhelming" against reservations that would force the president to resubmit the treaty to the Allies and Germany. Wilson thus had every reason to be "satisfied with the results" of his tour, Grasty concluded, and he had "no doubt of ratification."[86]

Toward the end of the week, Wilson had even more reason for confidence. Following his appearance before tens of thousands of flag-waving supporters in San Diego, the *New York Times* reported that the people of Southern California not only wanted to see the League of Nations "given a chance," but wanted to see the United States as "one of its leading members." In the same edition, the *Times* also reported that Senator Johnson had given up his anti-League tour, claiming that he was needed back in Washington. Two days later the president left California in one "continuous ovation," the *Los Angeles Times* reported, with "dense throngs" of cheering people lining his entire way out of the state. California, the *LA Times* concluded, had gone "Wilson-Mad."[87]

The opposition's efforts, if anything, had only helped Wilson's cause. Shadowed by hostile senators and heckled in San Francisco, Wilson won sympathy from many who considered such tactics disrespectful. As Wilson toured California, the *Atlanta Constitution* called it "humiliating and shameful" enough that the president was being "stalked and dogged" by his Senate opponents. Now his detractors had resorted to the even more "shameful expedient" of "marshaling the roughs and toughs" of San Francisco to deny the president "the courtesy of a respectful hearing." Heckled by a "hooting, howling, jeering and insulting crowd of street ruffians and water-front hoodlums," Wilson's treatment in San Francisco, the *Constitution* opined, made "common American decency shudder!" Calling the "hectoring and hissing of the president of the United States" beyond "all bounds of reason" and simply "beyond toleration," the *Constitution* concluded that the president was "entitled at all times to be treated with respect" and blamed those who had been "snapping and snarling at the president's heels" for the "disrespectful and uncivil" display.[88]

Not everyone blamed the opposition for the tone of the debate. On September 17, the *Chicago Daily Tribune* complained that Wilson himself had done little to encourage a "reasoned conclusion" and complained: "His appeals are of the vaguest and most general order .... This is mere stump speaking which can be intended only to bring emotional pressure to bear on the senate." In an editorial reprinted in the *Chicago Daily Tribune,* the Kansas City *Star* went even further, calling Wilson's claims "extravagant" and "grotesque" and observing that he sounded like a man "fighting desperately for what he knows is a lost cause." Americans were "too level headed" to be "carried off their feet" by promises that war could be prevented "by treaty," nor could they be "frightened" by the "bogies of bolshevism and Hun propaganda." Americans wanted peace, the *Star* concluded, but not at the cost of "entangling alliances" with Europe.[89]

As Wilson entered the home stretch of his Western tour, the newspapers thus remained split on his performance. Some, like the *Chicago Daily Tribune,* wondered why the president had toured at all. Even if he were "clarifying our mind ... and disposing by reasoned argument of our doubts and objections," the *Tribune* editorialized, he could have done so back in Washington, where he had access to the "widest and most conspicuous publicity." More importantly, while Wilson was "away from his desk," domestic problems of the "most urgent importance" had gone unsolved.[90] Yet the reporters on the train tended to be more sympathetic. Charles H. Grasty, for example, claimed that among the reporters there was "universal admiration" for the president's "qualities as a stayer." Proclaiming his "gameness" all the more remarkable because of his "splitting headache," Grasty conceded that Wilson lacked the "exuberance" and "animal heat" of some politicians. Yet in conversations with the president, reporters found him utterly free of "any Presidential consciousness" or "petty vanity." Some thought him cold, but those who got to know him attributed that aloofness to "excessive shyness." The president, Grasty concluded, had an "Englishman's reserve."[91]

For the reporters on the train, the real drama of the Western tour revolved not around the treaty but the 1920 presidential election. Ratification seemed a foregone conclusion. With Wilson refusing to disclose his plans in 1920, however, reporters were left to speculate about the president's plans and to comment on the plight of Democrats confused and "embarrassed" by his silence.[92] Then, to add insult to injury, the president chose mostly Republicans to head his local reception committees and introduce his speeches. As Robert T. Small reported, the president's tour had only increased the "depression" among Democrats. They had hoped for a "few words of encouragement," but with Wilson saying nothing about his plans for a third term there could be "no [D]emocratic plans."[93]

In the closing days of the tour, Wilson might not only have reassured Democrats but also laid the groundwork for compromise with the Senate. Instead, he remained obstinate, refusing to disclose his plans for 1920 and even threatening to kill the treaty himself if the Senate did not capitulate to his demands. In his final speech in Pueblo, he hardly sounded like a man committed to oratorical statesmanship and the rhetoric of "common counsel." To the contrary, he tried to bully his critics by questioning their patriotism and exploiting fears of another world war. To some, the Pueblo speech was the highlight of the Western tour and one of the best performances of Wilson's career. In many ways, however, it marked the culmination of Wilson's drift toward demagoguery and portended some of the worst tendencies of the modern rhetorical presidency.

The Legend of Pueblo

And I want to say—I cannot say it too often—any man
who carries a hyphen about with him carries a dagger
that he is ready to plunge into the vitals of this republic
whenever he gets the chance.

PUEBLO, COLORADO, SEPTEMBER 25, 1919

"President Wilson seeks for the United States the leadership of the world," Robert T. Small reported from Cheyenne, Wyoming, on September 25. For that reason, he stubbornly opposed any amendments or reservations to the Treaty of Versailles. If the United States refused to embrace the League "whole-heartedly and unreservedly," it could hardly aspire to world leadership, and the president was struggling to "keep his temper" with those who failed to grasp that point. Since there was no time limit on ratification, Small speculated that Wilson might even "pigeonhole" the treaty if the Senate insisted upon "serious reservations." But that would carry the issue into the next campaign and destroy the League's nonpartisan character. Faced with that dilemma, Wilson could only point to the large, enthusiastic crowds that greeted him on his Western tour and claim a public mandate. Yet while Small deemed him "unquestionably . . . correct" that the "overwhelming sentiment in the country" favored the idea of a League of Nations, he concluded that most people understood "little or nothing of the technicalities of the fight for reservations."[1]

Perhaps that explains why Wilson spent more and more time talking about the proposed amendments and reservations toward the end of the tour. In California, he emphasized two issues that had inspired talk of amendments: the Shantung provision and the alleged British voting advantage. At almost every stop he also discussed three other issues behind the so-called Lodge reservations: the Monroe Doctrine, the right of withdrawal from the League, and the League's authority to intervene in America's domestic affairs. As Wilson reached Salt Lake City, however, he began to focus on just one of the Lodge reservations: the proposed reservation to Article X. Complaining that this reservation would cut the "heart" out of the treaty, Wilson equated it with rejection and declared that he would rather see the treaty defeated than ratified with qualifications. In Utah and Wyoming, the increasingly defiant Wilson won "huge ovations . . . sometimes reminiscent of his receptions in Europe," and as he arrived in Colorado he displayed "rejuvenated confidence" that he would prevail.[2] Yet there also was a note of desperation in Wilson's voice. Vilifying the opposition and predicting another world war, he did not sound at all like a man confident of victory.

When Wilson reached Pueblo, Colorado he delivered what was, "by common consent," the "most moving" speech of the Western tour—a speech that historian Thomas Bailey called the "high point of the entire trip."[3] Yet Wilson's speech in Pueblo also revealed his growing frustration, as he again lashed out at the mild reservationists and accused his critics of betraying those who had died in Europe. With thinly veiled threats of political retaliation, Wilson not only risked undermining bipartisan support for the treaty but also damaged his carefully cultivated image as an orator-statesman who relied upon principled argument rather than emotional appeal. For Bailey, the Pueblo speech may have been a "fitting climax" to an "inspired speaking tour" and to a "world-shaking speaking career—perhaps the most memorable in history."[4] In the final analysis, however, the speech betrayed Wilson's own principles of oratorical statesmanship and foreshadowed some of the worst tendencies of the modern rhetorical presidency.

I begin this chapter by charting Wilson's growing intransigence, even belligerence, in the two days leading up to his famous speech in Pueblo. Picking up the story with his declaration of war against the reservationists in Salt Lake City, I show how Wilson became even more defiant in Cheyenne and Denver, threatening to kill the treaty himself if the Senate approved reservations. Next, I offer a close reading of Wilson's address in Pueblo—a speech that has lived on in history and public memory but has attracted surprisingly little critical attention. Neither original nor eloquent by Wilson's own standards, the Pueblo speech sidestepped the controversy over reservations and substituted name-calling and threats for reasoned explication of the treaty. Above all, it betrayed Wilson's own admonitions against excess emotion, as the president devoted much of the speech to recalling the sacrifice of those who had died in the Great War. Finally, I investigate the legend of Pueblo, tracing the roots of the speech's mythic historical status to the memoirs of Wilson's closest confidants, his wife Edith and Joseph Tumulty. I argue that the Pueblo address is remembered not so much because of what Wilson said but because of the dramatic events surrounding the speech. Immortalized in Hollywood film and popular history, the Pueblo speech lives on as part of a larger story of personal courage and heroic self-sacrifice. In the legend of Pueblo, Wilson was not only "right" about the League of Nations but was also willing to sacrifice his own life to convince his fellow citizens.

The War on Reservationists

Not everybody viewed Wilson's speech in Salt Lake City as a declaration of war against the mild reservationists. Writing in the *Washington Post*, Small reported that while Wilson was "thoroughly wrought up over the situation in Washington," he was "trying to keep his temper." It had been expected that the president would "make some senatorial fur fly" in Utah, but instead he made "very earnest appeals to the senators to stop and consider anew what it is they propose to do."[5] Similarly, Philip Kinsley reported in the *Chicago Daily Tribune* that Wilson had been expected to "lash out" against the Democratic senators who were "deserting him," but instead he invoked public opinion, "practically warning them that they were going against the majority sentiment of the west in seeking to take the 'heart' out of the covenant."[6]

In retrospect, Wilson may well have restrained himself in Salt Lake City. Although he proclaimed them misguided, he also called the reservationists "high-minded, patriotic Americans" and professed to "respect them as much as I respect any man." They had arrived at their misguided conclusion only because they had "not looked into the matter" sufficiently, Wilson suggested in Salt Lake City.[7] In Cheyenne and Denver, however, Wilson had nothing at all good to say about the reservationists. Trying to shame them into submission, he characterized the Lodge reservations as a "base betrayal of our boys" and presented the Senate with a clear choice: either ratify the treaty without amendments or reservations of any kind or see it rejected altogether. He then warned of the dire consequences of rejection by imagining the horrors of the next, even more deadly world war.

Following a cavalry escort through the city, Wilson began his speech in Cheyenne with an extended discussion of the sacrifice and larger meaning of the "war to end all wars." Recalling the American soldiers who "saved the liberties of the world," Wilson directly contrasted their courage with the cowardice of the reservationists, utilizing the language suggested by Tumulty: "The men who went to Château-Thierry, the men who went into Belleau Wood, the men who did what no other troops had been able to do in the Argonne, never thought of turning back, they never thought of any *reservations* to their service." Declaring himself on a mission to "complete the task" that those "who died upon the battlefields of France" had begun, Wilson implied that the opposition was not only cowardly but also disloyal, serving the purposes of "hyphenated" and "pro-German" Americans. The vast majority of patriotic Americans understood why the nation had gone to war, Wilson suggested, and they also supported the peace settlement. "I have crossed the continent now, my friends, and am a part of my way back," Wilson began. "I can testify to the sentiment of the American people. It is unmistakable. The overwhelming majority of them demand the ratification of this treaty. And they demand it because, whether they have analyzed it or not, they have a consciousness of what it is that we are fighting for."[8]

Even as he conceded that few had "analyzed" the treaty closely, Wilson thus claimed a public mandate, and he increasingly substituted that claim for deliberative argument. In Cheyenne, he offered yet another long defense of the Shantung settlement, but he simply refused to debate the other objections raised against the proposed League of Nations. Claiming to have cleared the deck of such "bugaboos," he dismissed the concern with America's right to withdraw from the League as "no longer a question." He flatly declared that the Monroe Doctrine was "properly recognized" in the covenant, and he noted that the covenant "expressly" excluded "interference with domestic questions." That left but one question in the debate—a question that, according to Wilson, went to "the heart of the whole Covenant": the proposed reservation to Article X. Declaring it time for a "showdown" on that issue, Wilson again read the text of the proposed reservation, this time making clear his opposition to the language. Calling the reservation "unworthy and ridiculous," he concluded that there was no room for compromise: "It means the rejection of the treaty, my fellow countrymen, nothing less."[9]

Wilson's stance in Cheyenne went beyond his earlier objection that reservations might require renewed negotiations. As Chief Executive of the United States, he warned, he would personally regard adoption of the proposed reservation to Article X "a rejection of the treaty." In other words, Wilson threatened to kill the treaty himself if the Senate refused to capitulate. He then tried to frighten the opposition with predictions that the next war would make World War I seem like "child's play." At the end of the last war, he noted, "new instruments of destruction had been invented," including shells that could "steer themselves" and "carry immense bodies of explosives a hundred miles into the interior of countries, no matter how great the serried ranks of their soldiers were at the border." Wilson thereby reduced the whole debate to a simple choice between war and peace and warned that the wrong choice meant another world war. He also made it clear that he was no longer in the mood to debate the matter. The time had come to make a choice:

> The issue is final. We cannot avoid it. We have got to make it now, and once made, there can be no turning back. We either go in with the other free peoples of the world to guarantee the peace of the world now, or we stay out and, on some dark and disastrous day, we seek admission to the League of Nations along with Germany.[10]

Wilson drew cheers from his audience in Cheyenne when he appealed to their patriotism. Many also seemed moved by his pleas on behalf of the children who would be "sacrificed upon the altar" of that next, more terrible world war.[11] Yet the real news to emerge out of Cheyenne was that Wilson had presented the mild reservationists with a fresh dilemma: either ratify the treaty without reservations or Wilson himself would kill it. In his speech in Cheyenne, Wilson left no doubt that he would regard adoption of the Lodge reservations as a rejection of the pact, and reporter Small sensed important political implications in that threat. "With a defeated or mangled treaty on his hands," Small reported from Cheyenne, the president would have no choice but to "stand for a third term in the White House."[12]

From Cheyenne, Wilson proceeded to Denver, arriving at 10:30 P.M. to a surprisingly enthusiastic welcome. As he paraded through "bright streets packed with people," Denver "roared a welcome" to Wilson that continued all along the route to the Brown Palace Hotel.[13] The next morning, the president again paraded through the streets of the city, winding up at the city auditorium where William Jennings Bryan had been nominated for president in 1908. With every seat filled and "many hundreds crowded in the rear of the hall and in the aisles," Wilson addressed another huge crowd of somewhere between 11,000 and 15,000 people.[14] "Denver seemed to be friendly territory," newspaperman Kinsley reported in something of an understatement, and Wilson responded with another remarkably combative speech.[15]

Sustaining his petulant and defiant tone, Wilson announced at the outset of his Denver speech that all the objections to the treaty had now been "cleared away." Giving short shrift to such issues as the alleged British voting advantage and the Shantung provision, he again equated opposition to the treaty with disloyalty and dramatically proclaimed:

"Hyphen is the knife that is being stuck into this document." Declaring the debate over, he insisted that the stage had been reached "when all the things that need to be debated have been debated" and all the doubts "cleared up." The contest had now boiled down to "adoption or rejection," and he left no doubt where he stood on reservations: "Qualifying the adoption is not adoption." Reservations meant "asking for special privileges," and the president deemed it "unworthy" of the United States to ask for such privileges. The choice was thus simple, according to Wilson: "We must either go in or stay out."[16]

Wilson elaborated on the consequences of rejection in familiar terms, worrying aloud about the fate of the children. "When I passed your state Capitol square this morning," he began, "I saw thousands of children there to greet me. And I felt a lump in my throat. . . . I thought these are the little people I am arguing for. These are my clients." Again following Tumulty's advice, he then asked his audience to imagine "the next war" and the terrible instruments of destruction that might be deployed. As the last war ended, the belligerents already had developed "great projectiles" capable of guiding themselves "one hundred miles or more" and "bursting tons of explosives on helpless cities." And these weapons were but "toys" compared to "what would be used in the next war." Should the United States refuse to join the League, it would need to build the "biggest army in the world," institute a draft, impose "taxes such as we have never seen," and establish a concentration of governmental authority that could threaten free speech and other personal liberties. "You cannot conduct a war or command an army by a debating society," Wilson explained. "You cannot determine the war in community centers." Should the United States refuse to join the League, it would be forced to militarize the nation, becoming no different from the autocratic regimes that it had fought so hard to defeat.[17]

In concluding his speech in Denver, Wilson announced that the time had come for "sober and immediate conclusions." Again he reduced the debate to a simple choice: "We must now either accept this arrangement or reject it." Challenging opponents of the treaty "to show cause why it should not be ratified," Wilson feigned ignorance of the reasons for hesitation and reminded the Senate that, as president, he would have the final say. "When the Senate has acted," he stated, "it will be up to me to determine whether its action constitutes an adoption or rejection." Calling on the senators to make their decision "perfectly clear," Wilson repeated his own view that any qualification or reservation constituted a rejection of the treaty. For the first time since Tacoma, Wilson also mentioned the 1920 election. "When it is election time," he observed, it is "easy for applause to go to the head." But on this occasion, he could "thank God" that this "whole issue" had "nothing to do with me." "I didn't carry any purpose of my own to Paris," Wilson explained. "I didn't carry any purpose that I did not know from the action of public opinion in the United States was the purpose of the United States."[18]

Reporters interpreted Wilson's reference to the upcoming election as a threat to carry the issue "into the next campaign," even though neither Republican nor Democratic leaders wanted it to be "an issue in the presidential contest."[19] For his part, however, Wilson claimed to be acting as a "spokesman" for public opinion, not as a partisan. In Paris, he had not advocated "any privately conceived idea of my own," but rather had tried to "absorb the influences" of public opinion and embody them in the treaty. Now that he was nearing the end of his tour, his reception in the West had validated those efforts. In concluding his speech in Denver, Wilson challenged his opponents to "show cause" why the treaty should not be ratified and flatly claimed "the right to say that I have the support of the people of the United States."[20]

Reporters covering the tour remained skeptical of Wilson's claim to a public mandate. As the president completed the "last lap" of his tour, Kinsley reported, his speeches had become "more definite" and "more challenging in tone," with the president warning the Senate that he might "throw the whole document into the wastepaper basket" if they insisted upon "serious qualifications." Yet Kinsley questioned Wilson's assumption that "applause" meant support for his uncompromising position, and he noted that many in the Senate remained "adamant" in their support for reservations.[21] Similarly, Small reported that the president had begun to "burn all his bridges behind him" by denouncing "even the mildest of the mild reservations." According to Small, it was "difficult to figure" how he could win ratification "without some form of reservation covering ... the right of Congress ... to decide when this country shall go to war." His "tremendous audience" in Denver "showed its approval" of his defiant stance, Small reported, but people generally were "not wildly excited" over the League of Nations. Most simply assumed that the president and his critics would soon tire of "playing politics" and find some "satisfactory method of adopting the league."[22]

Whatever the public's actual views, Wilson took his enthusiastic reception in Denver as further "evidence that he had the people with him." And so, seemingly more confident than ever, he set out for Pueblo at 11:00 A.M. A steel strike was underway in that city, but this had "no effect" on the visit, according to Dr. Grayson; the president's reception was "cordial in the extreme." Wilson's health was another matter, however, as he had suffered all day from a "splitting headache" and was "practically at the limit of his physical powers."[23] Arriving in Pueblo, the president reluctantly agreed to be driven around the state fairgrounds where a big crowd waited to cheer him. He then proceeded to the new city auditorium, where an enthusiastic crowd of more than 3,000 people awaited his formal address. In the legend that has grown up around the speech, the president had planned to deliver just a few brief remarks in Pueblo that afternoon. Instead, he delivered one of the longest and most passionate speeches of the entire tour—a speech that did much to shape his historical legacy as a martyr to the cause of world peace.

Demagoguery Unleashed: The Pueblo Speech

It turned out to be the last speech that Woodrow Wilson would deliver on his Western tour. Indeed, it proved to be the last "extended public utterance" of his life—the "closing lines of one of the greatest speaking careers in American history," according to historian John Milton Cooper Jr.[24] The schedule called for five more major addresses—in Wichita, Oklahoma City, Little Rock, Memphis, and Louisville. Yet in one of the great dramas of American political history, Wilson fell ill after his speech in Pueblo, and a week later a stroke would leave him virtually incapacitated for the remainder of his term. As the presidential special sped back toward Washington, journalists fueled the drama by speculating about the president's condition. Only one thing seemed clear: the Western tour was over. Wilson had delivered thirty-three major addresses and about half a dozen minor speeches, but the Pueblo speech would be his last.

It was a little after 3:00 P.M. on Thursday, September 25, when Wilson rose to speak at the new civic auditorium in Pueblo. "This will have to be a short speech," he told reporters who already had heard him speak more than thirty times. "Aren't you fellows getting pretty sick of this?"[25] Yet inspired by ten minutes of cheering, Wilson somehow found the strength to deliver a 6,152-word address that touched on virtually every theme he had addressed over the course of the tour. Perhaps the president was energized by the warmth of the welcome. Or perhaps he somehow sensed that this would be his last speech. Whatever his inspiration, Wilson delivered a passionate speech that, according to some observers, left many in the audience in tears. It was a dramatic finale to Wilson's Western tour and the birth of one of the great legends of American political history.

Wilson broke no new ground in his speech in Pueblo. Summarizing the past few weeks, he began by claiming that he had gotten "a more inspiring impression" of public opinion since he began his tour. At the same time, however, he confessed to some "unpleasant impressions," as he had been forced to respond to critics who had created "an absolutely false impression" of the settlement and the proposed League of Nations. The "organized propaganda" against the League, he repeated, had come from "exactly the same sources" that had revealed their "disloyalty" before the war. He then delivered perhaps the most famous lines of the address, inspiring applause from an audience packed with supporters: "And I want to say—and I cannot say it too often—any man who carries a hyphen about with him carries a dagger that he is ready to plunge into the vitals of this republic whenever he gets the chance. If I can catch any man with a hyphen in this great contest, I will know that I have caught an enemy of the republic."[26]

If Wilson did not mean to question the loyalty of all who opposed him, he might have acknowledged—as he had in Salt Lake City—that some high-minded and patriotic Americans had legitimate concerns about the treaty. Instead, he set out to "clear away the mists," remove the "misapprehensions," and "do away" with the "false impressions" that had been created by the treaty's critics, including the mild reservationists. Returning to his earlier emphasis on the great principles behind the document, Wilson reviewed how the treaty affirmed the right of self-determination, provided a "great international charter for the rights of labor," and mobilized the "moral forces of the world" against aggression and war. He also addressed the concern with Britain's alleged voting advantage, emphasizing that the British colonies had but "speaking parts" in the Assembly and concluding: "Let us sweep aside all this language of jealousy." Finally, he repeated his usual defense of the Shantung provision, attributing the injustice of that settlement to the "state of international law" under the old world order. Under the League of Nations, he concluded, China would, for the first time, be afforded "a standing before the jury of the world." Only then could China reestablish its legitimate claim to the Shantung province.

About halfway through the speech Wilson came to what he now defined as the "heart of the whole matter": the controversy over Article X. All the other objections had been "blown away like bubbles," he declared, and the nation now had to make a choice: either "accept or reject" the treaty, including its promise to "respect and preserve the territorial integrity and existing political independence of every other member of the League as against external aggression." In Pueblo, Wilson again suggested that the League of Nations would be worthless without this guarantee, and he again made it clear that he was in no mood to compromise. Article X struck at the "taproot of war," he concluded, and to qualify or reject it would undermine the whole League.[27]

Wilson sounded exasperated as he once again responded to the treaty's critics. Reacting to fears that Article X might force the United States to take military action, he noted that the Council of the League could only "advise what steps, if any, are necessary to carry out" the article's guarantee of territorial integrity and independence for member nations. "I do not know any other meaning for the word 'advise' except 'advise,'" Wilson exclaimed. The Council merely "advised," and it could not even "advise" without the affirmative vote of the United States. Conceding that this provision might "impair somewhat the vigor of the League," Wilson seemed puzzled over objections to the provision: "Why gentlemen should fear that the Congress of the United States would be advised to do something that it did not want to do, I frankly cannot imagine, because they cannot even be advised to do anything unless their own representative has participated in the advice."[28]

Like all of the ideas he championed at Paris, Wilson claimed that Article X embodied American ideals and public opinion. "I would have felt very lonely . . . if, sitting at the peace table in Paris, I had supposed that I was expounding my own ideas," Wilson explained. He had "proposed nothing whatever" that he did not know with certainty "embodied the moral judgment of the citizens of the United States." In effect, he had gone to Paris with "explicit instructions," just as he had earlier expressed the "thought of the people of the United States" in his Fourteen Points. Recalling that earlier statement, Wilson claimed that he had "every assurance" that the Fourteen Points expressed the "moral judgment of the United States and not my single judgment." After the fourteen points became the basis for peace, he "crossed the ocean under bond to my own people and to the other governments with which I was dealing." He and the other negotiators were merely "architects" building on "specifications" established beforehand. Insisting that "men whose judgment the United States has often trusted" were of "exactly the same opinion," he quoted from an editorial by Theodore Roosevelt calling for collective security in October of 1914. "The one effective move for obtaining peace," Roosevelt had written, "is by an agreement among all the great powers in which each should pledge itself not only to abide by the decisions of a common tribunal, but to back its decisions by force."[29]

Then Wilson turned on his critics. Claiming that there was "not a leg for these gentlemen to stand on," he recalled how he had first presented a draft of the Covenant to the Senate in March. Then he had met with the Foreign Relations Committee and carried back to Paris a number of their suggestions, "every one" of which was "adopted." Venting his frustration, Wilson exclaimed, "What more could I have done? What more could have been obtained?" He then left little doubt about where he stood on reservations. Inasmuch as he already had responded to the Senate's concerns, we now have to do "one or other of two things—we have got to adopt it or reject it. There is no middle course." Equating reservations with entering the League "on a special-privilege basis," he pronounced the American people "too proud to ask to be exempted from responsibilities which the other members of the League will carry." We had to go into the League "upon equal terms" or "we do not go in at all." Finally, he described the "tragedy" that would result if "dangerous pride" led the Senate to reject the treaty. Should that happen, Wilson argued, the people of the United States would need to stand "ready to take care of ourselves," which meant maintaining "great standing armies and an irresistible navy." It also meant having "the organization of a military nation," with a "general staff, with the kind of power that the General Staff of Germany had, to mobilize this great manhood of the nation when it pleases." Under such a regime, he warned, "all the energy of our young men" would be "drawn into the thought and preparation for war."[30]

Wilson began the long, emotional peroration of his Pueblo speech with a rhetorical question: "What of our pledges to the men that lie dead in Europe?" Then marshaling his entire repertoire of pathetic proofs, he declared his "clients" to be "the children"—the "next generation"—and pledged to redeem his promise to those children that they should never have to go "upon a similar errand." He also recalled the story of the grieving mother who had "blessed" him despite losing her son—this time suggesting that he had met many such mothers on the tour. "Again and again," he said, "mothers who lost their sons in France" had come up to him, taken his hand, and with tears in their eyes had said: "God bless you, Mr. President!" Why, Wilson asked, "should they pray to God to bless me? I advised the Congress . . . to create the situation that led to the death of their sons. I ordered their sons overseas. I consented to their sons being put in the most difficult parts of the battle line, where death was certain, as in the impenetrable difficulties of the forest of Argonne." Why would such women bless the president? Wilson's answer, of course, was that they understood better than anyone the larger purposes and meaning of the war. They believed that their boys died for a cause "that vastly transcends any of the immediate and palpable objects of the war." They believed, and "rightly" so, that "their sons saved the liberty of the world." They believed that, "wrapped up with the liberty of the world," was the "continuous protection of that liberty by the concerted powers of all civilized people." And, above all, they believed that "this sacrifice was made in order that other sons should not be called upon for a similar gift—the gift of life, the gift of all that died."[31]

In effect, Wilson claimed that the boys who had died in Europe died for the League of Nations. And to reject the League now would not only diminish their sacrifice but also tarnish their memory. If the treaty were rejected, Wilson asked, "would not something of the halo go away from the gun over the mantelpiece, or the sword? Would not the old uniform lose something of its significance?" Those men were "crusaders," and "their transcendent achievement" had made "all the world believe in America as it believes in no other nation . . . in the modern world." Picturing soldiers lined up beside their president as he battled for the League of Nations, Wilson imagined even the dead rallying to the cause: "There seems to me to stand between us and the rejection or qualification of this treaty the serried ranks of those boys in khaki—not only those boys who came home, but those dear ghosts that still deploy upon the fields of France."[32]

Finally, Wilson took his Pueblo audience to that "beautiful hillside near Paris"—the American cemetery at Suresnes, where he had spoken on Memorial Day. "Behind me on the slopes," he recalled, "was rank upon rank of living American soldiers. And, lying before me upon the levels of the plain, was rank upon rank of departed American soldiers." As he spoke, Wilson recalled, a "little group of French women" stood nearby, paying their respects to the American boys they had adopted as their own. Becoming "mothers to these dear boys," the French women put flowers on the graves of American boys every day "because they had died to save France." Implying that his critics lacked both sympathy and understanding, Wilson declared, "I wish that some men in public life who are now opposing the settlement for which these men died could visit such a spot as that. I wish that the feeling which came to me could penetrate their hearts." If only they could "feel the moral obligation that rests upon us not to go back on those boys," they would "see the thing through" and "make good their redemption of the world. For nothing less depends upon us, nothing less than the liberation and salvation of the world."[33]

Wilson conceded that the League of Nations provided no "absolute guarantee" against future wars. But sounding a theme he had emphasized throughout the tour, he insisted that some "insurance" against war was better than "no insurance at all." He then sounded an ironic note. "Now that the mists of this great question have cleared away, I believe that men will see the truth, eye to eye and face to face." In Pueblo, of course, it was Wilson himself who fogged the whole debate in the mists of war sentimentality. And in closing, he awkwardly conjured up an especially foggy, dreamlike image, as he wistfully envisioned peaceful pastures and a world without war: "We have accepted [the] truth, and we are going to be led by it, and it is going to lead us, and, through us, the world, out into pastures of quietness and peace such as the world never dreamed of before."[34]

At the time, the reporters traveling with the president sensed nothing special about his speech in Pueblo. Reporting for the *Chicago Daily Tribune,* Kinsley observed that the president's emotional appeals were "effective as everywhere," and he noted that Mrs. Wilson had "tears on her cheeks" as the president finished his address. He also noticed that one "working man" in the front row had "wept" as the president "told of the graves in France." Yet Kinsley led his story with news of the steel strike in Pueblo, and he described Wilson's reception in that city as "respectful and friendly" but "not particularly enthusiastic."[35] Similarly, the *Los Angeles Times* only briefly paraphrased Wilson's pledge to fight for the children while emphasizing his attacks on hyphenated Americans and his call for a "showdown" in both Denver and Pueblo.[36] Instead of noting Wilson's sentimental reflections on war, the newspapers emphasized his defiance, highlighting how in both his speeches in

Colorado he had threatened to kill the treaty himself.[37] Several years later reporter David Lawrence would recall the Pueblo speech as a "masterpiece of eloquence."[38] At the time, however, nobody seemed to imagine that the Pueblo speech would be remembered as one of the great presidential speeches in history.

That would come later, after some of Wilson's closest confidants told the dramatic behind-the-scenes story of the Pueblo speech in their published memoirs. Later still, popular historians and even Hollywood filmmakers would get into the act, embellishing the story of Pueblo with still more dramatic turns and elevating Wilson to the status of a heroic martyr. In 1956, the one-hundredth anniversary of Wilson's birth afforded yet another opportunity to honor the man and to celebrate the League of Nations as among his "greatest contributions to the welfare of mankind."[39] By the 1960s, the revisionist portrait of Wilson—a portrait that placed Wilson among a handful of the great-est U.S. presidents—would become firmly entrenched. Despite his humiliating defeat in the League of Nations debate, Wilson would be remembered as a prophetic champion of collective security and a courageous crusader for world peace. In the revisionist view, Wilson proved "right" about the League of Nations and willingly risked his own life to convince his fellow Americans.

The Pueblo Speech in History and Public Memory

Wilson was very tired and "suffering" when he returned to his railroad car following his speech in Pueblo, Grayson noted in his diary on September 25, 1919. So twenty miles outside of town, Grayson ordered the train stopped so that the president could take a walk and get some fresh air. Accompanied by his doctor and Mrs. Wilson, the president walked for about an hour, first encountering an elderly farmer driv-ing a small car along a dusty country road. The farmer presented the president with a head of cabbage and some apples, expressing his hope that the president might have them for dinner. Later, Wilson spied a "very plainly ill" army private sitting in his uniform on the porch of a farmhouse. Climbing over a fence, the president went to shake hands with the boy, then chatted with his family. After the walk, the president ate better than he had in days, and he even defied doctor's orders by greeting a large crowd of well-wishers when the train stopped in Rocky Ford, Colorado.[40]

The next day Grayson's diary told a very different story. Awakened from his sleep at 2:00 A.M., Grayson recalled being told that the president was very sick and "suffering very much." Proceeding "at once" to the president's private car, he found Wilson "unable to sleep and in a highly nervous condition," the muscles in his face "twitching." The president was "extremely nauseated" and could "hardly get his breath," and the doctor was "obliged to give him every possible care and attention." Concerned that the president's condition could prove fatal, Grayson felt it his "duty" to recommend that the remainder of the trip be canceled. After consulting with Tumulty and Mrs. Wilson, Grayson recalled breaking the news to Wilson himself. The president "rebelled and said that he wanted to go on," fearing that his enemies would call him a quitter. But he finally gave in. "If you feel that way about it," Grayson quoted Wilson as saying, "I will surrender." Grayson concluded his account with a memorable image of a dejected Wilson, staring out the window and "almost overcome by his emotions." As the president came to accept his fate, he "choked and big tears fell from his eyes as he turned away."[41]

The treaty debate would go on, but the Western tour was over. As the presidential special sped back toward Washington, news of Wilson's illness caused a "sensation." All along the route crowds gathered in solemn respect, with "no cheering or noise of any kind."[42] When the presidential special finally arrived at Union Station on Sunday, September 28, Wilson was greeted by his daughter Margaret and perhaps a thousand well-wishers. He reportedly walked unaided to a waiting car. Most apparently assumed that a few days of rest would have the president back on his feet. But then, on October 2, the president suffered a stroke and collapsed on the bathroom floor, where Edith found him "bloody and unconscious."[43] For the remaining seventeen months of his presidency, Wilson remained virtually incapacitated, with Mrs. Wilson jealously guarding his privacy and the fate of the treaty in doubt.

During this time, the Senate twice voted to reject the Versailles treaty—first, on November 19, then again on March 19 of the following year. As Wilson regained a measure of his health, he concocted two fantastic schemes for fighting back, first by challenging the fifty-seven senators who opposed him to resign and stand for reelection in special elections, and then by proposing that the 1920 presidential campaign be made into a "great and solemn referendum" on the treaty.[44] To many observers, these fanciful proposals only confirmed that Wilson was a "petulant and sick man" and had become "the principal obstacle to ratification."[45] Before long, even the most devoted treaty supporters gave up the fight, and Wilson's great crusade—indeed, his "great political career"—came to a "pitiful end."[46]

The Western tour might have been remembered as a lesson in failed presidential leadership—as an illustration of Wilson's own principle that public opinion "must not be outstripped" but "kept pace with."[47] Or it might be viewed as a case study in the limitations of a rhetorical presidency.[48] Yet whatever their judgment of the tour itself, historians tend to agree that Wilson was right about the end of isolationism and the need for collective security. Had the nation only listened to Wilson, the conventional wisdom holds, the tragedy of a second world war might have been avoided.

Wilson's speech in Pueblo represents a key moment in this tragic narrative of lost opportunity. Not only has the speech itself been celebrated as the highest expression of Wilsonian idealism, but also the events surrounding the address have been dramatized as an inspirational tale of personal courage and heroic self-sacrifice. Published just two years after the tour, Joseph Tumulty's memoir, *Woodrow Wilson as I Know Him*, played a major role in shaping this legendary tale. Celebrating the Pueblo speech as the highlight of the tour and also as the greatest speech ever delivered by the twenty-eighth president, Tumulty penned the first "insider" account of the president's courageous determination to prevail in the League of Nations debate.

It should come as no surprise that Joseph Tumulty would praise the Pueblo speech as "one of the best and most passionate" of Wilson's entire career. With its long, emotional peroration, it was, after all, the fullest expression of Tumulty's own speech-making advice. Recalling how the speech left Mrs. Wilson with "tears in her eyes" and prompted even the men in the audience to "wipe the tears from their eyes," Tumulty reveled in Wilson's portrait of that "beautiful hillside near Paris" and his reflections on "the purposes for which those departed American soldiers had given their lives." Recalling the "great wave of emotion" that swept through the auditorium, Tumulty noted that even "hard-boiled" newspapermen appeared "deeply moved" by the speech. In a memorable simile, Tumulty compared the president to a "great organist" playing upon the "heart emotions" of his audience, leaving them "spell-bound" by his words. Praying to God that Pueblo would not be Wilson's last public speech, Tumulty reprinted the entire peroration of the speech in his memoir, quoting nearly 1,000 words over two full pages. The passage began with the rhetorical question that Tumulty himself had suggested: "What of our pledges to the men that lie dead in France?"[49]

Tumulty's account of events later that night further shaped the legend of Pueblo. Recalling how he was awakened by Dr. Grayson at 4:00 A.M., Tumulty first saw the president "fully dressed and seated in his chair" but obviously sick: "With great difficulty he was able to articulate. His face was pale and wan. One side of it had fallen, and his condition was indeed pitiful to behold." Agreeing that the trip could "end fatally," Tumulty endorsed Grayson's recommendation that the tour be canceled, and he, like Grayson, recalled the president vigorously resisting: "Don't you see that if you cancel this trip, Senator Lodge and his friends will say that I am a quitter and that the Western trip was a failure, and the Treaty will be lost." As the president continued to protest, Tumulty realized that his "whole left side was paralyzed," and that settled the matter. He immediately issued a statement to the "inquiring newspaper men that the Western trip was off." Concluding the story, Tumulty pictured a sick but still-determined Wilson—a martyr to the cause of world peace:

Suffering the greatest pain, paralyzed on his left side, he was still fighting desperately for the thing that was so close to his heart—a vindication of the things for which he had so gallantly fought on the other side. Grim old warrior that he was, he was ready to fight to the death for the League of Nations.[50]

Twenty years later, Mrs. Edith Bolling Wilson would add more brush-strokes to this tragic yet heroic portrait of Woodrow Wilson. She too remembered the Pueblo speech as the highest expression of Wilsonian eloquence, and she told an even more dramatic story of Wilson's gallant struggle to finish the trip. Recalling the president's promise to make only a "short speech" in Pueblo, Mrs. Wilson wrote of a surprising, even mysterious burst of energy and passion that seemed to overtake the ailing president as he took the stage. "Strangely," she wrote, the speech that he delivered that day—a day in which he suffered terribly from exhaustion and headaches—"was one of the longest, one of the most vigorous and touching he made on the tour." As he "warmed to his subject," Mrs. Wilson recalled that "the President's weariness seemed to leave him. New and undiscovered reservoirs of strength seemed to reinforce his efforts." As the president talked about being blessed by grieving mothers and pictured the scene at Suresnes, Mrs. Wilson recalled that tears began running down her cheeks—"and not mine alone." "Such was Woodrow Wilson's valedictory," Mrs. Wilson concluded in marking September 25, 1919, as the president's finest hour. After the Pueblo speech, she knew that "life would never be the same."[51]

Edith's account of the president's subsequent collapse differed in only minor details from those of Grayson and Tumulty. She began by recounting how the president had come back "much refreshed" from his walk in the "fresh Colorado air." Dinner that night was "cheerful," she recalled, as the president ate well and his "head was easier than it had been for days." At 11:30 that night, however, the president knocked on Mrs. Wilson's door and informed her that he was "very sick." Finding him in "unbearable" pain, she sent for Grayson, but there was little the doctor could do. According to Mrs. Wilson, it was she, not Tumulty or Grayson, who finally convinced the president that "the fight was over," and she quoted the president protesting in somewhat different words: "No, no, no. I must keep going." She also did not recall her husband sobbing, instead insisting that he "accepted the decree of Fate as gallantly as he had fought the fight," never once voicing a "syllable of self-pity or regret." Edith's version of the story was no less tragic, however. That night proved "the longest and most heartbreaking" of her life, she recalled, and as she "sat there watching the dawn break slowly," she sensed that from that moment forward she would have to "wear a mask," not only in public, but even around "the one I loved best in the world."[52]

Over the years, the legend of Pueblo would continue to be embellished by popular historians and even Hollywood filmmakers. In 1944, for example, Oscar-winning producer Darryl F. Zanuck released a lavish 20th Century Fox production, *Wilson,* that portrayed the twenty-eighth president as the greatest chief executive since Washington and Lincoln.[53] Biographer Ray Stannard Baker served as a technical adviser on the film, but that did not stop Zanuck from exercising his dramatic license, particularly in retelling the story of the Western tour and the Pueblo speech. At one point in the film, Zanuck had Tumulty begging Wilson not to tour out of concern for his health, even though Tumulty was, in fact, the most vocal advocate of the tour. At another point, the film had Edith passionately urging Wilson to accept the Lodge reservations—"for my sake." To this Wilson supposedly replied, "I have no right to accept any changes. It's just a scheme to kill the League entirely." As flashes of the train, the crowds, and the local headlines chart the tour's progress from Columbus through the Midwest and on to California, we hear Wilson's voice delivering lines that he never actually delivered. "The isolation of the United Slates is at an end," Zanuck had him declaring in Los Angeles. Finally, the presidential special slowly rolls into Pueblo, with Wilson slumped in a chair, suddenly looking old and gray. As Edith and Grayson beg him to stop, Wilson appears dazed, his eyes barely open. "I can't stop now," he mumbles. "I must go on." The president then stumbles out the door to deliver his famous Pueblo address. Standing on the rear platform of the *Mayflower* (rather than in the city's new civic auditorium), he speaks for less than three minutes before being struck down by some sort of seizure. In a slight variation upon remarks that Wilson actually delivered in St. Louis three week earlier,[54] Wilson begins a very different speech than he actually delivered in Pueblo—a dark, fatalistic speech that seemed to reflect that he already had lost the debate:

> People of Pueblo. . . . I feel like asking the Secretary of War to get the boys who went across the water to fight together on some field where I could go and see them. And I will stand up before them and say, "Boys, I told you before you went across the seas that this was a war against wars. And I did my best to fulfill that promise, but I am obliged to come to you with mortification and shame and say I have been unable to fulfill that promise."
>
> "You are betrayed! You fight for something that you did not get!" And the glory of the armies and the navies of the United States is gone like a dream in the night and there ensues upon it, in the suitable darkness of the night, the nightmare of dread which lay upon the nations before this war came.
>
> And there will come some time in the vengeful providence of God another struggle in which not a few hundred thousand fine young men from America will have to die but as many millions as are necessary to accomplish the final freedom of the peoples of the world.
>
> I will . . .

At this point, Wilson gasps and is visibly jolted. Unable to continue, he meekly thanks the audience for coming and is helped back into the train, where he collapses as the musical score sounds an ominous note.

Wilson won critical claim and several Oscars for writing and production, but it bombed at the box office, losing about $2 million.[55] Nevertheless, it inspired something of a Wilson revival and helped solidify public support for the new United Nations.[56] It also helped etch into public memory some of the most enduring myths about Wilson's Western tour. Even today, one online educational site has Wilson collapsing during his speech in Pueblo, either from a "mild

stroke" or a "nervous breakdown."⁵⁷ Meanwhile, textbooks and antholo-
gies continue to celebrate the Pueblo address as a model of Wilsonian
eloquence—indeed, as one of the "top 100 speeches of the twentieth
century."⁵⁸ Reflecting an emerging historical consensus that Wilson
was right and his critics were wrong, Zanuck's film contributed to a
revisionist portrait of Wilson as a prophetic crusader for world peace.
In the revisionist view, the Pueblo speech was not a demagogic attempt
to bully or scare people into deferring to his uncompromising position. Rather, it was the highest expression of Wilsonian idealism and
a courageous, even heroic act of personal self-sacrifice.

The revisionist perspective on Wilson received official, bipartisan
sanction in 1956, when the U.S. Congress created the Woodrow Wilson
Centennial Celebration Commission. Charged with developing "suit-
able plans" for celebrating the one-hundredth anniversary of Wilson's
birth, the Commission worked closely with other organizations
dedicated to the memory of Wilson, creating educational programs,
sponsoring commemorative services, and overseeing production of an
up-to-date record of his letters and papers. It also oversaw production
of "a body of distinguished literature" about Wilson. Unabashedly cel-
ebratory, the Commission aspired to place Wilson "high on the list of
great American Presidents," and toward that end it set out to "educate"
the nation about his "mastery of lucid prose," his "deep humanitarian
instincts," and his "realistic vision of instrumentalities to promote world
peace." Scarcely a generation before, Wilson had been a "highly controversial figure," a president at "the center of the bitterest of political
battles," and a man who suffered a "calamitous defeat" in the League
of Nations debate. Yet "momentous events," including a "second and
more devastating world war," had dictated a reassessment of Wilson.
By "nationwide accord," the Commission concluded, Wilson was now
"recognized as one of America's greatest Presidents."⁵⁹

Since the 1950s, the revisionist portrait of Wilson has been reinforced
in popular as well as scholarly histories. In 1964, for example, Gene
Smith, a journalist with a "strong sense of history's drama," crafted a
version of the Western tour "straight out of Greek tragedy."⁶⁰ In recon-
structing the Pueblo speech, Smith wrote of the look of "terror" on the

First Lady's face when the president stumbled over a sentence early in his remarks, then stood mute for a few moments. Somehow he "gathered himself together," however, and he went on to speak eloquently of "Memorial Day at Suresnes, of the soldiers alive and dead at the cemetery, and of how he wished that some of the Senators opposing the League might have been there on that day." According to Smith, "men and women alike" reached for handkerchiefs "to wipe their eyes" during the speech—a slight embellishment of Tumulty's recollection. Then, after speaking of the "dear ghosts who still deploy upon the fields of France," Wilson again lost focus. "He halted," Smith wrote. "The people looked at him and he at them." Smith then invented a dramatic scene that not even Hollywood had imagined: "The President of the United States, standing before an audience of some several thousands of his fellow citizens, was crying. . . . He turned away and the First Lady came to him. Their tears mixed." In Smith's version of the story, Wilson also "burst into tears" later when told that the trip had to be cancelled.[61] Yet the most enduring image from Smith's account was no doubt that portrait of the president of the United States, standing before a crowd of thousands and weeping over his own words. Unfortunately, it simply never happened. It was, by all accounts, a complete fabrication.

Not all historians have praised the Pueblo speech as a masterpiece of Wilsonian eloquence. "The words did not come," historian Robert H. Ferrell wrote in one of the more critical assessments of the speech. Quoting Wilson's closing line about "pastures of quietness and peace," Ferrell concluded, "These were tired words, not Wilsonian; they were patched-up street phrases."[62] Similarly, biographer Kendrick A. Clements has called Wilson's language in Pueblo "tired and ordinary" and has described the whole speech as not "especially inspired."[63] The president's stop in Pueblo may have been "the emotional high point of the trip," with a "large, spirited audience standing and cheering for ten minutes before Wilson could even begin." Yet the speech itself, in Clements's assessment, was simply "not very good."[64]

Nevertheless, the Pueblo speech generally lives on in history and public memory as the "most moving" speech of the Western tour—the "high point of the entire trip."[65] Even the most careful historian of the treaty debate, John Milton Cooper Jr., has praised the speech as among the "best performances" of the tour.[66] Why do we remember the Pueblo speech as a "great" presidential address? Why does it so overshadow the thirty-two other major addresses that Wilson delivered on the tour? The easy answer, of course, is that we remember the Pueblo speech more for what happened afterward than for what Wilson said—his dramatic collapse, the long and agonizing incapacitation, and the Senate's rejection of the treaty. Yet there may be more to our celebration of the Pueblo speech than sympathy for Wilson, as I will suggest in the Epilogue to this book. Not only did we later decide that Wilson was "right" about the League of Nations, but we also changed our standards of presidential eloquence.

Conclusion

When Woodrow Wilson arrived back in Washington following his Western tour, he was driven home to the White House through deserted streets. Along the way he lifted his hat and bowed in what historian August Heckscher would later describe as a "pathetic gesture"—the "last time as President that he would have even the illusion of acclaim." From the standpoint of pure drama, as Heckscher suggests, it might have been better if Wilson had collapsed and died while delivering the Pueblo speech. That would have solidified his reputation as a "martyr," and his life would have "held something of the mystery and awe that surrounds Lincoln."[67] Instead, Wilson returned to Washington to wither away while his enemies had their way with his beloved League of Nations. Following that humiliating defeat, Wilson quietly left the White House and faded into retirement at his house on S Street in Washington, D.C.

The Pueblo speech turned out to be Wilson's last major public utterance, the culmination of a career of public speaking that spanned many decades and brought him international fame. Ironically, the speech bore little resemblance to most of the speeches he had delivered over the course of his career. Indeed, not only was it not typical of his speeches, but it also violated the principles of oratorical statesmanship that he had championed as a scholar. As a deliberative speech, the Pueblo speech did little to illuminate the principles and provisions of the treaty. It also lacked the constructive and magnanimous tone of some of his better speeches on the tour, such as his speech in Des Moines. Wallowing in bitter memories of the war and questioning the sympathy and even the patriotism of all who disagreed, the Pueblo speech contributed little to the debate over America's rights and obligations under the League of Nations. Nobody wanted war. Nobody wanted the next generation of children to die in another devastating conflict. The debate was over how best to avoid war while protecting America's interests. Wilson's maudlin emotionalism in Pueblo contributed little to that debate.

Woodrow Wilson no doubt deserves credit for his determination and courage in fighting for what he believed. One cannot help but sympathize with a man who worked so diligently for a cause, only to have his efforts come to such a tragic end. Yet there seems to be more to our celebration of the Pueblo speech than personal sympathy for Wilson. The speech also gave voice to a philosophy of American internationalism that increasingly gained favor with the coming of the second world war, and it promoted that philosophy in a recognizably modern style of presidential rhetoric. In other words, Wilson's Pueblo speech may be remembered as a great speech because it anticipated both the international politics and the popular rhetorical leadership of the postwar era. In that sense, Wilson indeed proved prophetic. Not only did he foresee the future of American foreign policy, but he also described it in the language of the modern rhetorical presidency.

Epilogue

The Legacy of Wilson's Western Tour

I do not believe that, ordinarily speaking,
[the presidency] is a speech-making office.
CLEVELAND, OHIO, JANUARY 29, 1916

On September 11, 1919, Dr. Cary Grayson commented in his diary on one of the many gifts presented to the president as he toured the West. As the presidential special prepared to depart Helena, Grayson reported, the governor of Montana, Samuel Vernon Stewart, placed onboard a forty-five-pound rainbow trout that he personally had caught that day in the mountains.[1] To this day, the world record for a rainbow trout stands at just 42 pounds, 2 ounces, so we have reason to suspect Grayson's account.[2] Yet Grayson's monster trout is but one of many "fish stories" to be handed down from Wilson's Western tour. Over the years the story of the tour has been dramatized and embellished by a variety of journalists, historians, and even Hollywood filmmakers. As perhaps the most famous example of a president "going public," it also has been a fertile source of larger political lessons about presidential leadership, the role of public opinion in American foreign policy, and America's responsibilities as a great world power.[3]

For some, Wilson's Western tour remains the best illustration of the limitations of the rhetorical presidency. According to Jeffrey Tulis, the

Western tour was destined to fail because "popular" speech—speech appealing to "passion," speech designed to "move a crowd"—inevitably undermines serious policy deliberations. Wilson was "keenly sensitive to the need not to appear demagogic," Tulis argues, yet his "entreaties" to the masses nevertheless angered senators and contradicted what he had told them in person. In speech designed to influence public opinion, Wilson made statements that, according to Tulis, should have been discounted. Yet in Wilson's day, people took the president's speeches seriously, confusing his "popular rhetoric" with his "true" position.[4]

In his scholarly writings, Wilson worried about many of the same problems that concern Tulis and other critics of the rhetorical presidency. Criticizing the spellbinders of his day, he too warned that an overly popular style of leadership might subvert deliberation, and he called upon the nation's leaders not to pander, but to nurture, cultivate, and uplift public opinion. When the public became aroused, Wilson even called upon the orator-statesman to moderate the "passions and the thoughtless impulses of the people."[5] Yet unlike Tulis, he did not equate all popular speech with demagoguery, nor did he consider ordinary citizens incapable of deliberating intelligently. Envisioning a public actively involved in great national debates, Wilson had faith in the ability of the common folk to govern themselves. Taking issue with those who doubted the public's ability to "exercise intelligent discretion," he argued that a "charlatan" could not long masquerade as a statesman, and he voiced confidence that the public's deliberations would be "deliberate and wise."[6]

Wilson's faith in public opinion resonated from his speeches and writings throughout the Progressive Era. In *Constitutional Government in the United States* (1908),[7] he finally found his answer to the problem of a government dominated by Congress. Taking inspiration from Theodore Roosevelt, he imagined how the "bully pulpit" might be used to facilitate public discussion and give voice to enlightened public opinion. At the same time, he recognized that "going public" was not always feasible or appropriate, and he cautioned that the president must never lead too far in advance of public opinion. Even in popular speech, Wilson's responsible rhetorical president upheld the neoclassical oratorical tradition, and he refrained from stirring up popular passions with emotional appeals. Wilson's orator-statesman deliberated with the people in "common counsel," defining the principles at stake, illuminating the issues and controversies involved, and ultimately giving voice to their collective judgment. He was both an educator-leader and an interpreter of public opinion, and, ultimately, the spokesman for the "whole people."

As a candidate for president in 1912, Wilson made his vision of a revitalized public sphere a campaign issue. Contrasting his vision of political and spiritual renewal "from below" with Theodore Roosevelt's alleged "paternalism," Wilson proclaimed revived public discussion one of the great "needs of the hour" and promised to "restore the processes of common counsel" to American politics.[8] As president, Wilson generally lived up to that promise, leading public opinion "in a careful and constructive manner" and bargaining constructively with Congress. Promoting his New Freedom reforms, he appealed to public opinion with "discretion," rarely criticizing the opposition and assuming the role of a "interlocutor and coordinator" of Congress rather than its "master."[9] During his preparedness tour in 1916, Wilson again cast himself as a spokesman for the "whole people," embracing the principles animating both sides in the debate and working with Congress to fashion a compromise.

The success of the Committee on Public Information during World War I, as Stephen Vaughn has argued, had an "unfortunate effect on public opinion theory." Arousing public opinion to a "white hot" intensity, the CPI's "calculated appeal to emotion" undermined faith in the rationality of the public, suggesting new ways to "manipulate opinion" and promoting "an unthinking loyalty to the state."[10] After the war, even George Creel agreed that propaganda had no "proper place in the national life in time of peace."[11] Yet Edward Bernays and other veterans of the CPI took the lessons they had learned during the war into civilian life, arguing that "efforts comparable to those applied by the CPI . . . could be applied with equal facility to peacetime pursuits."[12] The result was the birth of the public relations industry and also a whole new attitude toward public opinion. By the mid-1920s, the "concept of a democratic public"—the concept that inspired many of the reform initiatives of the Progressive Era—had been displaced by "scientific" theories of mass persuasion, and the progressive ideal of a freely deliberating democratic public was no longer "a key element in the American political imagination."[13]

Wilson's Western tour reflected the tensions and contradictions of this transitional moment in the nation's history. At times, the president embodied his neoclassical ideals, "expounding" on the principles and provisions of the treaty and engaging the people in "common counsel." Especially early in the tour, he delivered a number of dispassionate, well-reasoned speeches, implicitly trusting in the ability of ordinary citizens to grasp complicated historical and philosophical arguments and to deliberate wisely. As he reached the West Coast, however, Wilson increasingly gave in to Joseph Tumulty's advice that he wave the bloody shirt and force a "showdown" with his critics. Drifting toward a more popular, even demagogic style, he finally proclaimed the debate over, declared "war" on the Senate reservationists, and threatened to kill the treaty himself if he did not get his way.

These rhetorical choices—not some inherent, institutional limitation of the rhetorical presidency—best account for Wilson's failure to reach some sort of compromise with the mild reservationists. In giving in to Tumulty's advice, Wilson chose to ignore his own prescriptions against an emotional, overly "popular" style of rhetorical leadership. He chose to abandon the rhetoric of "common counsel" and instead to defy and even threaten all who opposed him. As Samuel Kernell has suggested, Wilson failed to "force the Senate to accept his version of the League" not because he decided to "go public," but because he went about it in the wrong way. Contrasting Wilson's attempt to "overpower his opposition" with Truman's successful campaign for the Truman Doctrine, Kernell concludes that Truman had more success because he was "less confrontational" than Wilson. Unlike Wilson, Truman identified "no individuals or blocs of politicians in Washington as opponents," nor did he threaten Congress with political retribution. Instead, he did just what the scholarly Wilson might have suggested:

first he cultivated a "climate of public opinion" that made his position "more palatable to the country," then he negotiated with Congress and struck a deal.[14]

Today, the presidency has become even more of a "speech-making office." Presidents now routinely "go public," both to promote themselves and their policy agendas. Yet the neoclassical tradition that informed Wilson's rhetorical leadership has largely been forgotten, and we no longer take the president's popular speeches as seriously as we once did. For Tulis, that is a good thing, for in his view a president cannot possibly be "candid and forthright in popular speech" and still deliberate seriously with Congress.[15] By this view, popular speech is, by definition, irrational and demagogic. For Tulis and other critics of the modern rhetorical presidency, the legacy of the Western tour is a legacy of skepticism about deliberative democracy.

Yet there is another, quite different lesson that one might learn from Wilson's Western tour—the lesson taught by Wilson's own writings and by his vision of a responsible rhetorical presidency. That lesson suggests at least the possibility that a president might educate and enlighten the citizenry. It suggests how a president might engage the public in "common counsel" and faithfully articulate "the will of the people." As Arthur S. Link suggested nearly fifty years ago, Wilson's Western tour was "one of the most notable forensic accomplishments in American history," not only because he traveled 8,000 miles and delivered more than thirty major speeches, but because, for the most part, he also spoke "not as a partisan, but as a leader who stood above party strife and advantage."[16] In today's political world, that sort of statesmanship might be hard to imagine. Yet that is precisely the rhetorical presidency that Woodrow Wilson both imagined and often embodied: a presidency of a genuine "orator-statesmen" dedicated to the public good.

A second, related legacy of Wilson's Western tour is persistent skepticism about the role of public opinion in American foreign policy. In the conventional view, Wilson lost the League of Nations debate despite public support for his position, and ever since scholars have downplayed the role of public opinion in the formulation and conduct of American foreign policy.[17] But what do historians mean when they characterize the League of Nations debate as a contest for public opinion? And in an age before polling, how do we know that Wilson had the public behind him? As this study has shown, the case can be made that it was Wilson, not his critics, who defied public opinion by pushing too fast for a dramatic change in American foreign policy and refusing to compromise on the proposed reservations. If so, the real lesson of the Western tour may be the lesson that Wilson himself taught in his scholarly writings: that a president should never lead too far in advance of public opinion.

As Thomas J. Knock has observed, few historians have doubted that the League of Nations, "at least until 1920," enjoyed "overwhelming public approval."[18] One student of the debate has even claimed that "polls" showed a public already favorable toward the League well before Wilson toured[19]—a decade-and-a-half before George Gallup even invented what he called the "sampling referendum."[20] That Wilson failed to capitalize on this public support, according to the conventional wisdom, not only revealed the limits of the modern rhetorical presidency but also the negligible impact of public opinion on American foreign policy. Yet how do we know that a majority of Americans favored ratification, as Allan Nevins has asserted, or that opponents of the treaty spoke for but "a minority of the people," as Link concluded. As Tulis reminds us, there were no "reliable survey data regarding the state of public opinion towards the League or the treaty."[21] Indeed, there were no survey data at all. Nor have retrospective studies of public opinion shed much light on the attitudes of ordinary Americans.[22] Wilson and his critics both claimed public support for their positions. But which portrait of public opinion carried the day? And what impact, if any, did public opinion have on the outcome of the debate?

Again, Wilson's own writings provide a starting point for answering these questions. In *Congressional Government,* Wilson reflected on how public opinion historically had been formed by the great orator-statesmen in Congress giving voice to the views of their constituents. With the decline of congressional oratory, however, the business of defining public opinion had fallen to the press, which spoke "entirely without authority," in Wilson's view, and privileged the "gossip of the street."[23] Wilson's solution to this problem, as we have seen, was an active, rhetorical presidency that both led and gave voice to public opinion. As the one political figure elected by the "nation as a whole," Wilson imagined the president engaging the people in "common counsel," then giving voice to the "real sentiment and purpose of the country."[24]

During his League of Nations tour, Wilson claimed to do just that. Throughout the debate he complained that the press had exaggerated opposition to the treaty, and he accused his critics of speaking only for special interests. Near the end of the tour, he even announced the people's decision. Pointing to the size and enthusiasm of his crowds, Wilson claimed a public mandate and declared the debate over. Yet as historian Kendrick Clements has argued, Wilson sometimes mistook his ability to "move and inspire an audience" for an "instinctive understanding of their wishes." According to Clements, Wilson's "power over an audience" may even have given him the "illusion that he was expressing unspoken popular wishes when in fact no such wishes existed."[25] As Wilson left California, even his critics conceded that he had drawn huge and enthusiastic crowds. Yet even at the time, many doubted that those crowds reflected some broader public opinion. After Wilson spoke in Des Moines, for example, an Iowan wrote to the *Chicago Daily Tribune* explaining why he remained skeptical of the president's claim that he had the people behind him:

1. It is but natural that meetings of such character would be attended by sympathizers with the purpose for which the meeting was called, and would be by no means representative of common sentiment for the league.

2. I know from personal experience that real opponents of any scheme of a like nature would invariably remain at home rather than suggest by their presence a sympathy with the side of the question to be presented.

3. An address by a president of the United States would undoubtedly be well attended, even though he were to speak on the "Peril of Petrified Prunes in Panama."[26]

Throughout the tour, the reporters covering the tour also seemed skeptical of Wilson's claim to a public mandate. Most reporters agreed that the public favored the idea of a League of Nations. Yet most Americans also supported reservations, according to the newspapers, and many apparently did not care all that much about the issue. Wilson's critics in the Senate seemed to sense this. Few senators seemed intimidated by Wilson's threat to punish them at the polls. Indeed, most seemed more worried about the electoral consequences of backing the president. In the end, even many Democrats deserted Wilson to vote for the so-called Lodge reservations. And interestingly, those who did abandon the president tended to be facing reelection in 1920.[27]

Thomas Bailey apparently got it right nearly sixty years ago: Wilson never had a public mandate, at least not for his defiant, uncompromising position on reservations. Many who turned out to cheer Wilson were probably just "curiosity seekers," and the convention halls were no doubt "packed with Wilson sympathizers." More importantly, the size and enthusiasm of the crowds did not prove that the country was "swinging to the treaty *without reservations.*" Some have suggested that, had the president not collapsed, he might have forced the Senate to bow to a "storm of public opinion." Yet, as Bailey concluded, the "length and volume of the ovations did not prove a great deal," and in any case Wilson's popular support did not change "a single vote" in the Senate.[28]

Perhaps the lesson to be learned from Wilson's Western tour is not that public opinion counts for nothing in American foreign policy. To the contrary, it appears that Wilson himself defied public opinion, and in the final analysis he paid a price for that defiance. By refusing to compromise, Wilson ignored the prevailing assumption that, in the end, he would find some way to accommodate the mild reservationists. Nobody at the time ever imagined that he would prove so stubborn— even at the cost of total defeat. Perhaps Wilson genuinely believed that he had the "great mass of people behind him" and that the power of public opinion would "crush any Senator or party who opposed him," as Link has suggested.[29] Yet Wilson proved wrong in predicting that voters would punish his critics, and it would be another two decades before most Americans embraced his vision of collective security.

After World War II Wilson's vision of American internationalism became his greatest legacy—a legacy that not only shaped cold war policies but that also continues to influence American foreign policy to this day. As Link articulated the postwar consensus, the "prophet of 1919" was "right in his larger vision."[30] He had been "fundamentally right in the one great principle at stake in the Treaty fight": that the "most immoral thing" a nation could do was to "refuse to exercise power responsibly when it possesses it." For two decades, Americans ignored that principle, retreating back into what Link characterized as an outmoded isolationism and spurning "the responsibility that accompanied its power." Only when the "second and more terrible" world war came in 1939 ("as Wilson prophesied it would") did Americans finally learn the lesson that Wilson had tried to teach in 1919. But now that lesson came "at a fearful cost." According to Link, Wilson proved "right in his vision," and the "challenge" he raised was "no less real and no less urgent" sixty years later than it had been in Wilson's own day.[31]

In recent years, other historians have echoed Link's assessment of Wilson's "vision" and his place in history. Knock, for example, has argued that the Wilson's internationalist vision continues to "command attention" because the world still faces critical problems that can be solved only "through the concerted action of the international community." Comparing Wilson to Washington and Lincoln, Knock praised the twenty-eighth president for the "good will and humanity" of his "progressive internationalism" and predicted that history would continue to remember Wilson for "his inclusive comprehension of the unfolding epoch," his "eloquence," and the "enduring relevance of his vision."[32] Still more recently, historian John Milton Cooper Jr. has proclaimed Wilson "absolutely right" in his determination to find some "insurance" against another world war, even if he "failed to be as flexible and persuasive" as he might have been. Wilson may not have been a true "prophet," according to Cooper, but "two facts" about the League of Nations debate remained "incontrovertible": "For all their decency and intelligence, Wilson's opponents were wrong. For all his flaws and missteps, Wilson was right. He should have won the League fight. His defeat did break the heart of the world."[33]

Perhaps if Wilson had "won" the League of Nations debate there would have been no Hitler, no Holocaust, no World War II. And perhaps, as several scholars have suggested, Wilson would have won the debate if only it had taken place later—in the age of radio or, later still, in the age of polling. Had there been a "nation-wide radio hookup," Bailey argued in his classic study of the treaty debate, Wilson might have delivered a series of "fireside chats" that would have "informed and aroused the people" without sacrificing his health. According to Bailey, Wilson "had a fine voice and splendid diction," and he "probably would have been even more persuasive over the radio than in person."[34] John G. Geer has taken such speculation one step further, imagining how Wilson's hand might have been "greatly strengthened" by polls showing strong public support for his position. Had that been the case, Greer speculates, the opposition would have hesitated to "fly in the face" of public opinion and "Henry Cabot Lodge's coalition might well have collapsed." Indeed, Wilson might not have toured at all had there been polls showing support for his position, freeing the president to stay in Washington and concentrate on lobbying the Senate.[35]

In one sense, Wilson did win the League of Nations debate. While rejected in his own time, as Jason C. Flanagan has argued, Wilson's "new vision" has largely defined American foreign policy since World War II, with "almost every American president since Franklin Roosevelt" adopting a "Wilsonian" approach to foreign affairs.[36] Today, we still assume that the United States has a right, even a moral obligation to "mind other peoples' business," as Wilson put it in Indianapolis, and Wilsonian internationalism has come to define the American diplomatic tradition.[37] Yet as Cooper has reminded us, there was another "hallowed tradition" given voice in the League of Nations debate—an isolationist tradition dating back to Washington's warnings against "permanent alliances." We most remember Wilson's call to international leadership, but the League of Nations debate also "elicited more thoughtful, well-rounded expressions of isolationist views than had come before."[38] In an age of widespread resentment toward American internationalism, perhaps those voices have something to teach us as well. Perhaps the time has come for another great debate over American foreign policy.

Notes

Introduction

Epigraph: Woodrow Wilson, "An Address in Pittsburgh on Preparedness," *The Papers of Woodrow Wilson,* ed. Arthur S. Link, et al., 6: 27. Hereafter cited as *PWW.*

1. Loren B. Chan, "Fighting for the League: President Wilson in Nevada, 1919," 115, 118–20.
2. Chan, "Fighting for the League," 123–25.
3. John Milton Cooper Jr., "Fool's Errand or Finest Hour? Woodrow Wilson's Speaking Tour in September 1919," 198–99.
4. Thomas A. Bailey, *Woodrow Wilson and the Great Betrayal,* 90.
5. Robert H. Ferrell, *Woodrow Wilson and World War I, 1917–1921,* 156.
6. This explanation emerged in the 1970s and is most prominent in *The Papers of Woodrow Wilson.* In reflecting on Wilson's behavior during this period, Link and his colleagues conclude that biographers and historians have written about Wilson "as if he had been a reasonably healthy person, one responsible for his actions." They called for a reassessment of Wilson's behaviors in light of the evidence of his "long struggle with cerebrovascular disease." See "Introduction," *PWW,* 64: ix.
7. See Alexander L. George and Juliette L. George, *Woodrow Wilson and Colonel House: A Personality Study;* and Sigmund Freud and William C. Bullitt, *Thomas Woodrow Wilson: A Psychological Study.*
8. Arthur S. Link, "Woodrow Wilson: The Philosophy, Methods, and Impact of Leadership," 10.
9. John Milton Cooper Jr., *The Warrior and the Priest: Woodrow Wilson and Theodore Roosevelt,* 392, n. 4.
10. Robert Alexander Kraig, "The Second Oratorical Renaissance," 31.
11. Robert C. Hilderbrand, *Power and the People: Executive Management of Public Opinion in Foreign Affairs, 1897–1921,* 190.
12. "From Joseph Patrick Tumulty," *PWW,* 58: 244; "From William Gibbs McAdoo, with Enclosure," *PWW,* 61: 459.
13. Woodrow Wilson, *Constitutional Government in the United States,* in *PWW,* 18: 109, 114.

14. The editors of the Wilson Papers take this position, insisting that it was "perfectly obvious" from the start that "Wilson could obtain ratification of the treaty only by accepting the procedure demanded by the so-called mild reservationists." See "From the Desk Diary of Robert Lansing," *PWW*, 62: 507, n. 2.
15. Jeffrey Tulis, *The Rhetorical Presidency*, 147–61.
16. See Daniel Stid, "Rhetorical Leadership and `Common Counsel' in the Presidency of Woodrow Wilson," 174.
17. Tulis, *Rhetorical Presidency*, 176, 130–32.
18. Mary G. McEdwards, "Woodrow Wilson: His Stylistic Progression," 28–38.
19. Stephen E. Lucas and Martin J. Medhurst, eds. *Words of a Century: The Top 100 American Speeches, 1900–1999*.
20. Sidney Blumenthal, *The Permanent Campaign: Inside the World of Elite Political Operatives.*

Chapter One

1. "From Wilson's Shorthand Diary: `My Journal,'" *PWW*, 1: 143, 148–49.
2. Richard Hofstadter, *The American Political Tradition and the Men Who Made It*, 261.
3. Woodrow Wilson, "Cabinet Government in the United States," *PWW*, 1: 506.
4. Tulis, *Rhetorical Presidency*, 20, 176.
5. Richard J. Ellis, "Introduction," 8.
6. See Terri Bimes and Stephen Skowronek, "Woodrow Wilson's Critique of Popular Leadership: Reassessing the Modern-Traditional Divide in Presidential History," 144–50.
7. Woodrow Wilson, "Democracy," *PWW*, 7: 350.
8. Ellis, "Introduction," 9.
9. Kraig, "Second Oratorical Renaissance," 32.
10. Woodrow Wilson, "The Ideal Statesman," *PWW*, 1: 243–44.
11. Kraig, "Second Oratorical Renaissance," 15.
12. Robert Alexander Kraig, *Woodrow Wilson and the Lost World of the Oratorical Statesman*, 13.
13. Kraig, "Second Oratorical Renaissance," 15.
14. The Eumenean Society, founded in 1837, was one of two debating and literary societies at Davidson College. As the editors of the Wilson Papers point out, the society had "a keen interest in political as well as social and cultural affairs." Shortly after his election to the society, Wilson participated in a debate on a question of great personal interest: "Which

is the better form of government Republicanism or Limited Monarchy."
See "From the Minutes of the Eumenean Society: Regular Meeting,"
PWW, 1: 32, n. 1; and "From the Minutes of the Eumenean Society," *PWW*,
1: 36–37.

15. Kraig, "Second Oratorical Renaissance," 16.
16. Cooper, *The Warrior and the Priest*, 22.
17. See "From Two Wilson Notebooks," *PWW*, 1: 78.
18. An *Index Rerum* is a book of commonplaces in which useful quotations
    are arranged alphabetically by subject. For more on the style and content
    of Wilson's *Index Rerum*, see "Editorial Note, Wilson's Commonplace
    Book: 'Index Rerum,'" *PWW*, 1: 83–87.
19. See "From the Minutes of the American Whig Society," *PWW*, 1: 75, n. 1;
    see "Editorial Note: The Liberal Debating Club," *PWW*, 1: 245.
20. See "Editorial Note: Wilson's Shorthand Diary," *PWW*, 1: 130.
21. "From Wilson's Shorthand Diary," *PWW*, 1: 161.
22. Cooper, *The Warrior and the Priest*, 22–23.
23. "To the Editor," *PWW*, 1: 238–39.
24. "Editorial in *The Princetonian*," *PWW*, 1: 294–96.
25. Woodrow Wilson, "William Earl Chatham," *PWW*, 1: 407–12. The essay
    was published in the *Nassau Literary Magazine* in October 1878.
26. Wilson, "Cabinet Government in the United States," 494–95, 500, 504–506.
27. J. Michael Hogan and James R. Andrews, "Woodrow Wilson," 114.
28. Woodrow Wilson, "John Bright," *PWW*, 1: 612, 614, 618.
29. Woodrow Wilson, "Congressional Government," *PWW*, 1: 565–66.
30. "Editorial Note: Government by Debate," *PWW*, 2: 155.
31. Daniel D. Stid, *The President as Statesman: Woodrow Wilson and the
    Constitution*, 21.
32. "Editorial Note: Congressional Government," *PWW*, 4: 6.
33. Woodrow Wilson, *Congressional Government: A Study in Politics*, in *PWW*,
    4: 55, 64, 107, 117–18.
34. Ibid., 162, 164, 166, 172, 174–75.
35. See Kendrick A. Clements, *Woodrow Wilson: World Statesman*, 23–25.
36. "Introduction," *PWW*, 10: vii.
37. Woodrow Wilson, "Princeton in the Nation's Service," *PWW*, 10: 30–31.
38. "Introduction," *PWW*, 10: vii.
39. Dayton David McKean, "Woodrow Wilson," 2: 972–73.
40. Woodrow Wilson, "University Training and Citizenship," *PWW*, 8: 589;
    Woodrow Wilson, "The Making of a Nation," *PWW*, 10: 233; Wilson,
    "University Training and Citizenship," 592.
41. "Three Editorials in the Princetonian," *PWW*, 1: 275.
42. Wilson, *Congressional Government: A Study in Politics*, in *PWW* 4: 166.

43. Wilson, "William Earl Chatham," 410.

44. Woodrow Wilson, *The New Freedom: A Call for the Emancipation of the Generous Energies of a People*, 5, 7.

45. Ray A. Billington and Martin Ridge, *American History after 1865*, 113, 125.

46. Richard Hofstadter, *The Age of Reform: From Bryan to F.D.R.*, 5, 12.

47. Gabriel Kolko, *The Triumph of Conservatism: A Reinterpretation of American History, 1900–1916*, 2, 280, 285–86.

48. Ellen Fitzpatrick, *Endless Crusade: Women Social Scientists and Progressive Reform*, xii.

49. Steven J. Diner, *A Very Different Age: Americans of the Progressive Era*, 13.

50. See David W. Southern, *The Malignant Heritage: Yankee Progressives and the Negro Question, 1901–1914*; Billington and Ridge, *American History after 1865*, 131.

51. Robert M. Crunden, "Progressivism," 869.

52. Peter Levine, *The New Progressive Era: Toward a Fair and Deliberative Democracy*, 18.

53. John Dewey, *The Public and Its Problems*, 208.

54. Diner, *A Very Different Age*, 201, 203.

55. Kraig, "Second Oratorical Renaissance," 2.

56. Kraig, *Woodrow Wilson and the Lost World of the Oratorical Statesman*, 99.

57. Kraig, "Second Oratorical Renaissance," 1.

58. Kevin Mattson, *Creating a Democratic Public: The Struggle for Urban Participatory Democracy*, 45.

59. Levine, *New Progressive Era*, 18–19.

60. Mattson, *Creating a Democratic Public*, 12.

61. Herbert Croly, *Promise of American Life*, 190.

62. Walter Lippmann, *Drift and Mastery*, 151.

63. Walter Lippmann, *Public Opinion*; Mattson, *Creating a Democratic Public*, 118.

64. David B. Danbom, *"The World of Hope": Progressives and the Struggle for an Ethical Public Life*, 113.

65. Levine, *New Progressive Era*, 20.

66. Hofstadter, *American Political Tradition*, 240.

67. Tulis, *Rhetorical Presidency*, 132.

68. Woodrow Wilson, *Constitutional Government in the United States*, in *PWW*, 18: 202.

69. Ibid., 109, 114.

70. Ibid., 114.

71. Stid, "Rhetorical Leadership and 'Common Counsel' in the Presidency of Woodrow Wilson," 165.

72. Quoted in David Lawrence, *The True Story of Woodrow Wilson*, 39.

73. Cooper, *The Warrior and the Priest,* 174.

74. Wilson, *Constitutional Government in the United States,* in *PWW,* 18: 122.

75. Stid, "Rhetorical Leadership and 'Common Counsel' in the Presidency of Woodrow Wilson," 166–67.

76. Wilson, *Constitutional Government in the United States,* in *PWW,* 18: 161.

77. Kraig, "Second Oratorical Renaissance," 32.

78. Woodrow Wilson, "Princeton for the Nation's Service," *PWW,* 14: 170.

79. Clements, *Woodrow Wilson,* 39; Cooper, *The Warrior and the Priest,* 94.

80. Woodrow Wilson, "Report on the Social Coordination of the University," *PWW,* 17: 185.

81. John Morton Blum, *Woodrow Wilson and the Politics of Morality,* 30.

82. Hogan and Andrews, "Woodrow Wilson," in *U.S. Presidents as Orators,* 12.

83. August Heckscher, *Woodrow Wilson: A Biography,* 57.

84. Cooper, *The Warrior and the Priest,* 105.

85. Clements, *Woodrow Wilson,* 40–41.

86. "Two News Reports of an Address in Pittsburgh to Princeton Alumni," *PWW,* 20: 365.

87. Ellis, "Introduction," 9.

88. Bailey, *Woodrow Wilson and the Great Betrayal,* 93.

89. Cooper, *The Warrior and the Priest,* 140–41.

90. Wilson, *New Freedom,* 93–95.

91. Ibid., 90–91.

92. Ibid., 101, 28.

93. Ibid., 104, 107–109.

94. Stid, *President as Statesman,* 163; Stid, "Rhetorical Leadership and 'Common Counsel' in the Presidency of Woodrow Wilson," 168–69.

95. Stid, *President as Statesman,* 93–94.

96. Woodrow Wilson, "An Address on Tariff Reform to a Joint Session of Congress," *PWW,* 27: 270.

97. Kraig, *Woodrow Wilson and the Lost World of the Oratorical Statesman,* 131, 134.

98. Cooper, *The Warrior and the Priest,* 229.

99. Blum, *Woodrow Wilson and the Politics of Morality,* 122.

100. Arthur S. Link, *Woodrow Wilson and the Progressive Era, 1910–1917,* 185.

101. Lloyd E. Ambrosius, *Wilsonian Statecraft: Theory and Practice of Liberal Internationalism during World War I,* 56; Woodrow Wilson, "An Address in Pittsburgh on Preparedness," *PWW,* 36: 26.

102. Blum, *Woodrow Wilson and the Politics of Morality,* 123.

103. Kendrick A. Clements, *The Presidency of Woodrow Wilson,* 128.

104. Woodrow Wilson, "An Address in New York on Preparedness," *PWW,* 36: 8.

105. Woodrow Wilson, "An Address in Milwaukee on Preparedness," *PWW,* 36: 57.

106. Woodrow Wilson, "An Address in Des Moines on Preparedness," *PWW,* 36: 80–81.

107. Woodrow Wilson, "An Address in Chicago on Preparedness," *PWW,* 36: 66; Wilson, "An Address in Des Moines on Preparedness," 78.

108. Woodrow Wilson, "An Address on Preparedness in Topeka," *PWW,* 36: 87; Woodrow Wilson, "An Address in St. Louis on Preparedness," *PWW,* 36: 116; Woodrow Wilson, "An Address on Preparedness in Kansas City," *PWW,* 36: 102.

109. Wilson, "An Address in New York on Preparedness," 14–15; Wilson, "An Address in Pittsburgh on Preparedness," 30; Wilson, "An Address in St. Louis on Preparedness, 119.

110. Wilson, "An Address in New York on Preparedness," *PWW,* 36: 8; Woodrow Wilson, "An Address in Cleveland on Preparedness," *PWW,* 36: 46.

111. Wilson, "An Address in Des Moines on Preparedness," 77, 79; Wilson, "An Address in Pittsburgh on Preparedness," 27–28.

112. Wilson, "An Address on Preparedness in Kansas City," 36, 102.

113. In Kansas City, for example, he exhorted: "Fellow citizens, get up on your hind legs and talk and tell the people who represent you . . . what it is that the nation desires and demands." In Pittsburgh he also concluded with a call to political action: "I do not want you merely to listen to speeches. I want you to make yourselves vocal. I want you to let everybody who comes within earshot of you know that you are a partisan for the adequate preparation of the United States for national defense. . . . I want you to go home determined that, within the whole circle of your influence, the President—not as a partisan, but as the representative of the national honor—shall be backed up by the whole force that is in the nation." Wilson, "An Address on Preparedness in Kansas City," 106; Wilson, "An Address in Pittsburgh on Preparedness," *PWW,* 36: 34–35.

114. Wilson, "An Address on Preparedness in Kansas City," *PWW,* 36: 107.

115. Wilson, "An Address in Milwaukee on Preparedness," 36: 57.

116. Wilson, "An Address in St. Louis on Preparedness," 120.

117. Thomas J. Knock, *To End All Wars: Woodrow Wilson and the Quest for a New World Order,* 62.

118. Hofstadter, *American Political Tradition,* 271.

119. Woodrow Wilson, "An Address to a Joint Session of Congress," *PWW,* 41: 526; Woodrow Wilson, "A Flag Day Address," *PWW,* 42: 504.

120. Knock, *To End All Wars,* 133.

121. Stephen Vaughn, *Holding Fast the Inner Lines: Democracy, Nationalism, and the Committee on Public Information,* xii.

122. Kraig, "Second Oratorical Renaissance," 27.

123. Tulis, *Rhetorical Presidency,* 132.

124. Clements, *Woodrow Wilson,* 87.

125. Levine, *New Progressive Era,* 20.

126. Danbom, *"The World of Hope,"* 112–49.

Chapter Two

1. Woodrow Wilson, "An Address in the St. Louis Coliseum," *PWW,* 63: 43.

2. Woodrow Wilson, "An Address in Convention Hall in Kansas City," *PWW,* 63: 66–67.

3. Cooper, *Breaking the Heart of the World,* 160, 172.

4. Hilderbrand, *Power and the People,* 194.

5. See, for example, Ferrell, *Woodrow Wilson and World War I,* 169.

6. Robert M. Saunders, *In Search of Woodrow Wilson: Beliefs and Behavior,* 219–20.

7. Bailey, *Woodrow Wilson and the Great Betrayal,* 107.

8. Cooper, *Breaking the Heart of the World,* 172, 181, 186. In an earlier study, Cooper recognized that there appeared to be little connection between Wilson's health and his speeches. "Curiously," he wrote, "the ups and downs of Wilson's speechmaking" did not seem to reflect "the variations in his physical condition." See Cooper, "Fools Errand or Finest Hour?" 207.

9. Cooper, "Fools Errand or Finest Hour?" 203–204.

10. Bailey, *Woodrow Wilson and the Great Betrayal,* 108.

11. "Introduction," *PWW,* 63: ix.

12. Heckscher, *Woodrow Wilson,* 604.

13. Arthur S. Link, *Wilson the Diplomatist: A Look at His Major Foreign Policies,* 140.

14. John M. Blum, *Joe Tumulty and the Wilson Era,* 208.

15. "From the Desk Diary of Robert Lansing," *PWW,* 62: 507, n. 2.

16. Kraig, *Woodrow Wilson and the Lost World of the Oratorical Statesman,* 165.

17. Blum, *Joe Tumulty and the Wilson Era,* 208.

18. "From William Gibbs McAdoo, with Enclosure," *PWW,* 61: 459.

19. Joseph P. Tumulty, *Woodrow Wilson as I Know Him,* 434.

20. See Kraig, *Woodrow Wilson and the Lost World of the Oratorical Statesman,* 166; and "Wants Senate Trailers Paid," *New York Times,* September 4, 1919, 2.

21. "A Comedy of Errors," *New York Times,* September 1, 1919, 6.

22. Cooper, "Fools Errand or Finest Hour?" 200.

23. Josephus Daniels, *The Life of Woodrow Wilson*, 326–27.

24. Bailey, *Woodrow Wilson and the Great Betrayal*, 90.

25. Hilderbrand, *Power and the People*, 191–92; Cooper, *Breaking the Heart of the World*, 119.

26. See Hilderbrand, *Power and the People*, 192–93; Woodrow Wilson, "An Address to the Senate," *PWW*, 61: 434, 436.

27. Tumulty, *Woodrow Wilson as I Know Him*, 438; Hilderbrand, *Power and the People*, 194.

28. Bailey, *Woodrow Wilson and the Great Betrayal*, 101.

29. Blum, *Joe Tumulty and the Wilson Era*, 209. Tumulty originally had hoped to include an even larger party on the president's train, including at least one labor representative, a suffrage leader, and an Irish American politician, but space limitations forced him to reduce the list to only the press contingent.

30. Small actually worked for the Philadelphia *Public Ledger*, although the *Atlanta Constitution* claimed him as their "exclusive" reporter with the president and his dispatches appeared in other papers as well.

31. Cooper, *Breaking the Heart of the World*, 163–64.

32. Blum, *Joe Tumulty and the Wilson Era*, 209.

33. M. L. Stein, *When Presidents Meet the Press*, 65.

34. Cooper, *Breaking the Heart of the World*, 164.

35. "Wilson Takes Stump for Peace Treaty," *Atlanta Constitution*, September 4, 1919, 1–2.

36. "Wilson on Long Trip," *Washington Post*, September 4, 1919, 1. The *New York Times* reported in virtually identical language that the president had "not prepared his addresses in advance because of the mass of other business at the White House." See "Wilson Begins Tour for Treaty, Sees Victory in the Senate Fight, Republicans Fear Party Setback," *New York Times*, September 4, 1919, 1.

37. "Wilson Takes Stump for Peace Treaty," 2.

38. Ibid.

39. See Ferrell, *Woodrow Wilson and World War I*, 176; and Kraig, *Woodrow Wilson and the Lost World of the Oratorical Statesman*, 152.

40. Lloyd E. Ambrosius, *Woodrow Wilson and the American Diplomatic Tradition: The Treaty Fight in Perspective*, 152.

41. "Wilson Begins Tour for Treaty," 1.

42. Lawrence, *True Story of Woodrow Wilson*, 274–75.

43. Tumulty, *Woodrow Wilson as I Know Him*, 446. Grayson noted in his diary how a variety of factors conspired to make Wilson's appearance in Columbus "very unsatisfactory." Wilson arrived at 11:00 A.M. on a gray, rainy day, according to Grayson, and a streetcar strike "made it impossible

for the people of the out-lying sections to get down town." Also, the president had "made a number of speeches in Columbus" before and "was pretty well known there." All of this, "combined with the fact that it was Thursday morning—a bad time for any kind of meeting"—had the effect of "holding down the number in attendance." See "From the Diary of Dr. Grayson" [September 4, 1919], *PWW*, 63: 3.

44. Tumulty, *Woodrow Wilson as I Know Him*, 439.

45. "From the Diary of Dr. Grayson" [September 4, 1919], 3. Wilson apparently was responding to a speech by Senator Philander C. Knox of Pennsylvania, who had declared the treaty too harsh on Germany.

46. Woodrow Wilson, "An Address to the Columbus Chamber of Commerce," *PWW*, 63: 7.

47. Ibid., 7–9.

48. Ibid., 8–9.

49. Lawrence, *True Story of Woodrow Wilson*, 275.

50. Wilson, "An Address to the Columbus Chamber of Commerce," 10–11.

51. Ibid., 10, 12.

52. Ibid., 12–14.

53. Ibid., 15–16.

54. Ibid., 17.

55. Ibid., 12.

56. Shantung had been a German protectorate before Japan conquered and occupied the province. Concerned that Japan might not join the League, Wilson agreed to a short-term cession of Shantung to Japan, later arguing that the League would compel Japan to honor its promise to withdraw within five years. That eventually did happen. Yet the Shantung provision provoked furious opposition in the United States. See Cooper, *Breaking the Heart of the World*, 88–89.

57. "Wilson Defends Treaty and League as Tour Begins; Challenges Senate Foes to Offer a Better Program; Senate Committee Adopts Four Treaty Reservations," *New York Times*, September 5, 1919, 1–2.

58. Tumulty, *Woodrow Wilson as I Know Him*, 439.

59. Lawrence, *True Story of Woodrow Wilson*, 275–76.

60. "From the Diary of Dr. Grayson" [September 4, 1919], 4. According to Grayson, the crowd in Indianapolis was "very much excited" and there was "much shuffling of feet" as the president began his address. Due to the commotion, many could not hear and headed for the doors, forcing Wilson to interrupt his speech until a "stentorian-voiced usher" was able to restore order.

61. Woodrow Wilson, "An Address in the Indianapolis Coliseum," *PWW*, 63: 19–21.

62. Ibid., 21–25.
63. Ibid., 22–23.
64. Ibid., 26–27.
65. Ibid., 27–28.
66. Ibid., 25–26, 28–29.
67. Bailey, *Woodrow Wilson and the Great Betrayal*, 117.
68. The *Washington Post* likewise emphasized Wilson's challenge to his "foes," paraphrasing the line in a headline: "Offer Something Better or 'Shut Up,' He Says." Wilson's challenge also provided the lead for the Associated Press account that appeared in newspapers across the nation. "Put Up or Shut Up" was the "advice given opponents of the League of Nations by the President," the AP began its story.
69. Philip Kinsley, "'Put Up or Shut Up': Wilson to Treaty Foes," *Chicago Daily Tribune*, September 5, 1919, 1, 4.
70. Arthur Sears Henning, "Vote to Ratify Treaty after Vital Changes," *Chicago Daily Tribune*, September 5, 1919, 1.
71. Albert W. Fox, "Reservations Win 9," *Washington Post*, September 6, 1919, 1.
72. Woodrow Wilson, "A Luncheon Address to the St. Louis Chamber of Commerce," *PWW*, 36: 34–36.
73. Wilson, "An Address in the St. Louis Coliseum," 43, 45–48, 50. In the transcript of the address, the usually careful editors of the *Papers of Woodrow Wilson* have the crowd shouting "read, read" after Wilson's offer to send a copy of the treaty to the "gentlemen" who were opposing it. The chant obviously was directed at the state's irreconcilable senator, James A. Reed.
74. Robert T. Small, "Wilson Scores All Who Oppose Treaty," *Washington Post*, September 6, 1919, 1.
75. Wilson, "An Address in Convention Hall in Kansas City," 72–73.
76. Clements, *Presidency of Woodrow Wilson*, 195.
77. The *New York Times* suggested the former interpretation in its headline on September 7: "Wilson Likens Treaty Obstructors to Bolsheviki." The headline in the *Los Angeles Times*, however, seemed to suggest the latter interpretation of Wilson's remarks: "President Fears Bolshevism from Treaty Delay."
78. Wilson, "An Address in Convention Hall in Kansas City," 71–72. The banner headline in the *Atlanta Constitution* the next day revealed how some newspapers presented Wilson's talk of gibbeting quite literally. "Wilson Predicts Gallows for Senators," blared the headline.
79. Woodrow Wilson, "An Address in the Des Moines Coliseum," *PWW*, 63: 81.

80. Ibid., 77–80, 83–85.
81. Ibid., 81, 85, 87–88.
82. McEdwards, "Woodrow Wilson: His Stylistic Progression," 37–38.
83. Quoted in A. Craig Baird, *American Public Addresses, 1740–1952*, 232.
84. Lawrence, *True Story of Woodrow Wilson*, 278.
85. "Poison of Red Terror Spreads in America, Says President at Des Moines," *Washington Post*, September 7, 1919, 1.
86. Bailey, *Woodrow Wilson and the Great Betrayal*, 117–18.
87. Newspapers differed in their assessment of Wilson's reception in Columbus. The *New York Times* reported that the crowds were unenthusiastic and "not as large as some had expected," while the *Los Angeles Times* reported that "big crowds" had welcomed the president in Columbus and were "wildly enthusiastic." See "Wilson Defends Treaty and League as Tour Begins; Challenges Senate Foes to Offer a Better Program; Senate Committee Adopts Four Treaty Reservations," *New York Times*, September 5, 1919, 1–2; and Philip Kinsley, "Significance of Treaty and League is Clarified by the President," *Los Angeles Times*, September 5, 1919, part 1, 2.
88. "'Put Up or Shut Up,' Says Wilson," *Atlanta Constitution*, September 5, 1919, 1.
89. Bailey, *Woodrow Wilson and the Great Betrayal*, 106–107.
90. "8,000 Out at St. Joseph," *New York Times*, September 7, 1919, 3; "Wilson Likens Treaty Obstructors to Bolsheviki; Says He Fights for Cause Greater than the Senate; Republican Claim Victory for Modified Reservations," *New York Times*, September 7, 1919, 1.
91. Robert T. Small, "President Well Satisfied with Results of Speeches to Date in League Tour," *Washington Post*, September 7, 1919, 6.
92. "Wilson Likens Treaty Obstructors to Bolsheviki," 1–2; "Keenness for Peace Shown by People on Wilson's Route," *New York Times*, September 8, 1919, 1, 3.
93. "Wilson Likens Treaty Obstructors to Bolsheviki," 1–2.
94. Ibid. The *Times* apparently did not see opposition to the Shantung settlement a major obstacle, however, reporting that the president already had made some progress in responding to the "propaganda" of treaty opponents. In any case, the paper concluded, it was not clear that "the people" were "willing to endanger the treaty merely on this issue."
95. Robert T. Small, "Wilson Willing to Fight to Die for the League," *Washington Post*, September 9, 1919, 1; "From the Diary of Dr. Grayson" [September 8, 1919], 93–94.
96. Philip Kinsley, "He Would Die to Win the Treaty, Wilson Asserts," *Chicago Daily Tribune*, September 9, 1919, 4.
97. Bailey, *Woodrow Wilson and the Great Betrayal*, 107.

98. "Pro-Germans Here Would Kill League Says President," *New York Times*, September 9, 1919, 1.

99. "From the Diary of Dr. Grayson" [September 9, 1919], 122–24.

100. "'War or Peace?' League Issue, Says Wilson," *Washington Post*, September 11, 1919, 11.

101. "From the Diary of Dr. Grayson" [September 11, 1919], 168–69; [September 12, 1919], 210–11.

102. Bailey, *Woodrow Wilson and the Great Betrayal*, 109.

103. "President Gets Greatest Ovation on Reaching Coast," *New York Times*, September 14, 1919, 1, 3; "Collision Imperils President in Packed Launch at Fleet Review in Seattle Harbor," *Washington Post*, September 14, 1919, 1.

104. "Big Overflow Halts Speech," *Los Angeles Times*, September 14, 1919, part 1, 3.

105. Arthur Sears Henning, "Tries to Stem Tide in Senate Against Pact," *Chicago Daily Tribune*, September 8, 1919, 1.

106. See Cooper, *Breaking the Heart of the World*, 167–68.

107. U.S., Congress, Senate, Committee on Foreign Relations, *Treaty of Peace with Germany: Hearings. . . .* 66th Cong., 1st sess., 1276–77.

108. Heckscher, *Woodrow Wilson*, 597, 603.

109. Woodrow Wilson, "An Address in the Marlow Theater in Helena," *PWW*, 63: 196.

110. Bailey, *Woodrow Wilson and the Great Betrayal*, 94.

111. Cooper, *Breaking the Heart of the World*, 160.

112. Woodrow Wilson, "An Address in the Auditorium in Omaha," *PWW*, 63: 99–100, 102–105. Wilson's speech at Omaha was also one of the few in which he mentioned both U.S. senators from the state by name. He was "proud . . . to stand alongside of Senator Hitchcock in this fight," Wilson declared, and he would be "just as glad to stand by Senator Norris if he would let me" (p. 106).

113. Woodrow Wilson, "An Address in the Coliseum in Sioux Falls," *PWW*, 63: 108–13.

114. Woodrow Wilson, "An Address in St. Paul to a Joint Session of the Legislature of Minnesota," *PWW*, 63: 129–30.

115. Woodrow Wilson, "An Address in the Minneapolis Armory," *PWW*, 63: 132, 134, 138.

116. Cooper, *Breaking the Heart of the World*, 162.

117. See "Pro German Specter Raised by President," *Chicago Daily Tribune*, September 9, 1919, 1; and "Pro-Germanism Lifts Its Head, Says the President," *Los Angeles Times*, September 9, 1919, part 1, 1.

118. Philip Kinsley, "Hyphen Lifts It's Ugly Head Again: Wilson," *Chicago Daily Tribune*, September 10, 1919, 1.

119. Woodrow Wilson, "An Address in the St. Paul Auditorium," *PWW*, 63: 140, 143, 147. At the end of Wilson's speech, St. Paul's Republican mayor, L. C. Hodgson, called for a vote. The crowd responded with a "great chorus" of "ayes" in support of the treaty and "only a few voices raised in dissent." See "Wilson Demands Treaty to Hasten Living Cost Cut," *New York Times,* September 10, 1919, 1.

120. Woodrow Wilson, "An Address at Bismarck," *PWW*, 63: 155–56, 160–62.

121. Bailey, *Woodrow Wilson and the Great Betrayal,* 109.

122. Woodrow Wilson, "An Address in the Billings Auditorium," *PWW*, 63: 172, 174–75, 177, 179–80. According to the *New York Times,* many in Wilson's audience in Billings wept as he spoke of his ideals and paid tribute to those who had died, and the president was "profoundly touched." See "Peace Alone, Says President, Will Quiet World Unrest," *New York Times,* September 12, 1919, 1, 4.

123. See "From the Diary of Dr. Grayson" [September 10, 1919], 152; and [September 25, 1919], 489.

124. Wilson, "An Address in the Marlow Theater in Helena," 180–83, 195.

125. Ibid., 190–93.

126. Ibid., 181, 197.

127. Robert T. Small, "Wilson Attack Mild," *Washington Post,* September 13, 1919, 1.

128. Woodrow Wilson, "An Address at Coeur d'Alene," *PWW*, 63: 219–20.

129. Wilson, "An Address in the Spokane Armory," 226, 231.

130. Ibid., 228, 234.

131. Robert T. Small, "Politics in League Fight, Wilson Finds," *Washington Post,* September 14, 1919, 1. Historian John Milton Cooper Jr. has echoed Small's assessment, arguing that such a declaration would have "rung out like a cannon blast" and cast Wilson as a "totally disinterested seeker of world peace." See Cooper, *Breaking the Heart of the World,* 176–77.

132. Small, "Politics in League Fight, Wilson Finds," 11.

133. See "Vance Criswell McCormick to Joseph Patrick Tumulty," *PWW,* 63: 235.

134. "Two Memoranda by Joseph Patrick Tumulty," *PWW*, 63: 221–24.

135. Woodrow Wilson, "An Address in the Tacoma Armory," *PWW*, 63: 242–44.

136. Ibid., 244, 247–50.

137. See "From the Diary of Dr. Grayson" [September 13, 1919], 240.

138. Woodrow Wilson, "An Address in the Seattle Arena," *PWW*, 63: 254, 260, 262–63.

139. "President Gets Greatest Ovation on Reaching Coast," *New York Times,* September 14, 1919, 1, 3.

140. Bailey, *Woodrow Wilson and the Great Betrayal,* 109.

141. Heckscher, *Woodrow Wilson*, 603.

142. Charles H. Grasty, "Economic Issues Stir Northwest," *New York Times*, September 14, 1919, 3.

143. "Radicals Call on Wilson," *New York Times*, September 15, 1919, 1–2.

144. Wilson, "An Address in the Indianapolis Coliseum," 25.

145. Wilson, "An Address in the St. Paul Auditorium," 139.

146. Link, *Wilson the Diplomatist*, 140.

147. Bailey, *Woodrow Wilson and the Great Betrayal*, 114.

148. Cooper, "Fool's Errand or Finest Hour?" 208–209.

149. Cooper, *Breaking the Heart of the World*, 162.

150. Ambrosius, *Woodrow Wilson and the American Diplomatic Tradition*, 179.

Chapter Three

1. Philip Kinsley, "Try to Cry Wilson Down," *Chicago Daily Tribune*, September 18, 1919, 1. See also "Wilson Offers Hope to China and to Ireland," *New York Times*, September 18, 1919, 1.

2. Heckscher, *Woodrow Wilson*, 604.

3. "From the Diary of Dr. Grayson" [September 17, 1919], 308–309; [September 23, 1919], 446.

4. Bailey, *Woodrow Wilson and the Great Betrayal*, 111.

5. "Wilson Gains League Support in California," *New York Times*, September 19, 1919, 1; "Wilson Shows England Has Not 6 Votes to Our 1," *New York Times*, September 22, 1919, 1; Charles H. Grasty, "Find Wilson Shy Only in Private," *New York Times*, September 22, 1919, 1, 3; "Senate Hears Rumbling against Treaty Delay," *Los Angeles Times*, September 21, 1919, part 1, 1.

6. Cooper, *Breaking the Heart of the World*, 179.

7. Cooper, "Fool's Errand or Finest Hour?" 213.

8. Cooper, *Breaking the Heart of the World*, 179–80, 180.

9. Cooper, "Fool's Errand or Finest Hour?" 214.

10. "Two Killed in President's Party," *Los Angeles Times*, September 16, 1919, 1; "2 Die on Wilson Trip," *Washington Post*, September 16, 1919, 1.

11. "Pins Lodge to League," *Los Angeles Times*, September 16, 1919, 1; "Warm Greeting Given to Wilson by Oregonians," *New York Times*, September 16, 1919, 1.

12. "Pins Lodge to League," 8.

13. "Arrest Two for Cursing Wilson," *Chicago Daily Tribune*, September 16, 1919, 2; "Warm Greeting Given to Wilson by Oregonians," 1.

14. Woodrow Wilson, "A Luncheon Address in Portland," *PWW*, 63: 279, 281–83.

15. Woodrow Wilson, "An Address in the Portland Auditorium," *PWW*, 63: 283–85, 289, 292.

16. Philip Kinsley, "Makes Two Addresses," *Chicago Daily Tribune*, September 16, 1919, 2.

17. "Warm Greeting Given to Wilson by Oregonians," 1.

18. "From the Diary of Dr. Grayson" [September 16, 1919], 300.

19. "Wilson Spends Day Traveling," *Los Angeles Times*, September 17, 1919, 1; "Wilson Reveals China to be Safeguarded by the League," *Los Angeles Times*, September 18, 1919, 9; "From the Diary of Dr. Grayson" [September 17, 1919], 308.

20. "From the Diary of Dr. Grayson" [September 17, 1919], 309.

21. Woodrow Wilson, "A Luncheon Address in San Francisco" [September 17, 1919], *PWW*, 63: 314, 320–21.

22. See "Notes for an Address," *PWW*, 63: 322–23.

23. See "Wilson Offers Hope to China and to Ireland," *New York Times*, September 18, 1919, 1; "San Francisco Roars Greeting to the President: Noon Rush for Seats," *Los Angeles Times*, September 18, 1919, 1; and "From the Diary of Dr. Grayson" [September 17, 1919], 310, n. 2.

24. Woodrow Wilson, "An Address in the San Francisco Civic Auditorium," *PWW*, 63: 326, 333–36.

25. "From the Diary of Dr. Grayson" [September 18, 1919], 340.

26. "League as Trade Aid," *Washington Post*, September 19, 1919, 1.

27. Woodrow Wilson, "A Luncheon Address in San Francisco" [September 18, 1919], *PWW*, 63: 350.

28. Woodrow Wilson, "An Address in the Greek Theater in Berkeley," *PWW*, 63: 351.

29. Woodrow Wilson, "An Address in the Oakland Auditorium," *PWW*, 63: 352–58, 360.

30. "Wilson Gains League Support in California," *New York Times*, September 19, 1919, 1.

31. Robert T. Small, "Johnson's Stronghold Gives Huge Ovation to President Wilson," *Atlanta Constitution*, September 19, 1919, 17.

32. "Big Crowd Greets Wilson," *Los Angeles Times*, September 20, 1919, part 1, 1.

33. "Orders President to Rest," *New York Times*, September 20, 1919, 3.

34. "From the Diary of Dr. Grayson" [September 19, 1919], 369.

35. Philip Kinsley, "San Diego Opens 100,000 Arms to Embrace Wilson," *Chicago Daily Tribune*, September 20, 1919, 5.

36. "From the Diary of Dr. Grayson" [September 19, 1919], 370; "T. R. Wilson's Guide," *Washington Post*, September 20, 1919, 1.

37. "President Quotes Roosevelt's Views to a Crowd of 50,000," *New York Times*,

September 20, 1919, 1; "From the Diary of Dr. Grayson" [September 19, 1919], 369; Kinsley, "San Diego Opens 100,000 Arms to Embrace Wilson," 5.

38. Woodrow Wilson, "An Address in the San Diego Stadium," *PWW*, 63: 371–76, 379–80.

39. "President Quotes Roosevelt's Views to a Crowd of 50,000," 1; Wilson, "An Address in the San Diego Stadium," 382.

40. Cooper, *Breaking the Heart of the World*, 180.

41. Woodrow Wilson, "An After-Dinner Speech in San Diego," *PWW*, 63: 384–85.

42. "President Is Greeted with Storm of Cheers," *Los Angeles Times*, September 21, 1919, part 2, 1.

43. "Loud Welcome to President," *Los Angeles Times*, September 21, 1919, part 2, 2.

44. "Mr. and Mrs. Wilson in Imperial Hotel Suite," *Los Angeles Times*, September 21, 1919, part 2, 1, 3.

45. "From Joseph Patrick Tumulty, with Enclosure," *PWW*, 63: 397–99; and "From Joseph Patrick Tumulty," *PWW*, 63: 399–400.

46. "Wilson Dinner Brilliant," *Los Angeles Times*, September 21, 1919, part 1, 1.

47. Woodrow Wilson, "An After-Dinner Speech in Los Angeles," *PWW*, 63: 400–402, 406–407. Italics added.

48. "Wilson Triumph Here as Coast Tour Ends," *Los Angeles Times*, September 21, 1919, part 1, 1.

49. Woodrow Wilson, "An Address in the Shrine Auditorium in Los Angeles," *PWW*, 63: 415–16.

50. Ibid., 408, 418.

51. According to the newspaper accounts, no fewer than 1,000 people were already waiting at the entrance to the auditorium at 6:00 A.M, and by 9:00 A.M. there were 5,000 people in line. By 6:30 P.M. all the streets and alleys leading to the auditorium were "jammed." Police were unable to control the crowds, heavy fences set up to channel their movements collapsed, and "in one hour twenty-three women fainted in front of the main entrance" to the auditorium. Some 50,000 people reportedly had to be turned away from the auditorium. See "Great Crowds Greet Wilson in Los Angeles," *New York Times*, September 21, 1919, 1, 3; and "Wilson Triumph Here as Coast Tour Ends," part 1, 1.

52. "Wilson Triumph Here as Coast Tour Ends," 1; "President Wins Los Angeles to His League Plan," *Chicago Sunday Tribune*, September 21, 1919, 7.

53. Robert B. Armstrong, "Senate Hears Rumbling against Treaty Delay," *Los Angeles Times*, September 21, 1919, part 1, 1, 10.

54. Grasty, "Find Wilson Shy Only in Private," 1, 3.

55. "President Quotes Roosevelt's Views to Crowd of 50,000," 3.

56. "Welcome, Mr. President," *Los Angeles Times*, September 20, 1919, part 2, 4.

57. Grasty, "Find Wilson Shy Only in Private," 3.

58. "Crowds Besiege President's Train, Now Speeding East," *New York Times,* September 23, 1919, 1, 3.

59. Philip Kinsley, "Wilson Reaches Half Way Point in League Tour," *Chicago Sunday Tribune,* September 21, 1919, part 1, 7.

60. Robert T. Small, "Wilson's Hopes Raised by Westerners, Who Tell Him People Favor the League," *Washington Post,* September 21, 1919, 1, 7.

61. "Executive Wins Strong Support," *Los Angeles Times,* September 22, 1919, part 2, 1; "From the Diary of Dr. Grayson" [September 21, 1919], 423.

62. Philip Kinsley, "President Fails to Make Dent in Johnson's Lair," *Chicago Daily Tribune,* September 23, 1919, 11.

63. "Crowds Besiege President's Train, Now Speeding East," *New York Times,* September 23, 1919, 1; "From the Diary of Dr. Grayson" [September 22, 1919], 426; Woodrow Wilson, "Remarks in Sacramento," *PWW,* 63: 426–27.

64. Bailey, *Woodrow Wilson and the Great Betrayal,* 112.

65. Chan, "Fighting for the League," 120–22. Chan argues that Wilson was "consistent in his argumentation" and appealed "in a definite way to his audience's logic." Yet he also claims that Wilson's discussion of Shantung "contradicted his earlier comments about nonintervention and self-determination," and he insists that Wilson did little to "soften his betrayal of China's national interests." In a "few lame last remarks," Chan concluded, Wilson promised to be a "helpful friend" to China, yet he already had "compromised his most lofty international political principles and betrayed China in his attempt to win Japan's support for his League of Nations Covenant." Chan thought it remarkable that Wilson "actually expected his Reno audience to endorse such a perfidious record."

66. "Not Like Vienna Conference," *New York Times,* September 23, 1919, 3.

67. Woodrow Wilson, "An Address in Reno," *PWW,* 63: 428, 435, 441.

68. Ibid., 432.

69. "Squaws Greet Wilson Speeding over Desert," *Los Angeles Times,* September 24, 1919, part 1, 2.

70. Woodrow Wilson, "To the People of Utah," *PWW,* 63: 447.

71. Woodrow Wilson, "Remarks in Ogden, Utah," *PWW,* 63: 448.

72. "Kill Reservations or Wreck Treaty, Says President," *New York Times,* September 24, 1919, 1, 5.

73. "From the Diary of Dr. Grayson" [September 23, 1919], 446.

74. Some historians have put the number in attendance at the Mormon Tabernacle at 15,000, but according to police estimates at the time there were only 12,000 present. See "'Cutting Heart' Out of League, President Says," *Atlanta Constitution,* September 24, 1919, 1.

75. Edith Bolling Wilson, *My Memoir,* 282.

76. Wilson received the news in several telegrams on September 22. See "From William Phillips," *PWW*, 63: 444; "Breckinridge Long to Joseph Patrick Tumulty," *PWW*, 63: 444–45; "Guy Mason to Joseph Patrick Tumulty," *PWW*, 63: 445; and "Rudolph Forster to Joseph Patrick Tumulty," *PWW*, 63: 445.

77. Wilson, "An Address in the Tabernacle in Salt Lake City," 449, 451–52.

78. Ibid., 451–52, 454, 456–57.

79. See "Joseph Patrick Tumulty to Rudolph Forster," *PWW*, 63: 447, n. 1.

80. Wilson, "An Address in the Tabernacle in Salt Lake City," 454.

81. Philip Kinsley, "Save Article X, Wilson Begs in Mormon Pulpit," *Chicago Daily Tribune*, September 24, 1919, 6.

82. Arthur S. Link, *Woodrow Wilson: Revolution, War, and Peace*, 120.

83. Heckscher, *Woodrow Wilson*, 606.

84. Cooper, *Breaking the Heart of the World*, 183.

85. Blum, *Joe Tumulty and the Wilson Era*, 212.

86. Charles H. Grasty, "Belief in League Found Nation-Wide," *New York Times*, September 18, 1919, 5.

87. "President Quotes Roosevelt's Views to Crowd of 50,000," 1, 3; "President's Departure from California is a Continuous Ovation," *Los Angeles Times*, September 23, 1919, part 1, 2.

88. "Badgering Wilson," *Atlanta Constitution*, September 20, 1919, 8.

89. "Editorial of the Day," *Chicago Daily Tribune*, September 17, 1919, 8.

90. "An Executive on Wheels," *Chicago Daily Tribune*, September 17, 1919, 8.

91. Grasty, "Find Wilson Shy Only in Private," 1.

92. "Political Foes," *Washington Post*, September 24, 1919, 6.

93. Robert T. Small, "Wilson Quits West with Section Full of Political Unrest," *Atlanta Constitution*, September 23, 1919, 13.

Chapter Four

1. Robert T. Small, "Wilson Prepared to Force League Fight into the Next Campaign If It Fails Now," *Washington Post*, September 25, 1919, 1, 10.

2. Hilderbrand, *Power and the People*, 195–96.

3. Bailey, *Woodrow Wilson and the Great Betrayal*, 113.

4. Ibid., 114.

5. Small, "Wilson Prepared to Force League Fight into the Next Campaign If It Fails Now," 1.

6. Philip Kinsley, "Amend League and Invite War, Wilson Warns," *Chicago Daily Tribune*, September 25, 1919, 6.

7. Wilson, "An Address in the Tabernacle in Salt Lake City," 454.

8. Woodrow Wilson, "An Address in the Princess Theater in Cheyenne," *PWW*, 63: 469–70.

9. Ibid., 474–76, 478–80.

10. Ibid., 478–80.

11. Ibid., 478.

12. Small, "Wilson Prepared to Force League Fight into the Next Campaign If It Fails Now," 10.

13. Philip Kinsley, "'Act, Then I'll Decide,' Wilson Word to Senate," *Chicago Daily Tribune*, September 26, 1919, 7.

14. "Wilson Will Hold Treaty Rejected by Senate Change," *New York Times*, September 26, 1919, 1, 3. As the editors of the Wilson Papers noted, "various newspapers" provided this range of estimates of Wilson's audience in Denver, but the figure of 12,000 persons in the *Rocky Mountain News* is "probably approximately correct." See "From the Diary of Dr. Grayson" [September 25, 1919], 490, n. 1.

15. Kinsley, "Act, Then I'll Decide," 7.

16. Woodrow Wilson, "An Address in the Denver Auditorium," *PWW*, 63: 490, 493–94, 497.

17. Ibid., 494–95.

18. Ibid., 498–99.

19. Small, "Wilson Prepared to Force League Fight into the Next Campaign If It Fails Now," 1.

20. Wilson, "An Address in the Denver Auditorium," 499–500.

21. Kinsley, "Act, Then I'll Decide," 7.

22. Robert T. Small, "Wilson's Plan to Fight All Reservations Means Delay in Action on Peace Treaty," *Washington Post*, September 26, 1919, 1.

23. "Wilson Will Hold Treaty Rejected by Senate Change," 1, 3; "From the Diary of Dr. Grayson" [September 25, 1919], 487–89.

24. Cooper, *Breaking the Heart of the World*, 187.

25. Wilson, *My Memoir*, 283.

26. Wilson, "An Address in the City Auditorium in Pueblo, Colorado," 501.

27. Ibid., 501–508.

28. Ibid., 508.

29. Ibid., 508–509.

30. Ibid., 509–11.

31. Ibid., 511.

32. Ibid., 511–12.

33. Ibid., 512.

34. Ibid., 512–13.

35. Kinsley, "Act, Then I'll Decide," 7.

36. "Treaty Finally Is Up to Wilson," *Los Angeles Times*, September 26, 1919, 2.
37. See, for example, "Wilson Will Hold Treaty Rejected by Senate Change," 1, 3.
38. Lawrence, *True Story of Woodrow Wilson*, 279.
39. Woodrow Wilson Centennial Celebration Commission, "Woodrow Wilson in Retrospect," 10–11.
40. "From the Diary of Dr. Grayson" [September 25, 1919], 488–90.
41. "From the Diary of Dr. Grayson" [September 26, 1919], 518–29.
42. "From the Diary of Dr. Grayson" [September 26, 1919], 520.
43. H. W. Brands, *Woodrow Wilson*, 125.
44. Blum, *Woodrow Wilson and the Politics of Morality*, 193–94.
45. Link, *Woodrow Wilson*, 126.
46. Ferrell, *Woodrow Wilson and World War I*, 156.
47. Wilson, "William Earl Chatham," *PWW*, 1: 410.
48. See Tulis, *The Rhetorical Presidency*, 147–61.
49. Tumulty, *Woodrow Wilson as I Know Him*, 448–51.
50. Ibid., 446–48.
51. Wilson, *My Memoir*, 283–84.
52. Ibid., 284–85.
53. Zanuck made this comparison directly at the start of the film, opening with two frames of written text: "Sometimes the life of a man mirrors the life of a nation. The destiny of our country was crystallized in the life and times of Washington and Lincoln . . . and perhaps, too, in the life of another president . . . Woodrow Wilson."
54. In his luncheon address to the St. Louis Chamber of Commerce on September 5, Wilson declared that should the treaty "in any important respect be impaired," he would feel like calling together "the boys who went across the water to fight" and telling them that they had been betrayed. In St. Louis, he elaborated on that sentiment in the exact language used in the movie, the only differences being the absence of the salutation to the "people of Pueblo" and the conditional phrasing of his remarks—*if* the treaty were impaired, he *would* feel like telling "the boys" that they had been betrayed. See Wilson, "A Luncheon Address to the St. Louis Chamber of Commerce," 42.
55. *Wilson* was the most expensive film ever made up to that time ($5.2 million), and Zanuck launched it with a million-dollar advertising campaign featuring 3,280 radio announcements, 32,000 billboards, and full-page magazine illustrations. Zanuck was bitterly disappointed when the film did not do well at the box office, and for years he reportedly forbade his associates from even mentioning the project in his presence. When he won the best picture Oscar in 1947 for *Gentlemen's Agreement*,

Zanuck bitterly told the audience, "Many thanks, but I should have won it for *Wilson*." After only seventy-five people viewed the film in Zanuck's hometown of Wahoo, Nebraska, a local doctor tried to explain the problem to Zanuck: "Why should you expect people to pay 75¢ to see a movie about Wilson when they wouldn't give 10¢ to see him alive?" See "Wilson," *Film Notes*, Department of History, University of San Diego, online at: http://history.acusd.edu/gen/filmnotes/wilsonnotes.html (accessed September 10, 2005).

56. Between 1937 and 1944, there was a dramatic increase in the number of Americans who said the United States should have joined the League of Nations after World War I, as well as in the number of Americans supporting U.S. participation in a new international peace-keeping organization. See Harry H. Field and Louise M. Van Patten, "If the American People Made the Peace," 500–504.

57. See "Wilson's Appeal to the Nation," *U-S-History.com*, online at http://www.u-s-history.com/pages/h1337.html (accessed September 10, 1005).

58. Lucas and Medhurst, eds., *Words of a Century.*

59. Woodrow Wilson Centennial Celebration Commission, *Woodrow Wilson Centennial*, 1–5.

60. Gene Smith, *When the Cheering Stopped: The Last Years of Woodrow Wilson*, x-xi.

61. Ibid., 77–78, 81.

62. Ferrell, *Woodrow Wilson and World War I*, 169.

63. Clements, *Woodrow Wilson*, 215.

64. Clements, *The Presidency of Woodrow Wilson*, 196.

65. Bailey, *Woodrow Wilson and the Great Betrayal*, 113.

66. Cooper, *Breaking the Heart of the World*, 186.

67. Heckscher, *Woodrow Wilson*, 611, 646

Epilogue

1. "From the Diary of Dr. Grayson" [September 11, 1919], 169.

2. According to the International Game Fish Association, David Robert White caught the world record rainbow trout at Bell Island, Arkansas, on June 22, 1970. See "World Freshwater Records," online at: http://www.schoolofflyfishing.com/resources/worldfreshrecords.htm (accessed September 10, 2005).

3. Samuel Kernell, *Going Public: New Strategies of Presidential Leadership*, 2.

4. Tulis, *Rhetorical Presidency*, 158–61.

5. Wilson, "Democracy," 350.

6. Woodrow Wilson, "Congressional Government," *PWW*, 1: 565–66.

7. Woodrow Wilson, *Constitutional Government in the United States*, in *PWW*, 18: 69–216.

8. Wilson, *New Freedom*, 90–91.

9. Stid, *President as Statesman*, 163: 93–94.

10. Vaughn, *Holding Fast the Inner Lines*, 235–36.

11. George Creel, *How We Advertised America*, 401.

12. Scott M. Cutlip, *The Unseen Power: Public Relations: A History*, 165, 168.

13. Mattson, *Creating a Democratic Public*, 115.

14. Kernell, *Going Public*, 26.

15. Tulis, *Rhetorical Presidency*, 161.

16. Link, *Wilson the Diplomatist*, 140.

17. Among the classic studies of public opinion and American foreign policy are Gabriel A. Almond, *The American People and Foreign Policy*; and Bernard C. Cohen, *The Public's Impact on Foreign Policy*. More recently, Page and Shapiro have argued that public opinion on foreign policy issues is more stable and "rational" than the conventional wisdom suggests, yet even they concede that elites "have held public opinion concerning foreign policy in especially low esteem" and that the public's level of information about foreign affairs is "indeed rather low." See Benjamin I. Page and Robert Y. Shapiro, *The Rational Public: Fifty Years of Trends in Americans' Policy Preferences*, 172.

18. Knock, *To End All Wars*, 239.

19. Leroy G. Dorsey, "Woodrow Wilson's Fight for the League of Nations: A Reexamination," 109.

20. See J. Michael Hogan, "George Gallup and the Rhetoric of Scientific Democracy," 161–79.

21. Allan Nevins, "Introduction," xvii; Link, *Woodrow Wilson*, 108; Tulis, *Rhetorical Presidency*, 158.

22. In the winter of 1967–68, *Public Opinion Quarterly* published a special issue on the "scientific study of past public opinion," with Wilson biographer Arthur S. Link as guest editor. The special issue included three essays on the League of Nations debate by students in Link's own seminar. Not surprisingly, none of those essays defined public opinion as it generally is understood today: as the aggregation of mass opinion measured by survey research. Instead, the essays focused on elite opinion within particular special interest groups assumed to have influence over mass opinion during the larger debate. See Wolfgang J. Jelbich, "American Liberals in the League of Nations Controversy," 568–96; James L. Lancaster, "The Protestant Churches and the Fight for Ratification of the Versailles

Treaty," 597–619; and Kenneth R. Maxwell, "Irish-Americans and the Fight for the Treaty," 620–41.

23. Woodrow Wilson, *Congressional Government: A Study in Politics,* in *PWW* 4: 172.

24. Wilson, *Constitutional Government in the United States,* in *PWW,* 18: 114.

25. Clements, *Woodrow Wilson,* 87–88.

26. "Voice of the People," *Chicago Daily Tribune,* September 20, 1919, 8.

27. Chan, "Fighting for the League," 127.

28. Bailey, *Woodrow Wilson and the Great Betrayal,* 120–22.

29. Link, *Woodrow Wilson,* 124.

30. Link, *Wilson the Diplomatist,* 156.

31. Link, *Woodrow Wilson,* 127–28.

32. Knock, *To End All Wars,* 275–76.

33. Cooper, *Breaking the Heart of the World,* 433.

34. Bailey, *Woodrow Wilson and the Great Betrayal,* 104.

35. John G. Geer, *From Tea Leaves to Opinion Polls: A Theory of Democratic Leadership,* 11. Geer is wrong, of course, to imply that "public opinion" did not play an important role in the League of Nations debate because polls had not yet been invented. As I have argued, Wilson may have "lost" the debate precisely because the prevailing portrait of public opinion undermined his claim to a public mandate.

36. Jason C. Flanagan, "Woodrow Wilson's 'Rhetorical Restructuring': The Transformation of the American Self and the Construction of the German Enemy," 115.

37. Wilson, "An Address in the Indianapolis Coliseum," 27; Ambrosius, *Woodrow Wilson and the American Diplomatic Tradition,* esp. 290–98.

38. Cooper, *Breaking the Heart of the World,* 5.

Bibliography

Almond, Gabriel. *The American People and Foreign Policy.* New York: Frederick Praeger, 1967.

Ambrosius, Lloyd E. *Wilsonian Statecraft: Theory and Practice of Liberal Internationalism during World War I.* Wilmington, Del.: Scholarly Resources, 1991.

———. *Woodrow Wilson and the American Diplomatic Tradition: The Treaty Fight in Perspective.* Cambridge: Cambridge University Press, 1987.

Bailey, Thomas A. *Woodrow Wilson and the Great Betrayal.* Chicago: Quadrangle Books, [1945] 1963.

Baird, A. Craig. *American Public Addresses, 1740–1952.* New York: McGraw-Hill, 1956.

Billington, Ray A., and Martin Ridge. *American History after 1865.* 9th ed. Totowa, N.J.: Littlefield, Adams, 1981.

Bimes, Terri, and Stephen Skowronek. "Woodrow Wilson's Critique of Popular Leadership: Reassessing the Modern-Traditional Divide in Presidential History." In *Speaking to the People: The Rhetorical Presidency in Historical Perspective,* ed. Richard J. Ellis, 134–61. Amherst: University of Massachusetts Press, 1998.

Blum, John M. *Joe Tumulty and the Wilson Era.* Boston: Houghton Mifflin, 1951.

———. *Woodrow Wilson and the Politics of Morality.* Boston: Little, Brown, 1956.

Blumenthal, Sidney. *The Permanent Campaign: Inside the World of Elite Political Operatives.* Boston: Beacon Press, 1980.

Brands, H. W. *Woodrow Wilson.* New York: Times Books, 2003.

Chan, Loren B. "Fighting for the League: President Wilson in Nevada, 1919." *Nevada Historical Society Quarterly* 22 (Summer 1979): 115–27.

Clements, Kendrick A. *The Presidency of Woodrow Wilson.* Lawrence: University Press of Kansas, 1992.

———. *Woodrow Wilson: World Statesman.* Chicago: Ivan R. Dee, [1987] 1999.

Cohen, Bernard C. *The Public's Impact on Foreign Policy.* Boston: Little, Brown, 1973.

Cooper, John Milton Jr. *Breaking the Heart of the World: Woodrow Wilson and the Fight for the League of Nations.* Cambridge: Cambridge University Press, 2001.

————. "Fool's Errand or Finest Hour? Woodrow Wilson's Speaking Tour in September 1919." In *The Wilson Era: Essays in Honor of Arthur S. Link,* ed. John Milton Cooper Jr. and Charles E. Neu, 198–220. Arlington Heights, Ill.: Harlan Davidson, 1991.

————. *The Warrior and the Priest: Woodrow Wilson and Theodore Roosevelt.* Cambridge: Belknap Press of Harvard University Press, 1983.

Creel, George. *How We Advertised America.* New York: Arno Press, [1920] 1972.

Croly, Herbert. *The Promise of American Life.* Boston: Northeastern University Press, [1909] 1989.

Crunden, Robert M. "Progressivism." In *The Reader's Companion to American History,* ed. Eric Foner and John A. Garraty, 868–71. Boston: Houghton Mifflin, 1995.

Cutlip, Scott M. *The Unseen Power: Public Relations, a History.* Hillsdale, N.J.: Lawrence Erlbaum, 1994.

Danbom, David B. *"The World of Hope": Progressives and the Struggle for an Ethical Public Life.* Philadelphia: Temple University Press, 1987.

Daniels, Josephus. *The Life of Woodrow Wilson.* Philadelphia: John C. Winston, 1924.

Dewey, John. *The Public and Its Problems.* Athens, Ohio: Swallow Press, [1927] 1991.

Diner, Steven J. *A Very Different Age: Americans of the Progressive Era.* New York: Hill and Wang, 1998.

Dorsey, Leroy G. "Woodrow Wilson's Fight for the League of Nations: A Reexamination." *Rhetoric and Public Affairs* 2 (Spring 1999): 107–35.

Ellis, Richard J. "Introduction." In *Speaking to the People: The Rhetorical Presidency in Historical Perspective,* ed. Richard J. Ellis, 1–15. Amherst: University of Massachusetts Press, 1998.

Ferrell, Robert H. *Woodrow Wilson and World War I, 1917–1921.* New York: Harper and Row, 1985.

Field, Harry H., and Louise M. Van Patten. "If the American People Made the Peace." *Public Opinion Quarterly* 8 (Winter 1944): 500–512.

Fitzpatrick, Ellen. *Endless Crusade: Women Social Scientists and Progressive Reform.* New York: Oxford University Press, 1990.

Flanagan, Jason C. "Woodrow Wilson's 'Rhetorical Restructuring': The Transformation of the American Self and the Construction of the German Enemy." *Rhetoric and Public Affairs* 7 (Summer 2004): 115–48.

Freud, Sigmund, and William C. Bullitt. *Thomas Woodrow Wilson: A Psychological Study.* Boston: Houghton Mifflin, 1967.

Geer, John G. *From Tea Leaves to Opinion Polls: A Theory of Democratic Leadership.* New York: Columbia University Press, 1996.

George, Alexander L., and Juliette L. George. *Woodrow Wilson and Colonel House: A Personality Study.* New York: Dover, [1956] 1964.

Heckscher, August. *Woodrow Wilson: A Biography.* New York: Collier, 1993.

Hilderbrand, Robert C. *Power and the People: Executive Management of Public Opinion in Foreign Affairs, 1897–1921.* Chapel Hill: University of North Carolina Press, 1981.

Hofstadter, Richard. *The Age of Reform: From Bryan to F.D.R.* New York: Vintage, 1955.

———. *The American Political Tradition and the Men Who Made It.* New York: Vintage, 1948.

Hogan, J. Michael. "George Gallup and the Rhetoric of Scientific Democracy." *Communication Monographs* 64 (June 1997): 161–79.

Hogan, J. Michael, and James R. Andrews. "Woodrow Wilson." In *U.S. Presidents as Orators: A Bio-Critical Sourcebook,* ed. Halford Ryan, 111–33. New York: Greenwood Press, 1995.

Jelbich, Wolfgang J. "American Liberals in the League of Nations Controversy." *Public Opinion Quarterly* 31 (Winter 1967–68): 568–96.

Kernell, Samuel. *Going Public: New Strategies of Presidential Leadership.* 3d ed. Washington, D.C.: Congressional Quarterly Press, 1997.

Knock, Thomas J. *To End All Wars: Woodrow Wilson and the Quest for a New World Order.* Princeton, N.J.: Princeton University Press, 1992.

Kolko, Gabriel. *The Triumph of Conservatism: A Reinterpretation of American History, 1900–1916.* New York: Free Press, 1963.

Kraig, Robert Alexander. "The Second Oratorical Renaissance." In *Rhetoric and Reform in the Progressive Era,* ed. J. Michael Hogan, 1–48. East Lansing: Michigan State University Press, 2003.

———. *Woodrow Wilson and the Lost World of the Oratorical Statesman.* College Station: Texas A&M University Press, 2004.

Lancaster, James L. "The Protestant Churches and the Fight for Ratification of the Versailles Treaty." *Public Opinion Quarterly* 31 (Winter 1967–68): 597–619.

Lawrence, David. *The True Story of Woodrow Wilson.* New York: George H. Doran, 1924.

Levine, Peter. *The New Progressive Era: Toward a Fair and Deliberative Democracy.* Lanham, Md.: Rowman and Littlefield, 2000.

Link, Arthur S. "Woodrow Wilson: The Philosophy, Methods, and Impact of Leadership." In *Woodrow Wilson and the World of Today,* ed. Arthur P. Dudden, 1–21. Philadelphia: University of Pennsylvania Press, 1957.

———. *Wilson the Diplomatist: A Look at His Major Foreign Policies.* Baltimore: Johns Hopkins University Press, 1957.

———. *Woodrow Wilson and the Progressive Era, 1910–1917.* New York: Harper and Brothers, 1954.

———. *Woodrow Wilson: Revolution, War, and Peace.* Arlington Heights, Ill.: AHM Publishing, 1979.

Link, Arthur S., et al., eds. *The Papers of Woodrow Wilson.* 69 vols. Princeton,
    N.J.: Princeton University Press, 1966–94.
Lippmann, Walter. *Drift and Mastery.* Englewood Cliffs, N.J.: Prentice-Hall,
    [1914] 1961.
————. *Public Opinion.* New York: Free Press Paperbacks, [1922] 1997.
Lucas, Stephen E., and Martin J. Medhurst, eds. *Words of a Century: The Top 100
    American Speeches, 1900–1999,* forthcoming. New York: Oxford University Press.
Mattson, Kevin. *Creating a Democratic Public: The Struggle for Urban
    Participatory Democracy.* University Park: Pennsylvania State University
    Press, 1998.
Maxwell, Kenneth R. "Irish-Americans and the Fight for the Treaty." *Public
    Opinion Quarterly* 31 (Winter 1967–68): 620–41.
McEdwards, Mary G. "Woodrow Wilson: His Stylistic Progression." *Western
    Journal of Speech Communication* 26 (Winter 1962): 28–38.
McKean, Dayton David. "Woodrow Wilson." In *History and Criticism of
    American Public Address,* ed. William Norwood Brigance, vol. 2: 968–92.
    New York: Russell and Russell, [1943] 1960.
Page, Benjamin I., and Robert Y. Shapiro. *The Rational Public: Fifty Years of Trends
    in Americans' Policy Preferences.* Chicago: University of Chicago Press, 1992.
Saunders, Robert M. *In Search of Woodrow Wilson: Beliefs and Behavior.*
    Westport, Conn.: Greenwood Press, 1998.
Smith, Gene. *When the Cheering Stopped: The Last Years of Woodrow Wilson.*
    New York: Time, 1966.
Southern, David W. *The Malignant Heritage: Yankee Progressives and the Negro
    Question, 1901–1914.* Chicago: Loyola University Press, 1968.
Stein, M. L. *When Presidents Meet the Press.* New York: Julian Messner, 1969.
Stid, Daniel D. *The President as Statesman: Woodrow Wilson and the
    Constitution.* Lawrence: University Press of Kansas, 1998.
————. "Rhetorical Leadership and 'Common Counsel' in the Presidency of
    Woodrow Wilson." In *Speaking to the People: The Rhetorical Presidency in
    Historical Perspective,* ed. Richard J. Ellis, 162–81. Amherst: University of
    Massachusetts Press, 1998.
Tulis, Jeffrey K. *The Rhetorical Presidency.* Princeton, N.J.: Princeton University
    Press, 1987.
Tumulty, Joseph P. *Woodrow Wilson as I Know Him.* Garden City, N.Y.:
    Doubleday, Page, 1921.
U.S., Congress, Senate, Committee on Foreign Relations. *Treaty of Peace with
    Germany: Hearings. . . .* 66th Cong., 1st sess. Washington, D.C.: GPO, 1919.
Vaughn, Stephen. *Holding Fast the Inner Lines: Democracy, Nationalism, and the
    Committee on Public Information.* Chapel Hill: University of North Carolina
    Press, 1980.

Wilson, Edith Bolling. *My Memoir.* Indianapolis: Bobbs-Merrill, 1938.

Wilson, Woodrow. *The New Freedom: A Call for the Emancipation of the Generous Energies of a People.* New York: Doubleday, Page, 1913.

Woodrow Wilson Centennial Celebration Commission. *Woodrow Wilson Centennial: Final Report of the Woodrow Wilson Centennial Celebration Committee.* Washington, D.C.: N.p., 1957.

Index